Property and Trust Law: Cape Town Convention

Property and Trust Law: Cape Town Convention

Second Edition

Sandie Calme

This book was originally published as a monograph in the International Encyclopaedia of Laws/Private International Law.

Founding Editor: Roger Blanpain
General Editor: Frank Hendrickx
Volume Editors: Alain Verbeke & Vincent Sagaert

Wolters Kluwer

Published by:
Kluwer Law International B.V.
PO Box 316
2400 AH Alphen aan den Rijn
The Netherlands
E-mail: lrs-sales@wolterskluwer.com
Website: www.wolterskluwer.com/en/solutions/kluwerlawinternational

Sold and distributed by:
Wolters Kluwer Legal & Regulatory U.S.
920 Links Avenue
Landisville, PA 17538
United States of America
E-mail: customer.service@wolterskluwer.com

ISBN 978-94-035-3617-0

e-Book: ISBN 978-94-035-3627-9
web-PDF: ISBN 978-94-035-3637-8

The Author

Sandie Calme has studied French and German Law at the Paris Ouest Nanterre La Défense University and at the Goethe University in Frankfurt am Main, Germany. She owns the Doctorate in Law from the Paris 1 Panthéon Sorbonne University. She has taken part in the activities of the Study Group on a European Civil Code. Her activity focuses, among other fields of interest, on international law, labour law, transport law and insolvency law. She is the author of 'L'évolution du droit des transports ferroviaires en Europe' (doctoral thesis, P. U. A. M., Collection de la Bibliothèque de Droit Maritime et des Transports), 'La réserve de propriété de droit français et de droit allemand dans le contexte européen – Une contribution au droit international de l'insolvabilité'/'Der Eigentumsvorbehalt des deutschen und französischen Rechts im europäischen Kontext – Zugleich ein Beitrag zum internationalen Insolvenzrecht' (bilingual publication, Peter Lang International Academic Publishers), 'L'essentiel du Droit des transports' (Gualino-Lextenso Editor), 'Droit international privé allemand' (EHV Academic Press), 'French Private International Law' (Vandeplas Publishing), 'Einführung ins Transport-und Speditionsrecht' (Diplomica Verlag), 'Französisches Gesellschaftsrecht' (Igel Verlag Recht Wirtschaft Steuer).

The Author

Table of Contents

Table of Contents

List of Abbreviations

COTIF	Convention concerning International Carriage by Rail
COTIF 1999	Convention concerning International Carriage by Rail (COTIF) of 9 May 1980 in the version of the Protocol of Modification of 3 June 1999
EBRD	European Bank for Reconstruction and Development
EC	European Community(ies)
EWHC	England and Wales High Court
ITU	International Telecommunications Union
OHADA	Organisation for the Harmonization in Africa of Business Law
UN	United Nations
UNCITRAL	United Nations Commission on International Trade Law
UNIDROIT	International Institute for the Unification of Private Law

List of Abbreviations

General Introduction

1. The Cape Town Convention and its Protocols root in the initiative of UNIDROIT, for high-value equipment crossing national borders. As a starting point, it is assumed that such high-value material must be subject to financial guarantees from banks and financial institutes. As far as financial institutions face difficulties, as to the difficult recognition of foreign credit securities over movable assets from one State to another (Gopalan Sandeep, 'Harmonization of Commercial Law: Lessons on the International Interests in Mobile Equipment', *Law and Business Review of the Americas* Vol. 9 (2003): 256), it is minded that the banks and financial institutes are reluctant when they are asked to offer credit guarantees for such high-value movable goods. These hypotheses are confirmed by the practitioners.

2. Concerning such concerns, the UNIDROIT Convention on International Financial Leasing, signed in Ottawa on 28 May 1988, has been considered the first step towards a solution, which may be the creation of a global legal system dedicated to international recognition of foreign credit securities over movable assets moving internationally.

3. As for maritime transport equipment, however, obviously, it has to be treated separately from other movable assets, as far as conventions such as the International Conventions for the Unification of Certain Rules Relating to Maritime Liens and Mortgages (Conventions of Brussels from 10 April 1926 and from 27 May 1967) or the International Convention on Maritime Liens and Mortgages (Convention from 6 May 1993) already intervene in this area.

4. Professor Cuming (UNIDROIT 1993, Etude LXXII, doc. 6, no. 3), from the University of Saskatchewan, had issued, for UNIDROIT, a report, according to which most of the national legal orders on credit securities over movables lack flexibility and predictability and tend to discriminate foreign credit securities (in particular, at the level of the recognition of foreign credit securities; *see*, for instance, concerning the aircraft equipment: *Blue Sky One Limited and Others v. Mahan Air and Another* (2010) EWHC 631 (Comm); *see* William J. Glaister, Robert Murphy, Marisa Chan, Elie Dunne & Julian Acratopulo, 'Lex Situs after Blue Sky: Is the Cape Town Convention the Solution?', *Cape Town Law Journal* (2013): 3–23), so that he considered the creation of an international legal instrument, containing substantial legal rules as well as rules of conflicts of laws, for this matter, as suitable. The study group (UNIDROIT 1993, Etude LXXII, doc. 6, no. 7), led by Professor Goode with Professor Cuming, has confirmed the convenience of such a project and recommended starting from a new international guarantee broadly defined in a new convention, which would be subject to an international registry system.

5. The techniques specific to the Cape Town Convention and its Protocols may come from the time of the creation of the UNIDROIT Conventions on International Financial Leasing and on International Factoring: these techniques are developed from 1974 (Martin Stanford, 'The UNIDROIT Convention on International Financial Leasing and the Preliminary Draft UNIDROIT Convention on International Interests in Mobile Equipment: Two Examples of UNIDROIT in Its Law-Making Role', *International Journal of Legal Information* (1999): 189).

6. The industry involvement is an advantage for the Cape Town Convention and its Protocols (Martin Stanford, 'From Ottawa to Cape Town: UNIDROIT's Role in the Modernisation of the Law Governing Leasing and the Taking of a Security'. In *Secured Interests in Mobile Equipment*, edited by Iwan Davies. 2002, 491). Specialists have been asked to express their points of view on this project. Dr Maier, from the Deutsche Aerospace (UNIDROIT 1993, Etude LXXII, doc. 6, no. 11), answered that, as far as the scope of application of the proposed international convention was concerned, it was difficult to define (*see* Ole Böger, 'A Possible Protocol to the Cape Town Convention on Renewable Energy Equipment', *Uniform Law Review* Vol. 23(2) (1 June 2018): 242–269; Ole Böger, 'The Case for a New Protocol to the Cape Town Convention Covering Security over Ships', *Cape Town Convention Journal* Vol. 5(1) (2016): 73–102; Teresa Rodríguez de las Heras Ballell, 'Complexities Arising from the Expansion of the Cape Town Convention to Other Sectors', *Uniform Law Review* Vol. 23(2) (1 June 2018): 214–241) which material crossing borders was at stake, but it was sure that aircraft objects and space assets may be included. He criticised the concept of the new global international guarantee subject to an international registration, because of the inevitable strong impact of national laws, and he pointed out the need for specifying the common characteristics of existing national laws on such subject. On this point, one may underline the work of the Study Group on a European Civil Code in the Working Team on Credit Securities led by Professor Ulrich Drobnig. He also referred to the experience of international conventions on intellectual property rights: in this area, one finds the most advanced forms of international registration of property rights governed by common juridical frames. Miss White, from the United Kingdom Civil Aviation Authority, underlined the need for preserving the legal privileges from any regulation in the future convention and expressed her satisfaction that these privileges had to remain unaffected by the project (UNIDROIT 1993, Etude LXXII, doc. 6, no. 12). The French Association Française des Sociétés Financières declared that it does not want the property right of the creditor in the frame of the crédit-bail (leasing) to be involved in the new project (UNIDROIT 1993, Etude LXXII, doc. 6, no. 13). As for railway rolling stock crossing the borders, Mr Howard Rosen insisted on the need for a European register permitting to identify the property rights on such goods. He preferred a European register, which would be encouraged by the European Commission, rather than a treaty on mutual recognition of local credit securities (UNIDROIT 1993, Etude LXXII, doc. 6, no. 15), but he was not against a combination of both solutions (UNIDROIT 1993, Etude LXXII, doc. 6, no. 16). In those times, the Secretary of UNIDROIT was in favour of a common solution for any kind of assets moved internationally, even though the Secretary recognised the possibility of emerging specificities for any category of material: it insisted on the fact that it was not convenient, in terms of legal certainty, to have numerous international systems for the numerous types of moving assets (UNIDROIT 1993, Etude LXXII, doc. 6, no. 16).

7. The history of the Cape Town Convention and its Protocols is a long-term lawmaking process inspired by the international legal instruments developing in the meantime.

8. This lawmaking process under the aegis of UNIDROIT gave rise to the Convention on International Interests in Mobile Equipment (Cape Town Convention), which has been signed in Cape Town on 16 November 2001. To date, it has entered into force in Afghanistan, Albania, Angola, Argentina, Australia, Bahrain, Bangladesh, Belarus, Bhutan, Brazil, Burkina Faso, Cabo Verde, Cameroon, China, Colombia, Congo, Costa Rica, Cuba, the Democratic Republic of the Congo, Denmark, Egypt, Eswatini, Ethiopia, European Union (as a Regional Economic Integration Organization), Fiji, Gabon, Ghana, Iceland, India, Indonesia, Ireland, Ivory Coast, Jordan, Kazakhstan, Kenya, Kuwait, Kyrgyzstan, Latvia, Luxembourg, Madagascar, Malawi, Malaysia, Malta, Mexico, Mongolia, Mozambique, Myanmar, Namibia, New Zealand, Niger, Nigeria, Norway, Oman, Pakistan, Panama, Paraguay, Qatar, Republic of Moldova, Romania, Russian Federation, Rwanda, San Marino, Saudi Arabia, Senegal, Sierra Leone, Singapore, South Africa, Spain, Sweden, Tajikistan, Togo, Turkey, Ukraine, United Arab Emirates, United Kingdom, United Republic of Tanzania, United States of America, Uzbekistan, Viet Nam, Zambia.

9. In its declaration pursuant to Article 48, 2. of the Cape Town Convention, the EU expressed itself accordingly, except for the Kingdom of Denmark. It declares (4.) that its declaration is not applicable in the case of the territories of the Member States in which the Treaty establishing the European Community does not apply and is without prejudice to such acts or positions as may be adopted under the Cape Town Convention by the Member States concerned on behalf and in the interests of those territories. It underlines the fact that the Member States of the European Community have transferred their competence to the Community as regards matters which affect (5.) Council Regulation (EC) No 44/2001 of 22 December 2000 – now Regulation (EU) No 1215/2012 of the European Parliament and of the Council of 12 December 2012 – on jurisdiction and the recognition and enforcement of judgments in civil and commercial matters, Council Regulation (EC) No 1346/2000 of 29 May 2000 – now Regulation (EU) No 2015/848 of the European Parliament and of the Council of 20 May 2015 – on insolvency proceedings and Regulation (EC) No 593/2008 of the European Parliament and of the Council of 17 June 2008 on the law applicable to contractual obligations (Rome I). It states that the Member States keep their competence concerning the rules of substantive law as regards insolvency (6.). In the declaration, the EU recalls that the exercise of the competence transferred by the Member States is subject to continuous development (7.).

10. In addition to that, the EU makes an important declaration following Article 55, according to which:

> Pursuant to Article 55 of the Cape Town Convention, where the debtor is domiciled in the territory of a Member State of the Community, the Member States bound by Council Regulation (EC) No 44/2001 of 22 December 2000 on jurisdiction and the recognition and enforcement of judgments in civil and commercial matters will apply Articles 13 (ensuring the possibility of relief pending final determination) and 43 (on jurisdiction concerning relieves pending final determination) of the Cape Town Convention for interim relief only in accordance with Article 31 of Regulation No 44/2001 as interpreted by the Court of Justice of the European Communities in the context of Article 24 of the Brussels Convention of 27 September 1968 on jurisdiction and the enforcement of judgments in civil and commercial matters.

11. According to Article 31 of Regulation No 44/2001, which has the same content as Article 24 of the Brussels Convention of 27 September 1968 on jurisdiction and the enforcement of judgments in civil and commercial matters, 'application may be made to the courts of a Member State for such provisional, including protective, measures as may be available under the law of that State, even if, under this Regulation, the courts of another Member State have jurisdiction as to the substance of the matter'.

According to Article 80 of Regulation (EU) No 1215/2012 of the European Parliament and of the Council of 12 December 2012 on jurisdiction and the recognition and enforcement of judgments in civil and commercial matters, Regulation No 1215/2012 shall repeal Regulation (EC) No 44/2001, so that references to the repealed Regulation shall be construed as references to Regulation No 1215/2012 and shall be read in accordance with the correlation table set out in its Annex III. Pursuant to Article 68 in fine of Regulation No 1215/2012, in so far as Regulation No 1215/2012 replaces the provisions of the 1968 Brussels Convention between the Member States, any reference to the 1968 Brussels Convention shall be understood as a reference to Regulation No 1215/2012.

Article 31 of Regulation No 44/2001 and Article 24 of the 1968 Brussels Convention have the same content as Article 35 of Regulation No 1215/2012.

12. The Protocol to the Convention on International Interests in Mobile Equipment on Matters Specific to Aircraft Equipment, which entered into force on 1 March 2006, has entered into force in Afghanistan, Albania, Angola, Argentina, Australia, Bahrain, Bangladesh, Belarus, Bhutan, Brazil, Burkina Faso, Cabo Verde, Cameroon, China, Colombia, Congo, Costa Rica, Cuba, Democratic Republic of the Congo, Denmark, Egypt, Eswatini, Ethiopia, European Union (as a Regional Economic Integration Organization), Fiji, Gabon, Ghana, Iceland, India, Indonesia, Ireland, Ivory Coast, Jordan, Kazakhstan, Kenya, Kuwait, Kyrgyzstan, Latvia, Luxembourg, Madagascar, Malawi, Malaysia, Malta, Mexico, Mongolia, Mozambique, Myanmar, Namibia, New Zealand, Niger, Nigeria, Norway, Oman, Pakistan, Panama, Paraguay, Qatar, Republic of Moldova, Romania, Russian Federation,

Rwanda, San Marino, Saudi Arabia, Senegal, Sierra Leone, Singapore, South Africa, Spain, Sweden, Tajikistan, Togo, Turkey, Ukraine, United Arab Emirates, United Kingdom, United Republic of Tanzania, United States of America, Uzbekistan, Viet Nam, Zambia.

13. The EU's Declaration pursuant to Article XXVII(2) concerning the competence of the European Community over matters governed by the Aircraft Protocol on matters specific to aircraft equipment ('Aircraft Protocol'), in respect of which the Member States have transferred their competence to the Community, contains the same rules as for the Cape Town Convention, but this way with one other additional declaration, according to which:

> In accordance with Article XXX, 5 of the Aircraft Protocol, Article XXI of that Protocol will not apply within the Community and Council Regulation (EC) No 44/2001 of 22 December 2000 on jurisdiction and the recognition and enforcement of judgments in civil and commercial matters will apply to this matter for the Member States bound by the said Regulation or by any other agreement designed to extend its effects.

14. Article XXX, 5 of the Aircraft Protocol, allows a State's Declaration as to the extent of the application of Article XXI, which states that 'For the purposes of Article 43 (on jurisdiction concerning relieves pending final determination) of the Convention and subject to Article 42 (on the choice of forum) of the Convention, a court of a Contracting State also has jurisdiction where the object is a helicopter, or an airframe pertaining to an aircraft, for which that State is the State of registry.'

15. The Luxembourg Protocol to the Convention on International Interests in Mobile Equipment on Matters Specific to Railway Rolling Stock and the Protocol to the Convention on International Interests in Mobile Equipment on Matters Specific to Space Assets have not yet entered into force.

16. The Rail Protocol has been approved by the EU on 18 December 2014. This approval has the same general content as the Cape Town Convention and the Aircraft Protocol. It specifies the following:

> 5. The Member States of the European Union have transferred competence to the Union as regards matters which may affect or alter the rules of Council Regulation (EC) No 44/2001, to be replaced as of 10 January 2015 by Regulation (EU) No 1215/2012 of the European Parliament and of the Council, Council Regulation (EC) No 1346/2000, Regulation (EC) No 593/2008 of the European Parliament and of the Council, Directive 2008/57/EC of the European Parliament and of the Council (Directive 2008/57/EC of the European Parliament and of the Council of 17 June 2008 on the interoperability of the rail system within the Community) and Regulation (EC) No 881/2004 of the

European Parliament and of the Council (Regulation (EC) No 881/2004 of the European Parliament and of the Council of 29 April 2004 establishing a European Railway Agency).

6. As far as the numbering system of vehicles is concerned, the Union has adopted, by way of Commission Decision 2006/920/EC, amended on 14 November 2012 by Commission Decision 2012/757/EU, a numbering system which is appropriate for the purpose of identification of railway rolling stock as referred to in Article XIV of the Rail Protocol.

In the meantime, Council Regulation (EC) No 1346/2000 on insolvency proceedings has been replaced by Regulation (EU) 2015/848 of the European Parliament and of the Council of 20 May 2015 on insolvency proceedings, Directive 2008/57/EC of the European Parliament of the Council of 17 June 2008 on the interoperability of the rail system within the Community has been replaced by Directive (EU) 2016/797 of the European Parliament and of the Council of 11 May 2016 on the interoperability of the rail system within the European, Regulation (EC) No 881/2004 of the European Parliament and of the Council of 29 April 2004 establishing a European Railway Agency has been replaced by Regulation (EU) 2016/796 of the European Parliament and of the Council of 11 May 2016 on the European Union Agency for Railways and repealing Regulation (EC) No 881/2004, Commission Decision of 11 August 2006 concerning the technical specification of interoperability relating to the subsystem Traffic Operation and Management of the trans-European conventional rail system (notified under document number C(2006) 3593) has been replaced by Commission Decision of 12 May 2011 concerning the technical specification for interoperability relating to the 'operation and traffic management' subsystem of the trans-European conventional rail system (notified under document C(2011) 3099).

Furthermore, as far as data exchange between Member States of the European Union and the International Registry is concerned, the Union has made considerable progress by way of Commission Decision 2007/756/EC, amended on 14 November 2012 by Decision 2012/757/EU. Under that Decision, the Member States of the European Union have implemented National Vehicle Registers, and duplication of data with the International Registry should be avoided. These rules have been improved by Commission Implementing Decision (EU) 2018/1614 of 25 October 2018 laying down specifications for the vehicle registers referred to in Article 47 of Directive (EU) 2016/797 of the European Parliament and of the Council and amending and repealing Commission Decision 2007/756/EC, with the European Vehicle Register.

17. So the EU is to be a decisive partner with regard to the Rail Protocol.

According to the doctrine, the consequence of the involvement of the EU will be harmonisation in European property law, with the predominance of two different levels of proprietary regimes for security agreements: the title reservation agreement and the lease agreement, so that the European property law reform is thus encouraged (B. Patrick Honnebier, 'The Convention on International Interests in Mobile Equipment and Aircraft Equipment Protocol Encourages European Property

Law Reform', *Edinburgh Law Review* Vol. 8(1) (2004): 124). As a legal instrument of Private international law (*see* Karl F. Kreuzer, 'Jurisdiction and Choice of Law under the Cape Town Convention and the Protocols Thereto', *Cape Town Law Journal* Vol. 2(1) (2013): 149–164), the Cape Town Convention with its 'two-instruments approach' has been qualified as the concretisation of a 'unification of laws process' (Iwan Davies, 'The New *Lex Mercatoria*: International Interests in Mobile Equipment', *International and Comparative Law Quarterly:* Vol. 52(1) (2003): 153) in order to fulfil the 'need for adherence to recognised standards and structures' expressed (not only concerning international space projects in Europe) by the industry (Lesley Jane Smith, *The Principles of International Space Law and Their Relevance to Space Industry Contracts, in Contracting for Space, Contract Practice in the European Space Sector* (2011), 46).

18. The Protocol to the Cape Town Convention on Matters Specific to Agricultural, Construction and Mining Equipment has not yet entered into force.

Part I. Structure of the Cape Town Convention and Its Protocols

19. The Convention on International Interests in Mobile Equipment (Cape Town Convention) is a basic international legal instrument linked to area-specific Protocols which aims at adapting the Cape Town Convention's rules to particular kinds of high-value mobile equipment.

Chapter 1. The Convention on International Interests in Mobile Equipment as Basic Structure

§1. The General Frame

20. The Convention on International Interests in Mobile Equipment (Cape Town Convention), which has been signed in Cape Town on 16 November 2001, has been conceived as a solution to the classical issues arising out of financing mobile equipment, in particular for air transport, for the railway transport and for space assets, and may be extended to agricultural, construction and mining equipment. In this frame, the fate of securities on movable assets where goods are moved internationally is at stake. The Convention targets to establish a legal framework for international interests in mobile equipment of high value or particular economic significance and creates for that purpose an international registration system for their protection.

21. The Convention states that it is needed to ensure that such interests are recognised and protected universally and wants to promote the autonomy of the parties. This legal frame aims at ensuring economic benefits (*see* Lorne S. Clark, 'The 2001 Cape Town Convention on International Interests in Mobile Equipment and Aircraft Protocol: Internationalising Asset-Based Financing Principles for the Acquisition of Aircraft and Engines', *Journal of Air Law and Commerce* Vol. 69 (2004): 15; Sir Roy Goode, 'Security Interests in Mobile Equipment: Lawmaking Lessons from the Cape Town Convention', *Adelaide Law Review* Vol. 35(1) (2014): 68) for the implied parties. It takes into account the 'principles enunciated in existing Conventions relating to such equipment'.

22. Article 2 of the Convention provides for a definition of international interests pursuant to the Convention, which 'provides for the constitution and effects of an international interest in certain categories of mobile equipment and associated rights' (Article 2, 1).

23. An international interest in mobile equipment is constituted (Article 2, 2) where, according to Article 7 of the Convention, the agreement creating or providing for the interest:

- is in writing;
- relates to an object of which the chargor, conditional seller or lessor has power to dispose;
- enables the object to be identified in conformity with the Protocol; and
- in the case of a security agreement, enables the secured obligations to be determined, but without the need to state a sum or maximum sum secured.

24. According to Article 29, 7 of the Cape Town Convention, this Convention does not affect the rights of a person in an item, other than an object, held prior to its installation on an object if under the applicable law those rights continue to exist after the installation and do not prevent the creation of rights in an item, other than an object, which has previously been installed on an object where under the applicable law those rights are created.

25. In the first case, as a principle, the installation or incorporation of the item does not affect pre-existing rights, except if the applicable law applies the doctrine of accession, but the rules in the second case are considered unnecessary because the Convention does not apply to items that are not installed or have ceased to be installed so that rights in these are ruled by the applicable law (Sir Roy Goode, 'Official Commentary on the Convention on International Interests in Mobile Equipment', (2014), no. 4.195, pp. 227 and 228).

26. The international interest must concern specific categories of goods specified in the Convention, such as airframes, aircraft engines and helicopters, railway rolling stock and space assets, according to Article 2, 3 of the Convention.

27. The Convention and its specific protocols are to be read and interpreted as a whole so that in cases of doubt, the Protocols shall prevail (Article 6).

28. The interest concerned must be granted by the chargor under a security agreement, vested in a person who is the conditional seller under a title reservation agreement or who is the lessor under a leasing agreement (Article 2, 2). If the interest is granted by the chargor under a security agreement, it shall be distinguished from the title reservation agreement (which is limited to the context of the contract of sale) or leasing agreement (Article 2, 2 in fine). In order to be precise on whether the interest is granted by the chargor under a security agreement or is related to a title reservation agreement or leasing agreement, the Convention expressly refers to the 'applicable law' (Article 2, 4).

29. Article 2, 5 of the Convention states that 'an international interest in an object extends to proceeds of that object'. So if the concerned object disappears or is damaged, the corresponding indemnity is linked to the international interest.

30. The application of the present Convention depends on the situation of the debtor while the agreement creating or providing for the international interest is concluded (Article 3). The Convention applies only if the debtor is located in a Contracting State at this time, no matter the location of the creditor. The debtor is considered as located in a Contracting State if it is incorporated or formed under the law of this State, or if it has its registered office, its statutory seat, its centre of administration or its place of business in this State (Article 4, 1). The place of business shall be the principal place of business, where the debtor has many places of business or the debtor's habitual residence if this debtor lacks a place of business (Article 4, 2).

31. The interpretation of the present Convention is presented as a matter of flexibility. So its interpretation has to be based on its general principles, on the purposes set up in its preamble, taking into account its internationality as well as the need for uniformity and predictability in the application of the Convention (Article 5, 1 and 2). Nevertheless, if no general principle of the Convention may intervene, the interpretation shall be made with due respect to the 'applicable law', that is to say, that the conflict of laws rules of the State of the tribunal seized shall apply (Article 5, 2 and 3). In the case of federal legal systems (Article 5, 4), lacking an indication of the territorial law applicable, the law of the concerned State, if any, designates the territorial law applicable; nevertheless, if the national law does not provide for specific rules on that matters, the law of the territorial unit most closely connected to the case shall apply.

32. According to Article 41, the present Convention shall apply to the sale or prospective sale of an object as provided for in the Protocols with any modifications therein.

§2. Default Remedies

33. According to Article 11 of the Convention, the debtor and the creditor may at any time agree in writing as to the events that constitute a default or otherwise give rise to the rights and remedies for a default (pursuant to Articles 8–1 and 13 of the Convention; Article 11, 1). If there is no agreement on the meaning of default between the debtor and the creditor, it means a default that is substantially depriving the debtors of their rights as provided for under the agreement (Article 11, 2).

34. In this frame, the chargee (the creditor under a security agreement, according to Article 1, (i)) may, with the agreement of the chargor (its debtor), and with due respect to possible State's declarations regarding remedies (Article 54), be entitled to take possession or control of any object charged to it, to sell or grant a lease of any such object and/or to collect or receive any income or profits arising from the management or use of any such object (Article 8, 1). The chargee may alternatively apply for a court order in order to exercise these remedies (Article 8, 2).

35. According to Article 54 of the Convention, a Contracting State may, while subscribing to a Protocol, declare that while the charged object is situated within or controlled from its territory, the chargee (as the creditor under the security agreement) shall not grant a lease of the object in its territory (Article 54, 1). The Contracting State may also specify whether a remedy for which the present Convention does not foresee a compulsory application to a court may be exercised only with leave of the court (Article 54, 2).

36. These remedies, as well as the speedy relief pending determination according to Article 13, which may be considered as a sui generis remedy to be interpreted autonomously (Anna Veneziano, 'Advanced Relief under the Cape Town Convention and Its Aircraft Protocol: A Comment on Gilles Cuniberti's Interpretative Proposal', *Cape Town Law Convention Journal* Vol. 2(1) (2013): 185–190) shall be exercised in a commercially reasonable manner; as a principle, it will be exercised in a commercially reasonable manner if it respects a specific provision of the security agreement which is not manifestly unreasonable (Article 8, 3). This concept of 'commercially reasonable manner' is subject to different interpretations (Sanam Saidova, 'The Cape Town Convention: Repossession and Sale of Charged Aircraft Objects in a Commercially Reasonable Manner', *Lloyd's Maritime and Commercial Law Quarterly* (2013): 180, 182).

37. The chargee wanting to sell or grant a lease of the concerned object is not deprived of duties. It shall give reasonable prior notice in writing of the proposed sale or lease to such interested persons (Article 8, 4):

- the debtor;
- any person who, for the purpose of assuring performance of any of the obligations in favour of the creditor, gives or issues a form of credit insurance such as a suretyship or demand guarantee or a standby letter of credit;
- any other person having rights in or over the object and having given notice of its rights to the chargee within a reasonable time prior to the sale or lease.

38. In order to avoid the enrichment of the chargee above the scope of its rights, the sum it collects or receives while exercising the remedies has to be applied towards the discharge of the amount of the secured obligations (Article 8, 5) and where the sums collected or received exceed the amount secured by the security interest and any reasonable costs incurred in the exercise of any such remedy, unless otherwise ordered by the court, the chargee has to distribute the surplus among holders of subsequently ranking interests which have been registered or of which the chargee has been given notice, in order of priority, and pay any remaining balance to the chargor (Article 8, 6).

39. There is also the possibility to vest an object covered by the security interest in the charge in or towards the satisfaction of the secured obligation (Article 9). It may result from an agreement between the chargee and all the interested persons (Article 9, 1), or from a judgment by a court (Article 9, 2). In the latter case, the court shall accept such a solution only if the amount of the secured obligations to be satisfied by such vesting is commensurate with the value of the object, taking into account any payment to be made by the chargee to any of the interested persons (Article 9, 3).

40. In case of default, before the sale of the charged object or the making of a court order in order to exercise the remedies set up in Article 8, the chargor (i.e., to say the debtor) or any interested person may discharge the security interest by paying in full the amount secured, subject to any lease granted by the chargee or ordered by a court according to Article 8, 1, b and Article 8, 2. If the payment is made in full by an interested person other than the debtor, this person is subrogated to the rights of the chargee (Article 9, 4).

41. If the object is sold under Article 8(1)(b) or if the object is vested in satisfaction through an agreement or through a court order pursuant to Articles 9, 1 and

2, the ownership or any other interest of the chargor is free from any other interest over which the chargee's security interest has priority under the provisions of Article 29.

42. In fact, according to Article 29, a registered interest has priority over any other interest subsequently registered and over an unregistered interest (Article 29, 1). This priority applies even if the first-mentioned interest was acquired or registered with actual knowledge of the other interest and even as regards the value given by the holder of the first-mentioned interest with such knowledge (Article 29, 2).

43. As a principle, 'priorities and other rights against third parties derived from a registration come to an end when the registration is discharged' (Sir Roy Goode, 'Official Commentary on the Convention on International Interests in Mobile Equipment', (2014), no. 4.190, p. 226). So, in the frame of sale and lease-back, if the sub-lessor's interest has been registered first, the sub-lessee is entitled to quiet possession both against the sub-lessor and the buyer as head lessor, in the application of Article 29, 4, (b) of the Convention (Sir Roy Goode, 'Official Commentary on the Convention on International Interests in Mobile Equipment', (2014), no. 4.191, p. 226).

44. In the case of the title reservation agreement as well as concerning the leasing agreement, the remedies for default shall be at least one of the following: on the one hand, there is the possibility to terminate the agreement and take possession or control of any object to which the agreement relates, with due respect to State's declarations of Article 54; on the other hand, the creditor may apply for a court order authorising or directing the remedies (Article 10). According to Sir Roy Goode, Article 10 does not apply to title reservation agreements and to some forms of lease under the laws of the United States, Canada and New Zealand, because these legal orders treat title reservation agreements and some specific forms of leases as security agreements (Sir Roy Goode, 'Official Commentary on the Convention on International Interests in Mobile Equipment', (2014), no. 4.101, p. 187).

45. The applicable law may authorise additional remedies (Article 12), for instance, remedies agreed upon by the parties, but with due respect to the mandatory rules of Article 15 of the present Convention, that is to say, Articles 8(3)–(6), 9(3) and (4), 13(2) and 14.

46. Relieves pending final determination (Article 13) may be subject to a State's declaration under Article 55, according to which the State partly or wholly derogates from Article 13 and/or Article 43. Pursuant to Article 13, a Contracting State may ensure that a creditor who adduces evidence of default by the debtor may, pending final determination of its claim and to the extent that the debtor has at any time so agreed, obtain from a court speedy relief, in order:

- to preserve the object and its value;
- to ensure the possession, control or custody of the object;
- to immobilise the object;

- in other cases than the three ones above mentioned, to manage the object and the income therefrom;
- to lease the object.

47. Other forms of interim relief are available (Article 13, 4).

48. The court is entitled to specifically protect the interested persons in its order, in the event that the creditor, in implementing any order granting such relief, fails to perform any of its obligations to the debtor under this Convention or the Protocol, or fails to establish its claim, wholly or in part, on the final determination of that claim (Article 13, 2).

49. Before making such an order, the court may require notice of the request to be given to any of the interested persons (Article 13, 3).

50. In the frame of Article 13, the remedies also have to be exercised in a commercially reasonable manner (Article 13, 4).

51. With due respect to Article 54, 2, the present remedies shall be exercised in conformity with the procedure of the law of the place where the remedy is to be exercised (Article 14).

§3. The International Registration System

52. The Cape Town Convention sets up an International Registry (*see* John Atwood, 'The Cape Town Convention: The New Dublin International Registration System in Practice', *Uniform Commercial Code Law Journal* Vol. 43(2) (2011): 637–653) for the following interests (Article 16, 1):

- international interests, prospective international interests and registrable non-consensual rights and interests (such as legal liens, statutory mortgages, preferential claims of employees for wages and of states for taxes, judicial attachments: Sir Roy Goode, 'Security Interests in Mobile Equipment: Lawmaking Lessons from the Cape Town Convention', *Adelaide Law Review* Vol. 35(1) (2014): 65; *see* John Pritchard & David Lloyd, 'Analysis of Non-consensual Rights and Interests under Article 39 of the Cape Town Convention', *Cape Town Law Journal* Vol. 2(1) (2013): 3–40);
- assignments and prospective assignments of international interests;
- acquisitions of international interests by legal or contractual subrogation under the applicable law (According to Professor Sir Roy Goode, the term 'applicable law' may refer to the right of subrogation given by Article 9, 4 of the Convention: Sir Roy Goode, 'Official Commentary on the Convention on International Interests in Mobile Equipment', (2014), no. 4.84, p. 185);
- notices of national interests; and
- subordinations of such interests.

53. It states that different international registries may be established for different categories of objects and associated rights (Article 16, 2).

54. There is an extensive conception of registration: the concept of registration may include an amendment, extension or discharge of a registration (Article 16, 3).

55. A Registry (Article 17) is led by a Supervisory Authority and a Registrar (Article 23): they enjoy specific privileges and immunities (Article 27). The liability of the Registrar is covered by a financial assurance (Article 28).

56. There are specific registration requirements (Article 18), for instance, in order to assume the required level of confidentiality: such requirements shall be specified in the Protocols.

57. Specific rules decide the validity and time of registration (Article 19): for instance, Article 19, 4, states that 'if an interest first registered as a prospective international interest becomes an international interest, that international interest shall be treated as registered from the time of registration of the prospective international interest provided that the registration was still current immediately before the international interest was constituted'.

58. Attention is paid to the consent to registration (Article 20), to the duration of registration (Article 21), to the electronic registry search certificate (Article 22), to the evidentiary value of certificates (Article 24), to the cases of discharge of registration (Article 25), to the access to the international registration facilities (Article 26).

§4. Effects of an International Interest as Against Third Parties

59. Article 29 provides for an extensive priority of the registered interest (it has priority over any other interest subsequently registered and over an unregistered interest even if it was acquired or registered with actual knowledge of the other interest and even as regards value given by the holder of the interest registered with such knowledge, pursuant to Article 29, 1 and 2. mentioned above): the buyer of an object acquires its interest in it subject to an interest registered at the time of its acquisition of that interest but free from an unregistered interest even if it has actual knowledge of such an interest (Article 29, 3); the conditional buyer or lessee acquires its interest in or right over that object subject to an interest registered prior to the registration of the international interest held by its conditional seller or lessor but free from an interest not so registered at that time even if it has actual knowledge of that interest (Article 29, 4.).

60. This priority may be varied by agreement between the holders of those interests, but an assignee of a subordinated interest is not bound by an agreement to subordinate that interest unless at the time of the assignment a subordination had been registered relating to that agreement (Article 29, 5).

61. Such priority to an interest in an object extends to proceeds (Article 29, 6).

62. Pursuant to the rule of priority, in insolvency proceedings against the debtor, an international interest is effective if, prior to the commencement of the insolvency proceedings, this interest was registered in conformity with the present Convention (Article 30, 1). But nothing in this article impairs the effectiveness of an international interest in the insolvency proceedings where that interest is effective under the applicable law (Article 30, 2) and nothing in this article affects any rule of law applicable in insolvency proceedings relating to the avoidance of a transaction as a preference or a transfer in fraud of creditors or any rule of procedure relating to the enforcement of rights to property which is under the control or supervision of the insolvency administrator (Article 30, 3).

§5. Assignment and Reassignment

63. An assignment of associated rights transfers the related international interest only if it is in writing, if it enables the associated rights to be identified under the contract from which they arise and, in the case of an assignment by way of security, if it enables the obligations secured by the assignment to be determined in accordance with the Protocol but without the need to state a sum or maximum sum secured (Article 32, 1).

64. An assignment of an international interest created or provided for by a security agreement is valid only if some or all related associated rights also are assigned (Article 32, 2).

65. Any assignment of associated rights which is not effective to transfer the related international interest is not concerned by the present Convention (Article 32, 3).

66. Except as otherwise agreed by the parties, any assignment of associated rights fulfilling the formal requirements set up in Article 32 also transfers to the assignee both the related international interest and all the interests and priorities of the assignor under this Convention (Article 31, 1).

67. In the case of a partial assignment, which is not forbidden under the present Convention, the assignor and assignee may agree as to their respective rights concerning the related international interest assigned, but not so as adversely to affect the debtor without its consent (Article 31, 2).

68. The debtor may at any time, by an agreement in writing, waive all or any of the defences and rights of set-off available to the debtor against the assignee other than defences arising from fraudulent acts on the part of the assignee (Article 31, 4). These defences and rights of set-off available to the debtor against the assignee are determined by the applicable law (Article 31, 3).

69. In the case of an assignment by way of security, the assigned associated rights retest in the assignor, to the extent that they are still subsisting when the obligations secured by the assignment have been discharged (Article 31, 5).

70. With due respect to the priority of competing assignments (Article 33, 3), when the associated rights and the related international interest have been transferred, the debtor in relation to those rights and that interest is bound by the assignment and has a duty to make payment or give other performance to the assignee, if but only if (Article 33, 1):

- the debtor has been given notice of the assignment in writing by or with the authority of the assignor; and
- the notice identifies the associated rights.

71. Under such circumstances, payment or performance is effective (Article 33, 2).

72. For the case of default by the assignor under the assignment of associated rights and the related international interest made by way of security, Article 34 foresees an application of Articles 8, 9 and 11–14 by analogy between the assignor and the assignee and that, in relation to associated rights, these articles shall apply in so far as those provisions are capable of application to intangible property (*see* Sir Roy Goode, 'The Treatment of Intangible Assets under the Cape Town Convention and Protocols', *Cape Town Journal* (2013): 41–49).

73. Where there are competing assignments of associated rights and at least one of the assignments includes the related international interest and is registered, Article 35, 1, provides for the application of Article 29 by analogy.

74. Article 30 on the priority of the registered interest in case of debtor's insolvency applies by analogy to an assignment of associated rights (Article 35, 2) and to the insolvency proceedings against the assignor (Article 37).

75. Nevertheless, the priority – pursuant to Article 35, 1 – of the assignee of associated rights and the related international interest whose assignment has been registered is limited to the following conditions (Article 36):

- the contract under which the associated rights arise shall state that they are secured by or associated with the object; and
- the associated rights shall be related to an object (Article 36, 1), to the extent that they consist of rights to payment or performance that relate to a sum advanced and utilised for the purchase of the object, a sum advanced and utilised for the purchase of another object in which the assignor held another international interest if the assignor transferred that interest to the assignee and the assignment has been registered, the price payable for the object, the rentals payable in respect of the object, or other obligations arising from a transaction referred to in any of the preceding sub-paragraphs (Article 36, 2).

76. In all other cases, the priority of the competing assignments of the associated rights shall be determined by the applicable law (Article 36, 3).

77. The acquisition of associated rights and the related international interest by legal or contractual subrogation, as far as the applicable law allows it, is not forbidden by the present Convention (Article 38, 1).

78. The priority between such interest and a competing interest may be varied by agreement in writing between the holders of the respective interests, but an assignee of a subordinated interest is not bound by an agreement to subordinate that interest unless at the time of the assignment a subordination had been registered relating to that agreement (Article 38, 2).

§6. Jurisdiction

79. As far as jurisdiction is concerned, priority is given to the courts of the Contracting State chosen by the parties to a transaction, in respect of any claim brought under this Convention, no matter whether this chosen forum has a connection with the parties or the transaction and such chosen jurisdiction shall be exclusive unless otherwise agreed between the parties (Article 42, 1). This agreement on jurisdiction shall be in writing or follow the formal requirement of the law of the chosen jurisdiction (Article 42, 2).

80. As for speedy relief pending final determination, Article 43 offers the parties a broad choice of competent courts.

81. As for the jurisdiction to make orders against the Registrar (Article 44), the principle is that the courts of the place in which the Registrar has its centre of administration have exclusive jurisdiction.

82. The present rules on jurisdiction do not apply to insolvency proceedings (Article 45).

§7. Relationship to Other Conventions

83. According to Article 45 bits of the present Cape Town Convention, this Convention shall prevail over the United Nations (UN) Convention on the Assignment of Receivables in International Trade, opened for signature in New York on 12 December 2001, as it relates to the assignment of receivables which are associated rights related to international interests in aircraft objects, railway rolling stock and space assets.

84. The relationship between this Convention and the UNIDROIT Convention on International Financial Leasing, signed in Ottawa on 28 May 1988, is to be ruled in the Protocols (Article 46).

§8. Declarations and Reservations

85. The present Convention may be subject to State's declarations and reservations, to the extent that it is admitted by its final provisions. For instance, some rights having priority without registration (Article 39) and registrable non-consensual rights or interests (Article 40) may be subject to declarations by Contracting States.

§9. Regional Economic Integration Organizations

86. This Convention is open to Regional Economic Integration Organizations (Article 48).

Chapter 2. The Protocol to the Convention on International Interests in Mobile Equipment on Matters Specific to Aircraft Equipment

§1. The General Frame

87. The Protocol to the Convention on International Interests in Mobile Equipment on Matters Specific to Aircraft Equipment (Aircraft Protocol) aims at implementing the Cape Town Convention in matters of aircraft equipment and is extended to contracts of sale of aircraft equipment, with due respect to the 'principles and objectives of the Convention on International Civil Aviation, signed in Chicago on 7 December 1944'.

88. This Protocol uses an aircraft-specific terminology (Article I). It applies to specific aircraft objects, which are not used in military, customs or police services and may be qualified as airframes, aircraft engines or helicopters and are submitted to the 'test of carrying capacity': they must be high-value units (Sir Roy Goode, 'Official Commentary on the Protocol to the Convention on International Interests in Mobile Equipment on Matters Specific to Aircraft Equipment', (2013), nos 5.3–5.5, p. 304). Professor Sir Roy Goode explains that an aircraft as such is not an object for the purposes of the Convention unless it is a helicopter, an engine installed on an airframe is a separate object which does not form part of the airframe, and an engine installed on a helicopter forms part of the helicopter, though any pre-installation rights and interests are preserved after installation (Sir Roy Goode, 'Official Commentary on the Convention on International Interests in Mobile Equipment', (2013), no. 4.27, p. 162). Furthermore, an aircraft engine does not form part of the airframe on which it is installed but is an independent object, and installed helicopter engines are neither separate objects nor aircraft objects within the definition in Article I, 2. (c) while installed on a helicopter (Sir Roy Goode, 'Official Commentary on the Protocol to the Convention on International Interests in Mobile Equipment on Matters Specific to Aircraft Equipment', (2013), no. 5.3, p. 304).

89. The Protocol is closely associated with the Cape Town Convention; hence, these two legal instruments as a whole are known as 'the Convention on International Interests in Mobile Equipment as applied to aircraft objects' (Article II).

90. Specifically, in matters of aircraft equipment, specific rules of the Convention apply to contracts of sales and prospective sales (Article III):

- Article 3 (sphere of application);
- Article 4 (where the debtor is situated);
- Article 16(1)(a) (according to which an International Registry shall be established for registrations of international interests, prospective international interests and registrable non-consensual rights and interests);

- Article 19(4) ('If an interest first registered as a prospective international interest becomes an international interest, that international interest shall be treated as registered from the time of registration of the prospective international interest provided that the registration was still current immediately before the international interest was constituted as provided by Article 7.');
- Article 20(1) (as regards registration of a contract of sale or a prospective sale: 'An international interest, a prospective international interest or an assignment or prospective assignment of an international interest may be registered, and any such registration amended or extended prior to its expiry, by either party with the consent in writing of the other');
- Article 25(2) (as regards a prospective sale: 'Where a prospective international interest or a prospective assignment of an international interest has been registered, the intending creditor or intending assignee shall, without undue delay, procure the discharge of the registration after written demand by the intending debtor or assignor which is delivered to or received at its address stated in the registration before the intending creditor or assignee has given value or incurred a commitment to give value.');
- Article 30 (effects of insolvency);
- the general provisions of Article 1 (sphere of application and general provisions);
- Article 5 (interpretation and applicable law);
- Chapters IV–VII (related to the International Registry: the international registration system, Chapter IV; Other matters relating to registration, Chapter V; Privileges and immunities of the Supervisory Authority and the Registrar, Chapter VI; Liability of the Registrar, Chapter VII);
- Article 29 (other than Article 29(3) which is replaced by Article XIV(1) and (2)), (Priority of competing interests);
- Chapter X (Rights or interests subject to declarations by Contracting States);
- Chapter XII (other than Article 43), (on Jurisdiction);
- Chapter XIII (Relationship with other Conventions);
- Chapter XIV (other than Article 60) (Final provisions).

91. A contract of sale is equivalent to an agreement according to Article 1(a) of the Convention, a sale is equivalent to an international interest, a prospective sale is equivalent to a prospective international interest, the seller replaces the debtor and the buyer replaces the creditor (Sir Roy Goode, 'Official Commentary on the Protocol to the Convention on International Interests in Mobile Equipment on Matters Specific to Aircraft Equipment', (2013), no. 5.19, p. 310).

92. In this frame, a person may have a registrable interest in an aircraft object in two different capacities, for example, if the lessee under a leasing agreement with an option to purchase grants a sub-lease, or if an aircraft object is sold for the purpose of being let under a leasing agreement: the prospective sale, the international interest as sub-lessor, the buyer's rights as such and the buyer's rights in the frame of the lease are registrable interests (Sir Roy Goode, 'Official Commentary on the Protocol to the Convention on International Interests in Mobile Equipment on Matters Specific to Aircraft Equipment', (2013), no. 5.23, p. 311).

93. With due respect to Article 3, 1. of the Cape Town Convention, according to which the 'Convention applies when, at the time of the conclusion of the agreement creating or providing for the international interest, the debtor is situated in a Contracting State', the Convention will also apply in relation to a helicopter, or to an airframe pertaining to an aircraft, registered in an aircraft register of a Contracting State which is the State of registry, and where such registration is made pursuant to an agreement for registration of the aircraft it is deemed to have been effected at the time of the agreement (Article IV, 1.).

94. Article 1(n) of the Cape Town Convention defines 'internal transaction' as a transaction related to an international interest in mobile equipment where the centre of the main interests of all parties to such transaction is situated, and the relevant object located (as specified in the Protocol: *see* Article IV of the Aircraft Protocol, Article XXIX of the Rail Protocol and Article I, 3. of the space Protocol) in the same Contracting State at the time of the conclusion of the contract, and where the interest created by the transaction has been registered in a national registry in that Contracting State which has made, while subscribing to the Protocol, a declaration under Article 50(1), according to which the Convention does not apply to a transaction which is an internal transaction in relation to that State with regard to all types of objects or some of them.

95. According to Article IV, 2. of the Protocol, as for the definition of 'internal transaction', an airframe is located in the State of registry of the aircraft of which it is a part, an aircraft engine is located in the State of registry of the aircraft on which it is installed or, if it is not installed on an aircraft, where it is physically located, and a helicopter is located in its State of registry, at the time of the conclusion of the agreement creating or providing for the interest.

96. In the frame of this Protocol, the contract of sale is a contract in writing, which relates to an aircraft object of which the seller has power to dispose and enables the aircraft object to be identified (following Article VII) in conformity with this Protocol (Article V, 1.). It transfers the interest of the seller in the aircraft object to the buyer (Article V, 2.). The registration of a contract of sale remains effective indefinitely, but the registration of a prospective sale remains effective unless discharged or until the expiry of the period specified in the registration, as the case may be (Article V, 3.). A contract of sale containing an express reservation of title is not concerned (Sir Roy Goode, 'Official Commentary on the Protocol to the Convention on International Interests in Mobile Equipment on Matters Specific to Aircraft Equipment', (2013), no. 5.30, p. 314).

97. Following Article VI, a person who enters into an agreement or a sale, and registers an international interest in, or a sale of, an aircraft object, in an agency, trust or other representative capacity is entitled to assert rights and interests under the Convention. This article is to be interpreted broadly and concerns both the disclosed and the undisclosed representation (Sir Roy Goode, 'Official Commentary on the Protocol to the Convention on International Interests in Mobile Equipment on Matters Specific to Aircraft Equipment', (2013), no. 5.33, p. 315).

98. Where a Contracting State has agreed to allow the choice of law through a declaration according to Article XXX, 1. (Article VIII, 1.), parties to an agreement, or a contract of sale, or a related guarantee contract or subordination agreement may agree on the law which is to govern their contractual rights and obligations, wholly or in part (Article VIII, 2.): the Parties may agree on a dépeçage solution, according to which different laws apply to different parts or issues of their contract (Sir Roy Goode, 'Official Commentary on the Protocol to the Convention on International Interests in Mobile Equipment on Matters Specific to Aircraft Equipment', (2013), no. 5.39, p. 317). As a principle, unless otherwise agreed, the law chosen by the parties consists of the domestic rules of law of the designated State or of the designated territorial unit (Article VIII, 3.).

§2. Default Remedies

99. In cases of Chapter III of the Cape Town Convention, in addition to the default remedies specified in this Chapter III, the creditor may, if the debtor has at any time so agreed, procure the deregistration of the aircraft and procure the export and physical transfer of the aircraft object from the territory in which it is situated (Article IX, 1.). If the chargee proposes to procure the deregistration and export of the aircraft otherwise than pursuant to a court order, it shall give reasonable prior notice in writing of the proposed deregistration and export to the debtor, to any person who, for the purpose of assuring performance of any of the obligations in favour of the creditor, gives or issues a suretyship or demand guarantee or a standby letter of credit or any other form of credit insurance, and to any other person having rights in or over the object, provided that, in this latter case, this interested person has given notice of their rights to the chargee within a reasonable time prior to the deregistration and export (Article IX, 6.).

100. According to Article IV, 3., the provisions of Article IX, 2., 3., and 4. are the only rules of the Protocol the parties are not allowed to derogate from.

101. The exercise of these remedies is subject to the prior consent in writing of the holder of any registered interest ranking in priority to that of the creditor (Article IX, 2.).

102. Article 8, 3 of the Convention shall not apply to aircraft objects, although any remedy given by the Convention in relation to an aircraft object shall be exercised in a commercially reasonable manner in the sense of Article 8, 3 (Article IX, 3.).

103. A chargee giving ten or more working days' prior written notice of a proposed sale or lease to interested persons shall be deemed to satisfy the requirement of providing 'reasonable prior notice' according to Article 8, 4 of the Convention, even though a chargee and a chargor or a guarantor may agree to a longer period of prior notice (Article IX, 4.).

104. Article IX, 5. specifies the conditions under which a Contracting State may honour a request for deregistration and export.

105. Article X of the Protocol on the modification of provisions regarding relief pending final determination applies only where a Contracting State has made a corresponding initial declaration under Article XXX, 2, and to the extent of this declaration. According to Article XXX, 2, the application so agreed may be partly.

106. As for the speedy relief of Article 13, 1 of the Cape Town Convention, 'speedy' means within such number of working days from the date of filing of the application for relief as is specified in the declaration made by the Contracting State in which the application is made, according to Articles XXX, 2 and X, 2. This rule does not affect any applicable aviation safety laws and regulations (Article X, 7).

107. As for speedy relief pending final determination of the claim of Article 13, 1 of the Cape Town Convention, Article X, 3 adds the possibility for the creditor to request from a court, if at any time the debtor and the creditor specifically agree, sale and application of proceeds therefrom.

108. The courts of a Contracting State chosen by the parties and the courts of the Contracting State on the territory of which the object is situated have jurisdiction to grant this relief with respect to this object (modification of Article 43, 2), according to Article X, 3.

109. The ownership or any other interest of the debtor passing on a sale according to Article X, 3, is free from any other interest over which the creditor's international interest has priority according to Article 29 of the Cape Town Convention (Article X, 4).

110. The creditor and the debtor or any other interested person may agree in writing to exclude the application of Article 13, 2 of the Convention, according to which, in making any order for speedy relief pending final determination, the court may impose such terms as it considers necessary to protect the interested persons in the event that the creditor, in implementing any order granting such relief, fails to perform any of its obligations to the debtor under this Convention or the Protocol, or if the creditor fails to establish its claim, wholly or in part, on the final determination of that claim (Article X, 5).

111. As to the additional remedies of Article IX, 1, they shall be made available by the registry authority and other administrative authorities in a Contracting State, no later than five working days after the creditor notifies such authorities that the relief specified in Article IX, 1, is granted, or, in the case of relief granted by a foreign court, recognised by a court of that Contracting State, and that the creditor is entitled to procure those remedies in accordance with the Convention (Article X, 6, (a)), and the applicable authorities shall expeditiously co-operate with and assist the creditor in the exercise of such remedies in conformity with the applicable aviation safety laws and regulations (Article X, 6, (b)), with due respect to any applicable aviation safety laws and regulations (Article X, 7.).

112. Especially concerning remedies on insolvency, according to Article XXX, 3, a Contracting State may, while subscribing to this Protocol, declare that it will apply the entirety of Alternative A, or the entirety of Alternative B of Article XI and, if so, shall specify the types of insolvency proceedings, if any, to which it will apply Alternative A and the types of insolvency proceedings, if any, to which it will apply Alternative B. A Contracting State making such shall specify the time period required by Article XI.

113. Where the Contracting State is the primary insolvency jurisdiction in a specific case and has made a corresponding declaration of acceptance, Article XI on remedies for insolvency will apply to the extent of such declaration (Article XI, 1).

114. Article XI provides for two alternatives in this matter.

115. Alternative A:

The first alternative is Alternative A.

In the frame of Alternative A (which is based on the US Bankruptcy Code: Sir Roy Goode, 'Security Interests in Mobile Equipment: Lawmaking Lessons from the Cape Town Convention', *Adelaide Law Review* Vol. 35(1) (2014): 67) in case of insolvency proceedings, the insolvency administrator or the debtor shall give possession of the aircraft object to the creditor no later than the earlier of the end of the waiting period and the date on which the creditor would be entitled to possession of the aircraft object if this article did not apply (Article XI, 2., Alternative A). This time limit is compulsory (Article XI, 9., Alternative A).

The 'waiting period' is specified in the declaration of the Contracting State which is the primary insolvency jurisdiction (Article XI, 3., Alternative A).

The 'insolvency administrator' is this person in its official, not in its personal, capacity (Article XI, 4., Alternative A).

Unless and until the creditor is given the opportunity to take possession of the object pursuant to Article XI, 2., Alternative A, the insolvency administrator or the debtor shall preserve the aircraft object and maintain it and its value in accordance with the agreement, and the creditor shall be entitled to apply for any other forms of interim relief available under the applicable law (Article XI, 5., Alternative A).

The duty of the insolvency administrator or of the debtor to preserve the aircraft object and maintain it and its value in accordance with the agreement shall not preclude the use of the aircraft object under arrangements designed to preserve the aircraft object and maintain it and its value (Article XI, 6., Alternative A).

The insolvency administrator or the debtor, as applicable, may retain possession of the aircraft object where, by the time the creditor is to be given possession of the aircraft object (Article XI, 7. Alternative A), it has cured all defaults other than a default constituted by the opening of insolvency proceedings and has agreed to perform all future obligations under the agreement, but there will be no second waiting period in respect of a default in the performance of such future obligations (Article XI, 7., Alternative A).

As regards to the case of modification of default remedies provisions according to Article IX, 1, the remedies shall be made available by the registry authority and the administrative authorities in a Contracting State, as applicable, no later than five working days after the date on which the creditor notifies such authorities that it is entitled to procure those remedies in accordance with the Convention, and the applicable authorities shall expeditiously co-operate with and assist the creditor in the exercise of such remedies in conformity with the applicable aviation safety laws and regulations (Article XI, 8., Alternative A).

Any modification of the debtor's obligations under the agreement requires the consent of the creditor (Article XI, 10., Alternative A).

The authority of an insolvency administrator, under the applicable law, to terminate the agreement is not affected by the present provisions (Article XI, 11., Alternative A).

Only non-consensual rights or interests of a category covered by a State's declaration pursuant to Article 39, 1, shall have priority in insolvency proceedings over registered interests (Article XI, 12., Alternative A).

Article IX of this Protocol on the modification of default remedies provisions applies together with the present rules of Alternative A (Article XI, 13., Alternative A).

116. Alternative B:

The second Alternative is Alternative B.

In the frame of Alternative B, in case of insolvency proceedings, the insolvency administrator or the debtor, upon the request of the creditor, shall give notice to the creditor within the time specified in the declaration of the Contracting State pursuant to Article XXX, 3., whether it will cure all defaults other than a default constituted by the opening of insolvency proceedings and agree to perform all future obligations, under the agreement and related transaction documents or give the creditor the opportunity to take possession of the aircraft object, in accordance with the applicable law (Article XI, 2., Alternative B). This applicable law may permit the court to require the taking of any additional step or the provision of any additional guarantee (Article XI, 3., Alternative B).

If the insolvency administrator or the debtor does not give notice in conformity with Article XI, 2., Alternative B, or when the insolvency administrator or the debtor has declared that it will give the creditor the opportunity to take possession of the aircraft object but fails to do so, the court may permit the creditor to take possession of the aircraft object upon such terms as the court may order and may require the taking of any additional step or the provision of any additional guarantee (Article XI, 5., Alternative B). The creditor has the duty to provide evidence of its claims and proof that its international interest has been registered (Article XI, 4., Alternative B). The aircraft object shall not be sold pending a decision by a court regarding the claim and the international interest (Article XI, 6., Alternative B).

Where a Contracting State has made a corresponding declaration pursuant to Article XXX, 1., the courts of a Contracting State in which an aircraft object is situated shall, in accordance with the law of this Contracting State, co-operate to the maximum extent possible with foreign courts and foreign insolvency administrators in carrying out the provisions of Article XI (Article XII).

Article XIII applies where a Contracting State has made a corresponding declaration pursuant to Article XXX, 1.

The debtor may issue an irrevocable deregistration and export request authorisation substantially in the form specified by the annex of this Protocol and submit such authorisation for recordation to the registry authority: in this case, the authorisation shall be so recorded (Article XIII, 2.).

The 'authorised party' (Article XIII, 3.), that is to say, the person in whose favour the authorisation has been issued, or its certified designee, shall be the sole person entitled to exercise the remedies specified in Article IX, 1., and only in accordance with the authorisation and applicable aviation safety laws and regulations. This authorisation may be revoked by the debtor only with the consent in writing of the authorised party. The authorised party is entitled to require the registry authority to remove an authorisation from the registry.

The registry authority and other administrative authorities in Contracting States have to expeditiously co-operate with and assist the authorised party in the exercise of the remedies specified in Article IX (Article XIII, 4.).

§3. Modification of Priority Provisions

117. Specifically, in the case of aircraft equipment, a buyer of an aircraft object under a registered sale acquires its interest in that object free from an interest subsequently registered and from an unregistered interest, even if the buyer has actual knowledge of the unregistered interest (Article XIV, 1.) and the buyer of an aircraft object acquires its interest in that object subject to an interest registered at the time of its acquisition (Article XIV, 2.). Article XIV, 2. is to be interpreted, according to Professor Sir Roy Goode, as follows: 'the buyer of an aircraft object under a registered sale acquires its interest in the object subject to an interest previously registered' (Sir Roy Goode, 'Official Commentary on the Protocol to the Convention on International Interests in Mobile Equipment on Matters Specific to Aircraft Equipment', (2013), no. 5.72, p. 334).

118. Ownership of or another right or interest in an aircraft engine shall not be affected by its installation on or removal from an aircraft (Article XIV, 3.).

119. Article 29, 7 of the Cape Town Convention, according to which this Convention does not affect the rights of a person in an item, other than an object, held prior to its installation on an object if under the applicable law those rights continue to exist after the installation and do not prevent the creation of rights in an item, other than an object, which has previously been installed on an object where under the applicable law those rights are created, applies accordingly to an item, other than an object, installed on an airframe, aircraft engine or helicopter (Article XIV, 4.).

§4. Modification of Assignment Provisions

120. Article XV adds a requirement to the debtor's duty to make payment or give other performance to the assignee under Article 33, 1: the debtor shall have consented in writing, whether or not the consent is given in advance of the assignment or identifies the assignee.

§5. Debtor's Protection

121. Article XVI cares for the debtor's protection. In the absence of a default pursuant to Article 11 of the Convention, the debtor shall be entitled to the quiet possession and use of the object in accordance with the agreement, as against its creditor and the holder of any interest from which the debtor takes free, pursuant to Article 29, 4 (conditional buyer or lessee) of the Convention, or, in the capacity of buyer, pursuant to Article XIV, 1. of this Protocol – the buyer of the aircraft object under a registered sale acquires its interest in that object free from an interest subsequently registered and from an unregistered interest, even if the buyer has actual knowledge of the unregistered interest -, unless and to the extent that the debtor has otherwise agreed, and as against the holder of any interest to which the debtor's right or interest is subject pursuant to Article 29, 4, (conditional sale or lease) of the Convention or, in the capacity of buyer, Article XIV, 2. – the buyer of the aircraft object acquires its interest in that object subject to an interest registered at the time of its acquisition – of this Protocol, but only to the extent, if any, that such holder has agreed (Article XVI, 1.).

122. The creditor remains liable for any breach of the agreement under the applicable law in so far as that agreement relates to the aircraft object (Article XVI, 2.).

§6. Registration

123. Chapter III (Articles XVII–XX) contains registry provisions relating to international interests in aircraft objects.

§7. Jurisdiction

124. As for jurisdiction, Article XXI of the Protocol states that a court of a Contracting State also has jurisdiction where the object is a helicopter, or an airframe pertaining to an aircraft, for which that State is the State of registry.

125. A waiver of sovereign immunity from jurisdiction of the courts specified in Article 42 or Article 43 of the Convention or relating to enforcement of rights and interests relating to an aircraft object under the Convention, which must be in writing and contain a description of the aircraft object, shall be binding and, if the other conditions to such jurisdiction or enforcement have been satisfied, shall be effective to confer jurisdiction and permit enforcement, as the case may be (Article XXII).

§8. Relationship with Other Conventions

126. The present Convention shall, for a Contracting State that is a party to the Convention on the International Recognition of Rights in Aircraft, signed in Geneva on 19 June 1948, supersede this latter Convention, but only as it relates to aircraft, as defined in this Protocol, and to aircraft objects, and not as for the rights or interests not covered or affected by the present Convention (Article XXIII). These Conventions may be considered complementary (Sir Roy Goode, 'Official Commentary on the Protocol to the Convention on International Interests in Mobile Equipment on Matters Specific to Aircraft Equipment', (2013), no. 5.106, p. 347) in the relations between Contracting States to the Cape Town Convention (Sir Roy Goode, 'Official Commentary on the Protocol to the Convention on International Interests in Mobile Equipment on Matters Specific to Aircraft Equipment', (2013), no. 5.108, p. 348).

127. The present Convention shall, for a Contracting State that is a Party to the Convention for the Unification of Certain Rules Relating to the Precautionary Attachment of Aircraft, signed in Rome on 29 May 1933, supersede that Convention in its entirety between two Contracting States (Sir Roy Goode, 'Official Commentary on the Protocol to the Convention on International Interests in Mobile Equipment on Matters Specific to Aircraft Equipment', (2013), no. 5.110, p. 349) as it relates to aircraft, as defined in this Protocol (Article XXIV, 1.), but this rule is not compulsory: a Contracting State Party to the above Rome Convention may declare, at the time of ratification, acceptance, approval of, or accession to this Protocol, that it will not apply the present rule (Article XXIV).

128. The present Convention shall supersede the UNIDROIT Convention on International Financial Leasing, signed in Ottawa on 28 May 1988 in its entirety between two Contracting States (Sir Roy Goode, 'Official Commentary on the Protocol to the Convention on International Interests in Mobile Equipment on Matters Specific to Aircraft Equipment', (2013), no. 5.111, p. 349), as it relates to aircraft objects (Article XXV).

Chapter 3. The Luxembourg Protocol to the Convention on International Interests in Mobile Equipment on Matters Specific to Railway Rolling Stock

§1. The General Frame

129. The Luxembourg Protocol to the Convention on International Interests in Mobile Equipment on Matters Specific to Railway Rolling Stock (Rail Protocol) implements the Cape Town Convention in this domain.

130. It uses a railway-specific terminology (Article I). In particular, the concepts of guarantee contract (Sir Roy Goode, 'Official Commentary on the Protocol to the Convention on International Interests in Mobile Equipment on Matters Specific to Railway Rolling Stock', (2014), no. 5.3, p. 395) and railway rolling stock (Sir Roy Goode, 'Official Commentary on the Protocol to the Convention on International Interests in Mobile Equipment on Matters Specific to Railway Rolling Stock', (2014), no. 5.6, p. 397) are understood in a broad sense. Nevertheless, vehicles which do not move on a fixed track are not qualified as railway rolling stock.

131. The Cape Town Convention and the present Protocol are associated and called Convention on International Interests in Mobile Equipment as applied to railway rolling stock (Article II).

132. Article VII, 3. and 4. of the present Protocol are the only prescriptions the parties are not allowed to derogate from (Article III).

§2. Representative Capacities

133. As for representative capacities, Article IV of these Protocols provides that a person may, in relation to railway rolling stock, enter into an agreement, effect a registration, including, where appropriate, an amendment, extension or discharge of a registration (Article 16, 3 of the Cape Town Convention), and assert rights and interests under the Convention, in an agency, trust or representative capacity. In order to facilitate the coordination of fractional ownership as to complex railway rolling stock financing systems, the registration made by the representatives on behalf of beneficiaries or principals does not permit the beneficiaries or principals to register the same interest again (Sir Roy Goode, 'Official Commentary on the Protocol to the Convention on International Interests in Mobile Equipment on Matters Specific to Railway Rolling Stock', (2014), no. 5.10, p. 399).

§3. Identification of Railway Rolling Stock in the Agreement

134. For the purposes of Article 7, (c), of the Cape Town Convention, on the conditions of the constitution of an international interest, and Article XVIII, 2. of this Protocol, on waivers of sovereign immunity, a description of railway rolling stock is sufficient to identify the railway rolling stock if it contains (Article V, 1.):

- a description of the railway rolling stock by item;
- a description of the railway rolling stock by type;
- a statement that the agreement covers all present and future railway rolling stock; or
- a statement that the agreement covers all present and future railway rolling stock except for specified items or types.

135. In the frame of Article 7 of the Cape Town Convention, an interest in future railway rolling stock identified pursuant to Article V, 1. shall be constituted as an international interest as soon as the chargor, conditional seller or lessor acquires the power to dispose of the railway rolling stock, without the need for any new act of transfer (Article V, 2.).

136. A unique identification of an object is considered as not necessary for the constitution of an international interest (Sir Roy Goode, 'Official Commentary on the Protocol to the Convention on International Interests in Mobile Equipment on Matters Specific to Space Assets', (2014), no. 5.31, p. 433), not only for railway rolling stock but also for space assets. This is a matter of the Model Rules on Permanent Identification of Railway Rolling Stock, adopted on 24 February 2023 by the Inland Transport Committee of the United Nations Economic Commission for Europe, which create a voluntary framework for permanently attaching a Unique Rail Vehicle Identification System identifier to railway rolling stock.

§4. Choice of Law

137. According to Article XXVII, 1., a Contracting State may, while subscribing to the present Protocol, declare that it will apply either or both of Articles VI on choice of law and X on insolvency assistance.

138. Where Article VI is applicable through such declaration (Article VI, 1.), the parties to an agreement or a related guarantee contract or subordination agreement may agree on the law which is to govern their contractual rights and obligations, wholly or in part (Article VI, 2.). Primarily, the choice of law refers to a national legal system (Sir Roy Goode, 'Official Commentary on the Protocol to the Convention on International Interests in Mobile Equipment on Matters Specific to Railway Rolling Stock', (2014), no. 5.13, p. 402) and not to rules of conflicts of laws, the *dépeçage* is also admitted (Sir Roy Goode, 'Official Commentary on the Protocol to the Convention on International Interests in Mobile Equipment on Matters Specific to Railway Rolling Stock', (2014), no. 5.15, p. 402) and the mandatory rules of the *lex fori* keeps applying (Sir Roy Goode, 'Official Commentary on the Protocol to the Convention on International Interests in Mobile Equipment on Matters Specific to Railway Rolling Stock', (2014), no. 5.12, p. 402).

139. Unless otherwise agreed, the law chosen by the parties is the domestic law of the designated State or, where that State comprises several territorial units, the domestic law of the designated territorial unit (Article VI, 3.).

§5. Remedies

140. Article VII on modification of default remedies provisions slightly differs from the corresponding Article IX in the Protocol dedicated to the aircraft.

141. According to Article VII, 1., in addition to the remedies specified in Chapter III of the Convention, the creditor may, to the extent that the debtor has at any time so agreed and in the circumstances specified in that Chapter, procure the export and physical transfer of railway rolling stock from the territory in which it is situated. With due respect to any applicable safety laws and regulations, a Contracting State shall ensure that the relevant administrative authorities expeditiously co-operate with and assist the creditor to the extent necessary for the exercise of these remedies (Article VII, 5.). The creditor shall not exercise those remedies without the prior consent in writing of the holder of any registered interest ranking in priority to that of the creditor (Article VII, 2.). It is not provided that the creditor may procure the deregistration like in Article IX, 1. (a) of the Protocol dedicated to the aircraft. The criteria of exercise of remedies in a commercially reasonable manner also apply for railway rolling stock (Article VII, 3.), in the same way as provided for the aircraft equipment in Article IX, 3. of the corresponding Protocol related to the aircraft. The period of the prior notice in writing of the proposed sale or lease to the interested persons is organised in the same way as for the aircraft, but it is extended to 'fourteen or more calendar days' in the frame of railway rolling stock, in comparison with the Protocol for aircraft equipment (Article VII., 4).

142. Similar to Article IX, 6. of the Protocol for the aircraft, a chargee proposing to procure the export of railway rolling stock, according to Article VII, 1., otherwise than pursuant to a court order, shall give reasonable prior notice in writing of the proposed export to the debtor, to any person who, for the purpose of assuring performance of any of the obligations in favour of the creditor, gives or issues a suretyship or demand guarantee or a standby letter of credit or any other form of credit insurance and to any other person having rights in or over the object; in this latter case, the interested person shall have given notice of their rights to the chargee within a reasonable time prior to the export (Article VII, 6.).

143. Article VIII of the Rail Protocol, on the modification of provisions regarding relief pending final determination, is similar to Article X of the aircraft Protocol: as a difference for railway rolling stock, the concept of working days is replaced by the term of calendar days and in Article VII, 6. of the Rail Protocol, the five working days are replaced by seven calendar days.

144. Article IX on remedies on insolvency applies upon a declaration of the Contracting State that is the primary insolvency jurisdiction, according to Article XXVII (Article IX, 1.).

145. According to Article XXVII, a Contracting State may, while subscribing to this Protocol, declare that it will apply the entirety of one of Alternatives A, B and C of Article IX and, if it so declares, it shall specify the type of insolvency proceeding, if any, to which it will apply such Alternative; the Contracting State shall specify the time-period required by Article IX under paragraph 4 of Alternative A, paragraph 3 of Alternative B or paragraphs 5 and 15 of Alternative C, as applicable (Article XXVII, 3.).

146. The courts of Contracting States shall apply Article IX in conformity with the declaration made by the Contracting State which is the primary insolvency jurisdiction (Article XXVII, 4.).

147. In the frame of this legal system, the 'insolvency administrator' is that person in its official, not in its personal, capacity (Article IX, 2.).

148. There are three alternatives.

149. The first one, Alternative A, is the same as for the aircraft, except that it is not provided for railway rolling stock that the remedies shall be made available by the registry authority.

150. The second alternative, Alternative B, is the same as Alternative B in the aircraft Protocol.

151. Alternative C:

The third alternative is Alternative C.

In the frame of Alternative C, in case of insolvency proceedings, the insolvency administrator or the debtor shall, within the cure period – as the period, commencing with the date of the insolvency-related event, specified in a declaration of the Contracting State which is the primary insolvency jurisdiction (Article IX, 15., Alternative C) – cure all defaults other than a default constituted by the opening of insolvency proceedings and agree to perform all future obligations, under the agreement and related transaction documents, or give the creditor the opportunity to take possession of the railway rolling stock in accordance with the applicable law (Article IX, 3., Alternative C).

The debtor or the insolvency administrator may be granted a suspension period according to Article IX, 4. of Alternative C, as follows. Before the end of the cure period, the insolvency administrator or the debtor may apply to the court for an order suspending its obligation to give the creditor the opportunity to take possession of the railway rolling stock in accordance with the applicable law, for a period commencing from the end of the cure period and ending no later than the expiration of the agreement or any renewal thereof, and on such terms as the court considers just. Thus, all sums accruing to the creditor during the suspension period shall be paid from the insolvency estate or by the debtor as they become due, and the insolvency administrator or the debtor shall perform all other obligations arising during the suspension period.

If a suspension period is required by the debtor or by the insolvency administrator, the creditor shall not take possession of the railway rolling stock pending an order of the court. But if the application is not granted within such number of calendar days from the date of filing of the application for relief as is specified in a declaration made by the Contracting State in which the application is made, the application will be deemed withdrawn unless the creditor and the insolvency administrator or the debtor, as applicable, otherwise agree (Article IX, 5., Alternative C).

Unless and until the creditor is given the opportunity to take possession under paragraph 3, the insolvency administrator or the debtor, as applicable, shall preserve the railway rolling stock and maintain it and its value in accordance with the agreement, for instance, by the use of the railway rolling stock under arrangements designed to preserve and maintain it and its value (Article IX, 7., Alternative C), and the creditor shall be entitled to apply for any other forms of interim relief available under the applicable law (Article IX, 6., Alternative C).

Where during the cure period or any suspension period, the insolvency administrator or the debtor, as applicable, cures all defaults other than a default constituted by the opening of insolvency proceedings and agrees to perform all future obligations under the agreement and related transaction documents, the insolvency administrator or debtor may retain possession of the railway rolling stock and any order made by the court as to the suspension period shall cease to have effect, but there will be no second cure period in case of a default in the performance of such future obligations (Article IX, 8., Alternative C).

As to the remedies in Article VII, 1., on the modification of default remedies provisions, they shall be made available by the administrative authorities in a Contracting State no later than seven calendar days after the date on which the creditor notifies such authorities that it is entitled to procure those remedies in accordance with the Convention, and the applicable authorities shall expeditiously co-operate with and assist the creditor in the exercise of such remedies in conformity with the applicable safety laws and regulations (Article IX, 9., Alternative C).

With due respect to the rules related to the suspension period (Article IX, 4., 5. and 8., Alternative C), no exercise of remedies permitted by the Convention may be prevented or delayed after the cure period (Article IX, 10., Alternative C), and no obligations of the debtor under the agreement and related transactions may be modified in insolvency proceedings without the consent of the creditor (Article IX, 11., Alternative C).

The authority of the insolvency administrator, under the applicable law, to terminate the agreement, is not affected (Article IX, 12., Alternative C).

No rights or interests, except for non-consensual rights or interests of a category covered by a declaration pursuant to Article 39, 1 of the Convention, shall have priority in insolvency proceedings over registered interests (Article IX, 13., Alternative C).

The Convention as modified by Articles VII, on the modification of default remedies provisions, and XXV, on public service railway rolling stock, of this Protocol, shall apply to the exercise of any remedies under the present Article (Article IX, 14., Alternative C).

152. The courts of a Contracting State in which railway rolling stock is situated shall, in accordance with the law of the Contracting State, co-operate to the maximum extent possible with foreign courts and foreign insolvency administrators in carrying out the provisions of Article IX on the three alternatives for remedies on insolvency, if the Contracting State has made a corresponding declaration (Article X).

153. According to Article XXV, 1., as an exception for public service railway rolling stock (*see* Howard Rosen, 'Public Service and the Cape Town Convention', *Cape Town Law Journal* Vol. 2(1) (2013): 131–147), a Contracting State may, at any time, declare that it will continue to apply, to the extent specified in its declaration, rules of its law in force at that time which preclude, suspend or govern the exercise within its territory of any of the remedies specified in Chapter III of the Convention and Articles VII to IX of this Protocol in relation to railway rolling stock habitually used for the purpose of providing a service of public importance as specified in that declaration notified to the Depositary.

154. Article XXV specifies that any person, including a governmental or other public authority, that, under rules of law of a Contracting State making a declaration under Article XXV, 1., exercises a power to take or procure possession, use or control of any public service railway rolling stock, shall preserve and maintain such railway rolling stock from the time of exercise of such power until possession, use or control is restored to the creditor (Article XXV, 2.). During this period of time, the person concerned shall also make or procure payment to the creditor of an amount equal to the greater of such amount as that person shall be required to pay under the rules of law of the Contracting State making the declaration and the market lease rental in respect of such railway rolling stock (Article XXV, 3.). The first such payment shall be made within ten calendar days of the date on which such power is exercised, and subsequent payments shall be made on the first day of each successive month thereafter. In the event that in any month the amount payable exceeds the amount due to the creditor from the debtor, the surplus shall be paid to any other creditors to the extent of their claims in the order of their priority and thereafter to the debtor.

155. If the rules of law of a Contracting State do not provide for the obligations specified in Article XXV, 2. and 3., this State may, to the extent specified in a separate declaration notified to the Depositary, declare that it will not apply (Article

XXV, 4.) those paragraphs with regard to railway rolling stock specified in that declaration. Nevertheless, any person may agree with the creditor to perform such obligations or affect the enforceability of any agreement so concluded.

156. Any initial or subsequent declaration made under this article by a Contracting State shall not adversely affect the rights and interests of creditors arising under an agreement entered into prior to the date on which that declaration is received by the Depositary (Article XXV, 5.).

157. A Contracting State making a declaration under this article shall take into consideration the protection of the interests of creditors and the effect of the declaration on the availability of credit (Article XXV, 6.).

§6. Debtor's Protection

158. Article XI on debtor's protection in the Rail Protocol contains the same rules as Article XVI of the aircraft Protocol, except that in the Rail Protocol, the contract of sale is not included.

§7. Registration

159. Chapter III (Articles XII to XVII) of the present Protocol is dedicated to international interests in railway rolling stock cares for special registry provisions.

§8. Jurisdiction

160. Article XVIII of the Rail Protocol on Waivers of sovereign immunity has the same meaning as the provisions of Article XXII of the Aircraft Protocol.

§9. Relationship with Other Conventions

161. The Convention shall, to the extent of any inconsistency, prevail over the UNIDROIT Convention on International Financial Leasing, signed in Ottawa on 28 May 1988 (Article XIX). So between two Contracting States which are also Parties to the Leasing Convention, the Cape Town Convention will supersede the Convention on International Financial Leasing in its entirety (Sir Roy Goode, 'Official Commentary on the Protocol to the Convention on International Interests in Mobile Equipment on Matters Specific to Railway Rolling Stock', (2014), no. 5.72, p. 439).

162. The Convention shall, to the extent of any inconsistency, prevail over the Convention concerning International Carriage by Rail (COTIF) of 9 May 1980 in the version of the Protocol of Modification of 3 June 1999 (COTIF 1999) (Article XX).

Chapter 4. The Protocol to the Convention on International Interests in Mobile Equipment on Matters Specific to Space Assets

§1. The General Frame

163. The Protocol to the Convention on International Interests in Mobile Equipment on Matters Specific to Space Assets (Space Protocol) aims at implementing the Cape Town Convention concerning space assets – as assets primarily designed for use in the outer space (Sir Roy Goode, 'Official Commentary on It Is Also Based on Protocol to the Convention on International Interests in Mobile Equipment on Matters Specific to Space Assets', (2014), no. 5.12, p. 422; *see* Martin J. Stanford, 'The Availability of a New Form of Financing Space Activities: The Extension of the Cape Town Convention to Space Assets', *Cape Town Convention* Vol. 1 (2013): 109–123). It is also based on 'the principles of space law', in particular, those principles laid down in international space treaties of the UN as well as in the instruments of the International Telecommunication Union, and recalls the pre-eminence of State Party rights and obligations under the international space treaties of the UN by which the States Parties concerned are bound. It is a matter of creating a uniform and predictable regimen governing interests in space assets and in related rights and facilitating asset-based financing of these space assets.

164. The present Protocol associated with the Cape Town Convention is known as 'the Convention on International Interests in Mobile Equipment as applied to space assets' (Article II, 2.).

165. Basically, it shall apply in relation to space assets, rights assignments and rights reassignments (Article II, 1.).

166. The Protocol will apply to aircraft objects primarily designed for use in space (Article II, 3.) but not to aircraft objects designed to be temporarily in space (Article II, 4.).

167. The ownership of a space asset, as well as other rights or interests in space assets, shall not be affected by the docking of the space asset with another space asset in space, by the installation of the space asset on or the removal of the space asset from another space asset, or by the return of the space asset from space (Article III).

168. The application of the Convention to sales related to space assets is organised in the same way as for sales of aircraft equipment, with due reference to the transitional provisions foreseen in Article XL (Article IV, 1.). In addition, for space assets, the rules related to rights assignments also apply to a transfer to the buyer of a space asset of rights to payment or other performance due or to become due to the seller by any person, with respect to the space asset, as if references to the debtor and the creditor were references to the seller and the buyer respectively (Article IV, 2.).

169. No legal or contractual right of an insurer to salvage – that is to say, a legal or contractual right or interest in, relating to or derived from a space asset that vests in the insurer upon the payment of a loss relating to the space asset – recognised by the applicable law is affected by the present rules (Article IV, 3.).

170. The formalities, effects and registration of contracts of sale (Article V) are the same as in Article V of the Protocol dedicated to aircraft equipment.

171. Similar to the frame of the Protocols dedicated to aircraft and railway equipment, a person may, as for space assets, enter into an agreement or a contract of sale, effect a registration as defined by Article 16, 3 of the Convention and assert rights and interests under the Convention in an agency, trust or representative capacity (Article VI).

172. Article VII on the identification of space assets has the same content as Article V of the Protocol for railway rolling stock.

173. Article VIII on the choice of law has the same content as Article VIII for the aircraft Protocol and Article VI for the Rail Protocol, with due reference to the contract of sale as for aircraft and space assets.

174. Especially for space assets (Article IX), as to the formal requirements for rights assignment, the transfer of debtor's rights is constituted as a rights assignment where it is in writing and enables the debtor's rights the subject of the rights assignment to be identified, the space asset to which those rights relate to be identified and in the case of a rights assignment by way of security, the obligations secured by the agreement to be determined, but without the need to state a sum or maximum sum secured.

175. Such rights assignment transfers to the creditor the debtor's rights the subject of the rights assignment to the extent permitted by the applicable law (Article X, 1.). The applicable law shall determine the defences and rights of set-off available to the obligor against the creditor (Article X, 2.), and the obligor may at any time by agreement in writing waive all or any of the defences and such rights of set-off other than defences arising from fraudulent acts on the part of the creditor (Article X, 3.).

176. A provision in a rights assignment by which future debtor's rights are assigned operates to confer on the creditor an interest in the assigned rights when they come into existence, without the need for any new act of transfer (Article XI). This article is inspired by Article 5 (b) of the Convention on International Factoring, according to which 'as between the parties to the factoring contract, a provision in the factoring contract by which future receivables are assigned operates to transfer the receivables to the factor when they come into existence without the need for any new act of transfer' (Sir Roy Goode, 'Official Commentary on the Protocol to the Convention on International Interests in Mobile Equipment on Matters Specific to Space Assets', (2014), no. 5.48, p. 439).

177. Article XII of the Protocol related to space assets offers the possibility of recording rights assignment or acquisition by subrogation as part of registration of international interest. In this frame, the following Articles 18, 19, 20(1)–(4), 25(1), (2) and (4) and 30 of the Cape Town Convention apply by analogy:

- Article 18 on registration requirements.
- Article 19 on validity and time of registration.
- Article 20, 1–4. on consent to registration.
- Article 25, 1, 2. and 4. on discharge of registration.
- Article 30 on the effects of insolvency.

178. A recorded rights assignment has priority over any other transfer of debtor's except a rights assignment previously recorded, whereas, following Article 29, 6 of the Convention, the priority in an object extends to proceeds (Article XIII, 1.).

179. Where a rights assignment is recorded in the registration of a prospective international interest, it shall be treated as unrecorded unless and until the prospective international interest becomes an international interest, in which event the rights assignment has priority from the time it was recorded provided that the registration was still current immediately before the international interest was constituted (Article XIII, 2.).

180. To the extent that the debtor's rights have been assigned to the creditor under a rights assignment, the obligor is bound by the rights assignment and has a duty to make payment or give other performance to the creditor, provided that the obligor has been given notice of the rights assignment in writing by or with the authority of the debtor and the notice identifies the debtor's rights (Article XIV).

181. Articles IX to XIV of the present space asset Protocol on rights assignment applies to rights reassignment by analogy (Article XV).

182. The provisions of Article XVII, 1. and 2. are the only ones the parties are not allowed to derogate from (Article XVI).

§2. Remedies

183. Article XVII, 1. on modification of default remedies provisions as regards space assets provides for the same rules as Article IX, 3. of the aircraft Protocol and Article VII, 3. of the Rail Protocol.

184. Article XVII, 2. has the same content as Article VII, 4. for railway assets in the related Protocol.

185. Specifically for space assets, according to Article XVII, 3., unless otherwise agreed, a creditor may not enforce an international interest in a space asset that is physically linked with another space asset so as to impair or interfere with the operation of the other space asset if an international interest or sale has been registered with respect to the other space asset prior to the registration of the international interest being enforced. A sale or an interest equivalent to an international interest made or arising before the effective date of the Convention, which is registered within three years from that date, is deemed to be an international interest or a sale registered at the time of the constitution of the international interest or the sale, as the case may be.

186. In case of default by the debtor under a rights assignment or reassignment by way of security, following Articles of the Cape Town Convention apply by analogy (Article XVIII):

- Article 8 on remedies for charge.
- Article 9 on vesting of object in satisfaction and redemption.
- Articles 11–14 on meaning of default (Article 11), additional remedies (Article 12), relief pending final determination (Article 13) and Procedural requirements (Article 14).

187. Technically, subject to Article XXVI on the preservation of powers of Contracting States, the parties to an agreement may specifically agree for the placement of command codes and related data and materials with another person in order to afford the creditor an opportunity to take possession of, establish control over or operate the space asset (Article XIX).

188. Pursuant to Article XXVI, the present Protocol does neither:

- affect the exercise by a Contracting State of its authority to issue licences, approvals, permits or authorisations for the launch or operation of space assets or the provision of any service through the use or with the support of space assets; nor
- render transferable or assignable any licences, approvals, permits or authorisations which, in accordance with the laws and regulations of the granting Contracting State or the contractual or administrative provisions under which they are granted, may not be transferred or assigned; nor
- limit the right of a Contracting State to authorise the use of orbital positions and frequencies in relation to space assets; nor
- affect the ability of a Contracting State in accordance with its laws and regulations to prohibit, restrict or attach conditions to the placement of command codes and related data and materials (pursuant to Article XIX of this Protocol); nor
- oblige a Contracting State to recognise or enforce an international interest in a space asset when the recognition or enforcement of such interest would conflict

with its laws or regulations concerning the export of controlled goods, technology, data and services or the national security.

189. Article XX on the modification of provisions regarding relief pending final determination recalls the rules provided for railway rolling stock in Article VIII of the related Protocol.

190. As for remedies on insolvency, there are two alternatives: Alternative A and Alternative B.

191. Alternative A:

According to Article XXI, Alternative A on the remedies on insolvency is organised in the same way as in the Protocols for aircraft and railway, except that, according to its third paragraph, in case of insolvency proceedings, the insolvency administrator or the debtor shall, subject to paragraph 8 (on the possibility for the debtor or insolvency administrator to cure the defaults and retain possession and control of the space assets and debtor's rights covered by the rights assignment) and to Article XXVI, 2. of this Protocol (on the preservation of powers of Contracting States), give possession of or control over the debtor's rights covered by a rights assignment to the creditor, no later than the earlier of the end of the waiting period and the date on which the creditor would be entitled to possession of or control over the debtor's rights covered by the rights assignment, and without reference to the modification of default remedies provisions.

192. Alternative B:

Alternative B is the same as this of the Aircraft and Rail Protocols.

193. The rules on insolvency assistance (Article XXII), which apply through a State's declaration, are extended: according to Article XXII, 1., the courts of a Contracting State in the territory of which the space asset is situated, from the territory of which the space asset may be controlled, in the territory of which the debtor is located, in the territory of which the space asset is registered, which has issued a licence in respect of the space asset, or otherwise having a close connection with the space asset, shall, in accordance with the law of the Contracting State, co-operate to the maximum extent possible with foreign courts and foreign insolvency administrators in carrying out the provisions of Article XXI of this Protocol (the two alternatives for remedies on insolvency).

194. Especially for space assets, Article XXVII limits the possibility of insolvency remedies as to public services (*see* Howard Rosen, 'Public Service and the Cape Town Convention', *Cape Town Law Journal* Vol. 2(1) 131–147), in particular through the concept of 'public service notice' registered by the public service provider of the Contracting State with the agreement of the parties and the Contracting State, where the debtor, or the entity controlled by the debtor and the public services provider, enter into a contract for space assets public services in the Contracting State.

195. Article XXIII on modification of priority provisions recalls Article XIV, 1. and 2. of the Protocol dedicated to the aircraft.

§3. Modification of Assignment Provisions

196. Article XXIV on modification of assignment provisions recalls Article XV of the Aircraft Protocol.

§4. Debtor's Protection

197. Article XXV on the debtor's protection has the same content as Article XVI of the Aircraft Protocol.

§5. Registration

198. Chapter III provides for registry provisions related to international interests in space assets.

§6. Jurisdiction

199. As for jurisdiction, the rules on waiver of sovereign immunity (Article XXXIII) are the same as for the Aircraft Protocol (Article XXII) and for the Rail Protocol (Article XVIII).

§7. Relationship with Other International Conventions

200. The Convention as applied to space assets shall completely (Sir Roy Goode, 'Official Commentary on the Protocol to the Convention on International Interests in Mobile Equipment on Matters Specific to Space Assets', (2014), no. 5.125, p. 483) supersede the UNIDROIT Convention on International Financial Leasing in respect of the subject matter of this Protocol, as between States Parties to both Conventions (Article XXXIV).

201. The present Convention, as applied to space assets, shall not affect State Party rights and obligations under the existing UN outer space treaties or instruments of the International Telecommunication Union (Article XXXV).

202. The UN outer space treaties are the following:

- the Outer Space Treaty (Treaty on Principles Governing the Activities of States in the Exploration and Use of Outer Space, Including the Moon and Other Celestial Bodies);
- the Rescue and Return Agreement (Agreement on the Rescue of Astronauts and the Return of Objects Launched into Space);
- the Liability Convention (Convention on International Liability for Damage Caused by Space Objects);
- the Registration Convention (Convention on Registration of Objects Launched into Outer Space);
- the Moon Agreement (Agreement Governing Activities of States on the Moon and Other Celestial Bodies).

203. Space law instruments which are not UN outer space treaties, such as the Declaration of Legal Principles Governing the Activities of States in the Exploration of Outer Space, which is a starting point for the creation of the Outer Space Treaty, should be treated according to the general principles of *Lex posterior* and lex *specialis* (Sundahl, Mark J., *The Cape Town Convention, Its Application to Space Assets and Relation to the Law of Outer Space*. 2013, 132).

204. The instruments of the International Telecommunications Union (ITU) are in particular the Constitution of the ITU, the Convention of the ITU and the Radio Regulations of the ITU. A party taking title or control of a satellite pursuant to the Space Protocol shall take into account the restrictions imposed by the ITU instruments to the use of the satellite (Sundahl, Mark J., *The Cape Town Convention, Its Application to Space Assets and Relation to the Law of Outer Space*. 2013, 184): the use of orbits or radio frequencies requires the granting of a licence which is submitted to specific duties such as the obligation to avoid harmful interference with other transmissions and may be duly terminated or suspended by the State granting this licence, foreign ownership of licences to use radio frequencies may be duly restricted by the State and attention is to be paid to certain priorities imposed through the ITU Constitution, such as the priority of Telecommunications Concerning Safety of Life (Article 40 of the ITU Constitution) and the priority of Government Telecommunications (Article 41 of the ITU Constitution).

205. As far as the Rescue and Return Agreement is concerned, it could be useful to the creditor under the Cape Town Convention, for four reasons (Sundahl, Mark J., *The Cape Town Convention, Its Application to Space Assets and Relation to the Law of Outer Space*. 2013, 162 and 163):

- it gives the creditor the possibility to locate the space asset it is interested in when a Contracting State notifies the launching authority and the UN about the landing of a space object;
- the State's duty to retrieve space objects preserves the space asset's value and the creditor's rights upon it;

- the duty to rescue personnel on board (which also applies in the frame of the Outer Space Treaty), by preserving their safety, also preserves the debtor's activity;
- when a State Party to this Agreement returns a space object to the launching authority, the application of the Cape Town Convention is to be preserved if the launching authority is a State Party to the Cape Town Convention (if not, or if this State is not friendly to the creditor, it may threaten the creditor's interests).

206. If the concerned good is to be qualified as an aircraft, the general principles of *lex posterior* and *lex specialis* have to keep applying (Sundahl, Mark J., *The Cape Town Convention, Its Application to Space Assets and Relation to the Law of Outer Space*. 2013, 166).

207. Concerning the Moon Agreement, the State's duty to return the space asset found on the Moon to the control of the launching State will benefit the creditor in the same way as for the Rescue and Return Agreement (Sundahl, Mark J., *The Cape Town Convention, Its Application to Space Assets and Relation to the Law of Outer Space*. 2013, 180). There may also be competition between the Cape Town Convention's rules on jurisdictions and those of the Moon Agreement, according to which the State which owns the concerned asset has primary jurisdiction concerning this asset (Sundahl, Mark J., *The Cape Town Convention, Its Application to Space Assets and Relation to the Law of Outer Space*. 2013, 180 and 181).

208. The question of jurisdiction is also at stake as to the Outer Space Treaty and the Registration Convention (Sundahl, Mark J., *The Cape Town Convention, Its Application to Space Assets and Relation to the Law of Outer Space*. 2013, 167–177).

209. The Cape Town Convention may also interfere with the Liability Convention (Sundahl, Mark J., *The Cape Town Convention, Its Application to Space Assets and Relation to the Law of Outer Space*. 2013, 148–158).

210. As to the Declaration of Legal Principles Governing the Activities of States in the Exploration of Outer Space as an authoritative primarily non-binding UN legal instrument, it is not directly addressed in Article XXXIV of the Space Protocol, but it is a substantive part of the principles of space law the Space Protocol is based on. It underlines the following principles:

- The exploration and use of outer space shall be carried on for the benefit and in the interests of all mankind.
- Outer space and celestial bodies are free for exploration and use by all States on the basis of equality and in accordance with international law.
- Outer space and celestial bodies are not subject to national appropriation by claim of sovereignty, by means of use or occupation, or by any other means.

- The activities of States in the exploration and use of outer space shall be carried on in accordance with international law, including the Charter of the UN, in the interest of maintaining international peace and security and promoting international co-operation and understanding.
- States bear international responsibility for national activities in outer space, whether carried on by governmental agencies or by non-governmental entities, and for assuring that national activities are carried on in conformity with the principles set forth in the present declaration. The activities of non-governmental entities in outer space shall require authorisation and continuing supervision by the State concerned. When activities are carried out in outer space by an international organisation, responsibility for compliance with the principles set forth in this declaration shall be borne by the international organisation and by the States participating in it.
- In the exploration and use of outer space, States shall be guided by the principle of co-operation and mutual assistance and shall conduct all their activities in outer space with due regard for the corresponding interests of other States. If a State has reason to believe that an outer space activity or experiment planned by it or its nationals would cause potentially harmful interference with the activities of other States in the peaceful exploration and use of outer space, it shall undertake appropriate international consultations before proceeding with any such activity or experiment. A State which has reason to believe that an outer space activity or experiment planned by another State would cause potentially harmful interference with activities in the peaceful exploration and use of outer space may request consultation concerning the activity or experiment.
- The State on whose registry an object launched into outer space is carried shall retain jurisdiction and control over such object, and any personnel thereon, while in outer space. Ownership of objects launched into outer space, and of their component parts, is not affected by their passage through outer space or by their return to the earth. Such objects or component parts found beyond the limits of the State of registry shall be returned to that State, which shall furnish identifying data upon request prior to return.
- Each State which launches or procures the launching of an object into outer space, and each State from whose territory or facility an object is launched, is internationally liable for damage to a foreign State or to its natural or juridical persons by such object or its component parts on the earth, in air space, or in outer space.
- States shall regard astronauts as envoys of mankind in outer space, and shall render to them all possible assistance in the event of accident, distress, or emergency landing on the territory of a foreign State or on the high seas. Astronauts who make such a landing shall be safely and promptly returned to the State of registry of their space vehicle.

211. It is a starting point of numerous resolutions and lawmaking activities of the United Nations Committee on the Peaceful Uses of Outer Space, and the broad acceptance of this declaration permits the comparison with the Universal Declaration of Human Rights (Karin Traunmüller, 'The Declaration of Legal Principles Governing the Activities of States in the Exploration of Outer Space: The Starting

Point for the UN Law of Outer Space'. In *Soft Law in Outer Space, The Function of Non-binding Norms in International Space Law*, edited by Irmgard Marboe. 2012, 153).

Chapter 5. The Protocol to the Convention on International Interests in Mobile Equipment on Matters Specific to Mining, Agricultural and Construction Equipment

§1. The General Frame

212. The Protocol to the Convention on international interests in mobile equipment on matters specific to mining, agricultural and construction equipment (Convention on International Interests in Mobile Equipment as applied to mining equipment, agricultural equipment and construction equipment, MAC Protocol) shall apply to such equipment as described in its Annexes 1, 2, 3, irrespective of any intended or actual use of the equipment (Articles I, II and III). It may be subject to some derogative declarations from any of its Contracting States.

213. According to the doctrine, there are different needs (Howard Rosen, 'Commentary on "A Comparison of the Position of Buyers under the Cape Town Convention, the Three Existing Protocols and the Draft MAC Protocol"', *Cape Town Law Journal* Vol. 6 (2017): 123), depending on the sector the specific Protocol is related to. For instance, similar to the Rail Protocol, the MAC Protocol takes a pragmatic approach, through which prospective purchasers or secured parties are enabled to search for any notices of sale in the registry. It is an inclusive and transparent notice system disarming the bona fide purchaser well known under the traditional civil law accession system (Howard Rosen, 'Commentary on "A Comparison of the Position of Buyers under the Cape Town Convention, the Three Existing Protocols and the Draft MAC Protocol"', *Cape Town Law Journal* Vol. 6 (2017): 135). The common approach makes sense, not only because some mining equipment can also be rolling stock (Howard Rosen, 'Commentary on "A Comparison of the Position of Buyers under the Cape Town Convention, the Three Existing Protocols and the Draft MAC Protocol"', *Cape Town Law Journal* Vol. 6 (2017): 135).

214. The present Protocol is not yet in force. Depositary is UNIDROIT. It is open to Regional Economic Integration Organizations, such as the EU (Article XXIV).

§2. Representative Capacities

215. The Protocol allows a person to enter into an agreement, effect a registration (as defined by Article 16(3) of the Convention) and assert rights and interests under the Convention in an agency, trust or representative capacity, in relation to equipment (Article IV).

§3. CHOICE OF LAW

216. Where a Contracting State has made, pursuant to Article XXVIII(1), a declaration in this sense, the parties to an agreement or a related guarantee contract or subordination agreement may agree on the law which is to govern their contractual rights and obligations, wholly or in part, that is to say, the domestic rules of law of a designated State or, where that State comprises several territorial units, the domestic law of the designated territorial unit (Article VI).

217. As to the impact of domestic laws, accession concerns are more likely to arise in the context of the MAC Protocol, for instance, where an object covered by the MAC Protocol is affixed to a larger object which is outside the scope of the Cape Town Convention regime (Marek Dubovec, 'Accessions and Non-Accessions under the Cape Town Convention: Special Focus on MAC Equipment', *Cape Town Law Journal* Vol. 6 (2017): 55). The traditional Civil Code notion of accession may be at stake (Marek Dubovec, 'Accessions and Non-Accessions under the Cape Town Convention: Special Focus on MAC Equipment', *Cape Town Law Journal* Vol. 6 (2017): 56).

218. On this point, the MAC Protocol focuses on immovable-associated equipment.

§4. ASSOCIATION WITH IMMOVABLE PROPERTY

219. Where immovable-associated equipment is situated in a non-Contracting State, this Protocol does not affect the application of any law of that State that determines whether an international interest in the immovable-associated equipment cannot be created, has ceased to exist, is subordinated to any other rights or interests in the immovable-associated equipment, or is otherwise affected by the association of the equipment with immovable property (Article VII, 1.). As to the international interest in immovable-associated equipment which is situated in a Contracting State, the Protocol offers the Contracting State a choice between three alternatives, Alternative A, B or C, which shall apply in full (Article VII, 2.).

220. Alternative A:

> According to Alternative A, if immovable-associated equipment is severable from the immovable property, its association with the immovable property does not affect the application of this Protocol, including the creation, existence, priority or enforcement of any international interest in that equipment. This Protocol does not apply to immovable-associated equipment that is not severable from the immovable property.

In particular, immovable-associated equipment is severable from the immovable property only if its estimated value after physical disconnection of the equipment from the immovable property would be greater than the estimated cost of the disconnection and of any restoration of the immovable property.

Furthermore, if immovable-associated equipment is severable from the immovable property at the time it becomes immovable-associated equipment or the time an international interest in the equipment is created, whichever is the latter, there is a rebuttable presumption that it continues to be severable from that immovable property.

221. Alternative B:

> Pursuant to Alternative B, this Protocol does not affect the application of any law of the State where immovable property is situated that determines whether an international interest in immovable-associated equipment cannot be created, has ceased to exist, is subordinated to any other rights or interests in the immovable-associated equipment, or is otherwise affected by the association of the equipment with immovable property if the equipment has lost its individual legal identity in accordance with the law of that State.

In addition to that, where equipment subject to a registered international interest is immovable-associated equipment and has not lost its individual legal identity in accordance with the law of the State where the immovable property is situated, an interest in the immovable property that extends to that equipment has priority over the registered international interest in the equipment only if the following conditions are fulfilled:

- the interest in the immovable property has been registered in accordance with the requirements of domestic law prior to the time of registration of the international interest in the equipment under this Protocol and registration of the interest in the immovable property continues to be effective; and
- the equipment became associated with the immovable property prior to the time of registration of the international interest in the equipment under this Protocol.

222. Alternative C:

> Alternative C foresees that this Protocol does not affect the application of any law of the State where immovable property is situated that determines whether an international interest in immovable-associated equipment cannot be created, has ceased to exist, is subordinated to any other rights or interests in the immovable-associated equipment, or is otherwise affected by the association of the equipment with immovable property.

§5. Default Remedies and Priorities

223. As far as default remedies and priorities are concerned, the Protocol provides for solutions subject to prior specific declaration from the Contracting States:

it extends to modification of default remedies provisions (Article VIII), modification of provisions regarding relief pending final determination (Article IX), remedies on insolvency (Article X), insolvency assistance (Article XI), provisions relating to inventory (Article XII).

224. Subject to State's declaration, in addition to the remedies specified in Chapter III of the Convention on default remedies, the creditor may, to the extent that the debtor has at any time so agreed and in the circumstances specified in that chapter, procure the export and physical transfer of equipment from the territory in which it is situated.

225. The creditor shall not exercise such remedies without the prior consent in writing of the holder of any registered interest ranking in priority to that of the creditor.

226. Article 8(3) of the Convention on the exercise of default remedies in a commercially reasonable manner shall not apply to equipment. Nevertheless, any remedy given by the Convention in relation to equipment shall be exercised in a commercially reasonable manner. Specifically, a remedy shall be deemed to be exercised in a commercially reasonable manner where it is exercised in conformity with a provision of the agreement except where such a provision is manifestly unreasonable.

227. A chargee giving fourteen or more calendar days' prior written notice of a proposed sale or lease to interested persons as provided by the Convention in its Article 8(4) shall be deemed to satisfy the requirement of giving the 'reasonable prior notice' specified therein. The foregoing shall not prevent a chargee and a chargor or a guarantor from agreeing to a longer period of prior notice.

228. Subject to any applicable safety laws and regulations, a Contracting State shall ensure that the relevant administrative authorities expeditiously co-operate with and assist the creditor to the extent necessary for the exercise of the default remedies. Nevertheless, a Contracting State may, at the time of ratification, acceptance, approval of, or accession to this Protocol, declare that it will not apply these co-operation and creditor assistance rules.

229. A chargee proposing to procure the export of equipment otherwise than pursuant to a court order shall give reasonable prior notice in writing of the proposed export to interested persons specified in Article 1(m)(i) – that is to say, the debtor –, and (ii) – that is to say, any person who, for the purpose of assuring performance of any of the obligations in favour of the creditor, gives or issues a suretyship or demand guarantee or a standby letter of credit or any other form of credit insurance – and in Article 1(m)(iii) – that is to say, any other person having rights in or over the object – of the Convention who have given notice of their rights to the chargee within a reasonable time prior to the export.

230. According to Article 13(1) of the Convention, a Contracting State shall ensure that a creditor who adduces evidence of default by the debtor may, pending final determination of its claim and to the extent that the debtor has at any time so agreed, obtain from a court speedy relief in the form of one or more of specified orders as the creditor requests. Article IX of the Protocol adds, as an additional order specific to mining, agricultural and construction equipment, if at any time the debtor and the creditor specifically agree, the possibility to proceed to the sale of the object and the application of proceeds therefrom.

231. Subject to State's declaration, for the purposes of Article 13(1) of the Convention on speed relief pending final determination, 'speedy' in the context of obtaining relief means within such number of calendar days from the date of filing of the application for relief as is specified in a declaration made by the Contracting State in which the application is made.

232. As to jurisdiction, the courts of a Contracting State chosen by the parties and the courts of the Contracting State on the territory of which the object is situated also have jurisdiction to grant relief under Article 13(1) (e).

233. Ownership or any other interest of the debtor passing on a sale under the preceding paragraph is free from any other interest over which the creditor's international interest has priority under the provisions on the priority of competing interests of Article 29 of the Convention.

234. The creditor and the debtor or any other interested person may agree in writing to exclude the application of Article 13(2) of the Convention, according to which, in making any order under Article 13(1), the court may impose such terms as it considers necessary to protect the interested persons in the event that the creditor, in implementing any order granting such relief, fails to perform any of its obligations to the debtor under this Convention or the Protocol; or fails to establish its claim, wholly or in part, on the final determination of that claim.

235. With regard to default remedies, as regulated in Article VIII(1):

- they shall be made available by the administrative authorities in a Contracting State no later than seven calendar days after the creditor notifies such authorities that the relief specified in Article 13 of the Convention is granted or, in the case of relief granted by a foreign court, recognised by a court of that Contracting State, and that the creditor is entitled to procure those remedies in accordance with the Convention; and
- the applicable authorities shall expeditiously co-operate with and assist the creditor in the exercise of such remedies in conformity with the applicable safety laws and regulations.

236. According to paragraph 7 of Article IX, paragraph 2, of Article IX on speedy relief and Paragraph 6 of Article IX shall not affect any applicable safety laws and regulations. The creditor shall not exercise the default remedies specified in the preceding paragraph without the prior consent in writing of the holder of any registered interest ranking in priority to that of the creditor and paragraph 6, according to which a Contracting State may, at the time of ratification, acceptance, approval of, or accession to this Protocol, declare that it will not apply the present rules on co-operation and assistance to the creditor, shall not affect any applicable safety laws and regulations.

237. Subject to State's declaration, as to remedies on insolvency, upon the occurrence of an insolvency-related event, the insolvency administrator, in its official capacity, or the debtor, as applicable, give possession of the equipment to the creditor not later than the earlier of the end of the waiting period and the date on which the creditor would be entitled to possession of the equipment if this article did not apply (Article X, paragraph 3).

238. The waiting period is defined as the period specified in a declaration of the Contracting State which is the primary insolvency jurisdiction (Article X, paragraph 4).

239. If the creditor is not given or not yet given the opportunity to take possession according to the present rules, the insolvency administrator or the debtor, as applicable, shall preserve the equipment and maintain it and its value in accordance with the agreement, and the creditor shall be entitled to apply for any other forms of interim relief available under the applicable law (Article X, paragraph 5).

240. In this framework, the use of the equipment under arrangements designed to preserve the equipment and maintain it and its value is possible (Article X, paragraph 6).

241. The insolvency administrator or the debtor, as applicable, may retain possession of the equipment (Article X, paragraph 7) where, by the time specified to give possession of the equipment to the creditor according to the present rules, it has cured all defaults other than a default constituted by the opening of insolvency proceedings and has agreed to perform all future obligations under the agreement and related transaction documents. A second waiting period shall not apply in respect of a default in the performance of such future obligations.

242. With regard to the specific remedies in Article VIII(1), they shall be made available by the administrative authorities in a Contracting State no later than seven calendar days after the date on which the creditor notifies such authorities that it is entitled to procure those remedies in accordance with the Convention, and the applicable authorities shall expeditiously co-operate with and assist the creditor in the exercise of such remedies in conformity with the applicable safety laws and regulations (Article X, paragraph 8).

243. No exercise of remedies permitted by the Convention or this Protocol may be prevented or delayed after the date foreseen in order to give possession of the equipment to the creditor (Article X, paragraph 9).

244. No obligations of the debtor under the agreement may be modified without the consent of the creditor (Article X, paragraph 10).

245. The present rules do not affect the authority, if any, of the insolvency administrator under the applicable law to terminate the agreement (Article X, paragraph 11).

246. No rights or interests, except for non-consensual rights or interests of a category covered by a State's declaration pursuant to Article 39(1) of the Convention, shall have priority in insolvency proceedings over registered interests (Article X, paragraph 12).

247. The Convention as modified by Article VIII relating to modified default remedies provisions shall apply to the exercise of all default remedies under Article VIII (Article X, paragraph 13).

248. Subject to State's declaration, the courts of a Contracting State in which equipment is situated shall, in accordance with the law of that State, co-operate (Article XI) to the maximum extent possible with foreign courts and foreign insolvency administrators in carrying out the provisions for remedies on insolvency (set up in Article X of the MAC Protocol).

249. According to Article XII, paragraph 2, on provisions relating to inventory, an interest in inventory created or provided for by an agreement under which the dealer is the debtor is not an international interest if the dealer is situated in a Contracting State having made the declaration to apply Article XII at the time the interest is created or arises.

250. In this context, as to mining, agricultural and construction equipment, Article 29(3)(b) and 29(4)(b) of the Convention do not apply to a buyer, conditional buyer or lessee of inventory from a dealer if the dealer is situated in a Contracting State which has made the required declaration that it will apply the present Article XII relating to provisions relating to inventory, at the time that a buyer, conditional buyer or lessee acquires its interest in or rights over the inventory (Article XII, paragraph 3).

251. For the purposes of this Article XII on provisions relating to inventory, a dealer is situated in a State where it has its place of business or, if it has more than one place of business in different States, its principal place of business (Article XII, paragraph 4).

§6. Debtor's Protection

252. Article XIII protects the debtor, which, in the absence of a default, shall be entitled to the quiet possession and use of the equipment in accordance with the agreement, while the creditor is liable for any breach of the agreement under the applicable law in so far as that agreement relates to equipment. Pursuant to Article VIII, Article 8(3) of the Cape Town Convention on the remedy of charge in a commercially reasonable manner does not apply to mining, agricultural and construction equipment; instead, a remedy shall be deemed to be exercised in a commercially reasonable manner where it is exercised in conformity with a provision of the agreement except where such a provision is manifestly unreasonable (Article VIII, 3).

§7. Registry Provisions

253. Chapter III of the Protocol provides for registry provisions relating to international interests in mining, agricultural and construction equipment, with a Supervisory Authority and a Registrar, as well as the possibility of notices of sale (Article XX).

§8. Jurisdiction

254. As to jurisdiction, with reference to Articles 42 and 43 of the Cape Town Convention, Article XXI of the Protocol specifies the modalities of waivers of sovereign immunity from the jurisdiction of courts or relating to equipment under the Convention: in particular, the waiver must be in writing and contain a description of the concerned equipment.

§9. Relationship with Other Conventions

255. As to the relationship with the UNIDROIT Convention on International Financial Leasing, the Convention on International Interests in Mobile Equipment as applied to mining equipment, agricultural equipment and construction equipment shall supersede the UNIDROIT Convention on International Financial Leasing in respect of the subject matter of this Protocol, as between States Parties to both Conventions (Article XXII).

Part II. Context of the Cape Town Convention and Its Protocols

256. The Cape Town Convention and its Protocols have to develop in a specific international legal environment, as far as they shall coexist with other international legal instruments. They may, to some extent, supersede some international Conventions which may remain in force outside of their scope of application, and it is not excluded that the Cape Town Convention and its Protocols refer to some rules of these Conventions or let to the parties the possibility to apply any of these 'competing' international Conventions.

Chapter 1. The UN Convention on the Assignment of Receivables in International Trade

257. First, the Cape Town Convention expresses its relationship to the UN Convention on the Assignment of Receivables in International Trade, which has not entered into force at the moment and specifies the priority of the Cape Town Convention juridical system, as for aircraft, rail and space equipment.

258. Both conventions roots in the recognition of the insufficiency of the lex situs conflict of laws rules, as for the determination of the law applicable to the case of intangibles: on the one hand, the UN Convention on the Assignment of Receivables in International Trade promotes the application of the law of the assignor's State; on the other hand, the Cape Town Convention conceives a new concept of registered international interest as a toolbox (N. Orkun Akseli, *International Secured Transactions Law, Facilitation of Credit and International Conventions and Instruments*. 2011, 54). One wonders whether there could be functional equivalences of the different available international instruments in this matter (Rudolf Claudia, *Einheitsrecht für internationale Forderungsabtretung*. 2005, 216–220). According to (Sir Roy Goode, 'Official Commentary on the Convention on International Interests in Mobile Equipment', (2014), nos 4.301, 4.302, pp. 269 and 270), the application of any of the two Conventions will usually lead to the same result, in particular due to the fact that Article 36, 3, which states that in some cases, the priority of the competing assignments of the associated rights shall be determined by the applicable law (Article 36, 3), may refer to the UN Convention on the Assignment of Receivables in International Trade as 'applicable law': the applicable law may be an international instrument or a domestic rule based on an international instrument such as a Model Law (N. Orkun Akseli, *International Secured Transactions Law, Facilitation of Credit and International Conventions and Instruments*. 2011, 112). It is also due to the contractual freedom granted both by the Cape Town Convention and the UN Convention on the Assignment of Receivables in International Trade. The contractual freedom, as part of the 'party autonomy culture' (N. Orkun Akseli, *International Secured Transactions Law, Facilitation of Credit and International Conventions and Instruments*. 2011, 121) laid down in the Cape Town Convention, is considered as 'crucial' for any modern secured transactions regimes, not only because it shall reduce transaction costs for the parties, which are in the position of identifying their commercial needs (N. Orkun Akseli, *International Secured Transactions Law, Facilitation of Credit and International Conventions and Instruments*. 2011, 113). In this frame, it is also a matter of protecting the week party (according to N. Orkun Akseli, *A* '"Conflict of Interest": The Principle of Debtor's Protection under the UN Convention on the Assignment of Receivables', In *International Arbitration and International Commercial Law,* edited by S. Kröll, L. A. Mistelis, P. Perales Viscasillas & V. Rogers. 2011, 510): whereas the Civil law systems focus on the numerous clausus system, the Common Law structure encourages a complete freedom of the parties to organise the law the contract is submitted to, provided that the choice is fair and does not infringe the law, for instance in the frame of the Uniform Commercial Code (N. Orkun Akseli, *International Secured Transactions Law, Facilitation of Credit and International*

Conventions and Instruments. 2011, 115); in the frame of the UN Convention on the assignment of Receivables in International Trade, attention is paid to the prohibition of affecting third parties rights through any agreement derogating from this Convention (Spiros Bazinas, 'UNCITRAL's Contribution to the Unification of Receivables Financing Law: The UN Convention on the Assignment of Receivables in International Trade', *Uniform Law Review* Vol. 7(1) (2002): 55 and 57; Elisabeth Schütze, *Zession und Einheitsrecht*. 2005, 128; N. Orkun Akseli, *International Secured Transactions Law, Facilitation of Credit and International Conventions and Instruments*. 2011, 117); this rule is not this of the Convention on the International Sales of Goods, which is nevertheless a model for the UN Convention on the assignment of Receivables in International Trade. Nevertheless, the Cape Town Convention does not contain this prohibition promoting certainty (Spiros Bazinas, 'UNCITRAL's Contribution to the Unification of Receivables Financing Law: The UN Convention on the Assignment of Receivables in International Trade', *Uniform Law Review* Vol. 7(1) (2002): 66): the party autonomy is a principle with a restricted scope under this Convention, for instance, because the parties' special agreements are to be in writing and because in cases of insolvency, the Cape Town Convention restricts the party autonomy (N. Orkun Akseli, *International Secured Transactions Law, Facilitation of Credit and International Conventions and Instruments*. 2011, 122). It has been written that the Cape Town Convention follows a non-unitary approach to security while the UN Convention on the Assignment of Receivables in International Trade has rather a unitary and functional approach (N. Orkun Akseli, *International Secured Transactions Law, Facilitation of Credit and International Conventions and Instruments*. (2011), 123). Similar to the Cape Town Convention system, the UN Convention on the Assignment of Receivables in International Trade provides for conflict of law rules, however only in the form of a few rules (as 'mini private international law Convention') Contracting States are expressly entitled to derogate from (Spiros Bazinas, 'UNCITRAL's Contribution to the Unification of Receivables Financing Law: The UN Convention on the Assignment of Receivables in International Trade', *Uniform Law Review* Vol. 7(1) (2002): 63; Hans Kuhne, 'Zur Neuordnung der grenzüberschreitenden Forderungsabtretung im Einheitsrecht UN-Abtretungsrecht', *Schweizerische Zeitschrift für Wirtschaftsrecht* (2002): 140 and 141). The UN Convention on the Assignment of Receivables in International Trade provides for serial default rules applicable if the parties do not agree otherwise (Spiros V. Bazinas, *Uniform Receivables Financing Law: Key Policy Aspects of the UN Convention on the Assignment of Receivables in International Trade, in Revue hellénique de droit International*, 2011, 37).

Chapter 2. The UNIDROIT Convention on International Financial Leasing

§1. The General Frame

259. The UNIDROIT Convention on International Financial Leasing has entered into force in Belarus, France, Hungary, Italy, Latvia, Nigeria, Panama, Russian Federation, Ukraine, and Uzbekistan.

260. It aims at removing some legal impediments to the international financial leasing of equipment, maintaining a fair balance of interests between the different parties to the transaction, making international financial leasing more available and adapting the rules of law governing the traditional contract of hire to the distinctive triangular relationship created by the financial leasing transaction. Its uniform rules relate primarily to the civil and commercial law aspects of international financial leasing. It is qualified as a 'minimal legal framework': (Martin Stanford, 'International Financial Leasing: The Status of the UNIDROIT Convention and an Analysis of Its Provisions', *Uniform Commercial Law Journal*, Vol. 32 (1999): 191), whose basic features are reflected in the 1988 Model Law on Leasing, which is primarily dedicated to developing countries businesses with a limited size (Herbert Kronke, 'Financial Leasing and Its Unification by UNIDROIT', *General reports on the XVIIIth Congress of the International Academy of Comparative Law*, edited by Karen B. Brown & David V. Snyder (2012): 331).

261. The present Convention applies to the financial leasing transaction by which the lessor, on the specifications of the lessee, enters into a supply agreement with the supplier under which the lessor acquires equipment, which is not to be used primarily for the lessee's personal, family or household purposes (Article 1, 4), on terms approved by the lessee so far as they concern its interests, and enters into a leasing agreement with the lessee, granting to the lessee the right to use the equipment in return for the payment of rentals (Article 1, 1). So there are both a supply agreement and a leasing agreement (Martin Stanford, 'International Financial Leasing: The Status of the UNIDROIT Convention and an Analysis of Its Provisions', *Uniform Commercial Law Journal* Vol. 32 (1999): 191).

262. In this frame (Article 1, 2):

- the lessee specifies the equipment and selects the supplier without relying primarily on the skill and judgment of the lessor;
- the equipment is acquired by the lessor in connection with a leasing agreement which, to the knowledge of the supplier, either has been made or is to be made between the lessor and the lessee; and
- the rentals payable under the leasing agreement are calculated so as to take into account, in particular, the amortisation of the whole or a substantial part of the cost of the equipment.

263. It does not matter whether or not the lessee has or subsequently acquires the option to buy the equipment or to hold it on lease for a further period, and whether or not for a nominal price or rental (Article 1, 3).

264. The scope of the present Convention is extended to sub-leasing transactions (Article 2).

265. The Convention applies when the lessor and the lessee have their places of business in different States and those States and the State in which the supplier has its place of business are Contracting States or both the supply agreement and the leasing agreement are governed by the law of a Contracting State (Article 3, 1).

266. In the presence of many places of business for one party, for the purpose of the present rule, the place of business which has the closest relationship to the relevant agreement and its performance, having regard to the circumstances known to or contemplated by the parties at any time before or at the conclusion of that agreement, is to be taken into consideration (Article 3, 2).

267. The present Convention keeps applying where the equipment has become a fixture to or incorporated in the land according to the law of the State where the land is situated (Article 4).

268. The parties both to the supply agreement and to the leasing agreement are entitled to exclude the application of the present Convention (Article 5, 1). If not, parties may derogate to the Convention in their relations with each other, provided that Articles 8, 3, and 13, 3, (b) and 4. are respected (Article 5, 2). According to Professor Sixto Sanchez Lorenzo, the Convention focuses on contractual issues rather than on property concerns and thus fails to contribute to the targeted legal harmonisation, ignoring even the question of ranking between leasing property rights and other property rights while precising that the present Convention does not apply compulsorily (Lorenzo Sanchez, 'Sixto, Aspectos Reales del Leasing Internacional', *Revista de la Corte Española de Arbitraje* 1992 (1992): 73–75).

269. By virtue of Article 6, in the interpretation of this Convention, regard is to be had to its object and purpose as set forth in the preamble, to its international character and to the need to promote uniformity in its application and the observance of good faith in international trade, and questions concerning matters governed by this Convention which are not expressly settled in it are to be settled in conformity with the general principles on which it is based or, in the absence of such principles, in conformity with the law applicable by virtue of the rules of private international law.

§2. Rights and Duties of the Parties

270. The lessor's real rights in the equipment shall be valid against the lessee's trustee in bankruptcy, including a liquidator, administrator or other person appointed to administer the lessee's estate for the benefit of the general body of creditors, and creditors, including creditors who have obtained an attachment or execution (Article 7, 1), with due respect to public notice requirements imposed by the applicable law (Article 7, 2), and with due respect to any other treaty under which the lessor's real rights in the equipment are required to be recognised (Article 7, 4).

271. As for this public notice requirement, the applicable law is the law of the following States at the time the public notice requirement rule is to be invoked (Article 7, 3):

- in the case of a registered ship, the State in which it is registered in the name of the owner, for instance, a bareboat charterer;
- in the case of an aircraft which is registered pursuant to the Convention on International Civil Aviation done at Chicago on 7 December 1944, the State in which it is so registered;
- in the case of other equipment of a kind normally moved from one State to another, including an aircraft engine, the State in which the lessee has its principal place of business;
- in the case of all other equipment, the State in which the equipment is situated.

272. The priority of any creditor having a consensual or non-consensual lien or security interest in the equipment arising otherwise than by virtue of an attachment or execution, or any right of arrest, detention or disposition conferred specifically in relation to ships or aircraft under the law applicable by virtue of the rules of private international law, is unaffected (Article 7, 5).

273. As a principle, except as otherwise provided by this Convention or stated in the leasing agreement, the lessor shall not incur any liability to the lessee in respect of the equipment save to the extent that the lessee has suffered loss as the result of its reliance on the lessor's skill and judgment and of the lessor's intervention in the selection of the supplier or the specifications of the equipment (Article 8, 1, (a)). The lessor as such shall not be liable to third parties for death, personal injury or damage to property caused by the equipment (Article 8, 1, (b)), but it may be liable in any other capacity, for example, as owner (Article 8, 1, (c)).

274. The lessor warrants that the lessee's quiet possession will not be disturbed by a person who has a superior title or right, or who claims a superior title or right and acts under the authority of a court, where such title, right or claim is not derived from an act or omission of the lessee (Article 8, 2). This rule applies compulsorily where the superior title, right or claim is derived from an intentional or grossly negligent act or omission of the lessor (Article 8, 3). Any broader warranty of quiet possession by the lessor, where this warranty is mandatory under the law applicable by virtue of the rules of private international law, is unaffected (Article 8, 4).

275. The lessee shall take proper care of the equipment, use it in a reasonable manner and keep it in the condition in which it was delivered, subject to fair wear and tear and to any modification of the equipment agreed by the parties, and when the leasing agreement comes to an end, the lessee, unless exercising a right to buy the equipment or to hold the equipment on lease for a further period, shall return the equipment to the lessor in such condition (Article 9).

276. The duties of the supplier under the supply agreement shall also be owed to the lessee as if it were a party to that agreement and as if the equipment were to be supplied directly to the lessee, but the supplier shall not be liable to both the lessor and the lessee in respect of the same damage (Article 10, 1).

277. The lessee may not terminate or rescind the supply agreement without the consent of the lessor (Article 10, 2).

278. The lessee's rights derived from the supply agreement under this Convention shall not be affected by a variation of any term of the supply agreement previously approved by the lessee unless it consented to that variation (Article 11).

279. Where the equipment is not delivered or is delivered late or fails to conform to the supply agreement, the lessee has the right as against the lessor to reject the equipment or to terminate the leasing agreement and the lessor has the right to remedy its failure to tender equipment in conformity with the supply agreement, as if the lessee had agreed to buy the equipment from the lessor under the same terms as those of the supply agreement (Article 12, 1).

280. Such right shall be exercisable in the same manner and shall be lost in the same circumstances as if the lessee had agreed to buy the equipment from the lessor under the same terms as those of the supply agreement (Article 12, 2).

281. The lessee shall be entitled to withhold rentals payable under the leasing agreement until the lessor has remedied its failure to tender equipment in conformity with the supply agreement or the lessee has lost the right to reject the equipment (Article 12, 3).

282. Where the lessee has exercised a right to terminate the leasing agreement, the lessee shall be entitled to recover any rentals and other sums paid in advance, less a reasonable sum for any benefit the lessee has derived from the equipment (Article 12, 4).

283. The lessee shall have no other claim against the lessor for non-delivery, delay in delivery or delivery of non-conforming equipment except to the extent to which this results from the act or omission of the lessor. (Article 12, 5).

284. Nothing in this article shall affect the lessee's rights against the supplier to invoke the supplier's duties and to terminate or rescind the supply agreement with the consent of the lessor under Article 10 (Article 12, 6).

285. In the event of default by the lessee, the lessor may recover accrued unpaid rentals, together with interest and damages (Article 13, 1).

286. Where the lessee's default is substantial, then the lessor may also require accelerated payment of the value of the future rentals, where the leasing agreement so provides, or may terminate the leasing agreement and, after such termination, recover possession of the equipment as well as such damages as will place the lessor in the position in which it would have been had the lessee performed the leasing agreement in accordance with its terms (Article 13, 2). In this frame, the lessor shall not be entitled to exercise its right of acceleration or its right of termination unless it has by notice given the lessee a reasonable opportunity of remedying the default so far as the same may be remedied (Article 13, 5).

287. The leasing agreement may provide for the manner in which the damages will place the lessor in the position in which it would have been had the lessee performed the leasing agreement in accordance with its terms of Article 13, 2, are to be computed (Article 13, 3, (a)). Such provision shall be enforceable between the parties unless it would result in damages substantially in excess of those damages as will place the lessor in the position in which it would have been had the lessee performed the leasing agreement in accordance with its terms provided for in Article 13, 2; the parties may not derogate from or vary the effect of such rule (Article 13, 3, (b)).

288. Compulsorily, where the lessor has terminated the leasing agreement, it shall not be entitled to enforce a term of that agreement providing for acceleration of payment of future rentals, but the value of such rentals may be taken into account in computing damages under Article 13, 2(b) and 3. (Article 13, 4).

289. The lessor shall not be entitled to recover damages to the extent that it has failed to take all reasonable steps to mitigate its loss (Article 13, 6).

290. The lessor may transfer or otherwise deal with all or any of its rights in the equipment or under the leasing agreement: such a transfer shall not relieve the lessor of any of its duties under the leasing agreement or alter either the nature of the leasing agreement or its legal treatment as provided in this Convention (Article 14, 1).

291. The lessee may transfer the right to the use of the equipment or any other rights under the leasing agreement only with the consent of the lessor and subject to the rights of third parties (Article 14, 2).

292. According to Article 20, a Contracting State may declare at the time of signature, ratification, acceptance, approval or accession that it will substitute its domestic law for Article 8, 3 if its domestic law does not permit the lessor to exclude its liability for its default or negligence. It is the case with France and the Russian Federation.

Chapter 3. The Convention for the Unification of Certain Rules Relating to the Precautionary Attachment of Aircraft

293. The Convention for the Unification of Certain Rules Relating to the Precautionary Attachment of Aircraft has entered into force in Belgium, Germany, Italy, Romania and Spain.

294. Among these States, only Spain is part of the Cape Town Convention and none is part of the Aircraft Protocol, so even though the Aircraft Protocol shall supersede this Convention for the Unification of Certain Rules Relating to the Precautionary Attachment of Aircraft in its entirety (Sir Roy Goode, 'Official Commentary on the Protocol to the Convention on International Interests in Mobile Equipment on Matters Specific to Aircraft Equipment', (2013), no. 5.110, p. 349), the latter is still in force at the moment.

295. The present Convention shall not apply to precautionary measures prescribed in bankruptcy proceedings, nor to precautionary measures taken in case of violation of customhouse, penal or police regulations (Article 7) and shall not prevent the application of international conventions between the High Contracting Parties which provide for more liberal exemptions from attachment (Article 8). The present Convention shall apply on the territory of any one of the High Contracting Parties to any aircraft registered in the territory of another High Contracting Party, including any territory under the sovereign power, suzerainty, protection, mandate or authority of the said High Contracting Party, for which the latter is a party to the Convention (Article 9).

296. In the frame of this Convention, a precautionary attachment is an act, whatever it may be called, whereby an aircraft is seized, in a private interest, through the medium of agents of justice or of the public administration, for the benefit either of a creditor, or of the owner, or of the holder of a lien on the aircraft, where the attaching claimant cannot invoke a judgment and execution, obtained beforehand in the ordinary course of procedure, or an equivalent right of execution (Article 2, 1).

297. Its scope is extended to the case where the applicable law gives the right of detention to the creditor who holds the aircraft without the consent of the operator (Article 2, 2).

298. Some aircraft are exempt from precautionary attachment (Article 3):

- any aircraft assigned exclusively to a Government service, the postal service included, commerce excepted;
- any aircraft actually put in service on a regular line of public transportation and indispensable reserve aircraft;
- any other aircraft assigned to transportation of persons or property for hire, when it is ready to depart for such transportation, except in a case involving a debt contracted for the trip which it is about to make or a claim arising in the course of

the trip, except in the case of a precautionary attachment made by the owner of an aircraft who has been dispossessed of the same by an unlawful act.

299. In case, attachment is not prohibited or in case the aircraft is exempt from attachment and the operator does not invoke such exemption, an adequate bond shall prevent the precautionary attachment or give a right to immediate release (Article 4, (1)). The bond shall be adequate if it covers the amount of the debt and the costs and is assigned exclusively to payment of the creditor, or if it covers the value of the aircraft in case this is less than the amount of the debt and costs (Article 4, (2)).

300. In every case, a judgment shall be rendered on a suit for release of the precautionary attachment in a summary and rapid procedure (Article 5).

301. If an aircraft has been attached which is exempt from attachment according to the provisions of the present Convention, or if the debtor has had to furnish a bond to prevent the attachment or to obtain the release thereof, the attaching claimant shall be liable in accordance with the law of the forum for the resulting damage to the operator or the owner (Article 6, (1)). The same rule applies in case a precautionary attachment has been made without just cause (Article 6, (2)).

Chapter 4. The Convention on the International Recognition of Rights in Aircraft, Signed in Geneva, on 19 June 1948

302. The Convention on the International Recognition of Rights in Aircraft, signed in Geneva on 19 June 1948 (Geneva Convention), refers to the recommendation of the International Civil Aviation Conference of Chicago from November–December 1944, to adopt shortly a Convention dealing with the transfer of title to aircraft. In view of the future expansion of international civil aviation, it purports to fulfil the need for an international recognition of rights in aircraft.

303. The present Convention, which is partly subject to State-specific special declarations, has entered into force in ninety-one States.

304. The present Convention applies in the Contracting States, for aircraft registered as to nationality in another Contracting State, and it applies partly to aircraft registered in the same Contracting State as to nationality (pursuant to Article XI: Articles II, III, IX, and Article IV, unless the salvage or preservation operations have been terminated within its own Territory).

305. National laws in immigration, customs and air navigation are unaffected (Article XII).

306. Aircraft used in military, customs or police services are not concerned (Article XIII).

307. For the purpose of this Convention, the competent judicial and administrative authorities of the Contracting States may, subject to any contrary provision in their national law, correspond directly with each other (Article XIV) and the Contracting States shall take such measures as are necessary for the fulfilment of the provisions of this Convention and shall forthwith inform the Secretary-General of the International Civil Aviation Organization of these measures (Article XV).

308. The concept of aircraft includes the airframe, engines, propellers, radio apparatus, and all other articles intended for use in the aircraft whether installed therein or temporarily separated therefrom (Article XVI).

309. If a separate register of aircraft for purposes of nationality is maintained in any territory for whose foreign relations a Contracting State is responsible, references in this Convention to the law of the Contracting State shall be construed as references to the law of that territory (Article XVII).

310. The Convention purports to assume the mutual recognition of the following rights (Article I, 1.):

- rights of property in aircraft;
- rights to acquire aircraft by purchase coupled with possession of the aircraft;
- rights to possession of aircraft under leases of at least six months;

– mortgages, hypothèques and similar rights in aircraft which are contractually created as security for payment of an indebtedness (according to Article V, the priority of such right extends to all sums thereby secured and the amount of interest included shall not exceed that accrued during the three years prior to the execution proceedings together with that accrued during the execution proceedings), provided that such rights have been constituted in accordance with the law of the Contracting State in which the aircraft was registered as to nationality at the time of their constitution and are regularly recorded in a public record of the Contracting State in which the aircraft is registered as to nationality.

311. And in this frame, the regularity of successive recordings in different Contracting States shall be determined in accordance with the law of the State where the aircraft was registered as to nationality at the time of each recording.

312. Although the recognition of any rights in aircraft under the law of any Contracting State is not prohibited, Contracting States shall not admit or recognise any right as taking priority over the rights the mutual recognition of is provided for according to the present Article (Article I, 2.).

313. The Convention organises a specific national recording system for the rights it concerns (Articles II and III).

314. In the event that any claims in respect of compensation due for salvage of the aircraft, or extraordinary expenses indispensable for the preservation of the aircraft give rise, under the law of the Contracting State where the operations of salvage or preservation were terminated, to a right conferring a charge against the aircraft, such right shall be recognised by the Contracting States and shall take priority over all other rights in the aircraft (Article IV, 1.).

315. These rights shall be satisfied in the inverse order of the dates of the incidents in connexion with which they have arisen (Article IV, 2.). Any of these rights may, within three months from the date of the termination of the salvage or preservation operations, be noted on the Record (Article IV, 3.). They shall not be recognised in other Contracting States after expiration of the three months period unless, within this period, the right has been duly noted on the record and the amount has been agreed upon or judicial action on the right has been commenced; as far as judicial action is concerned, the law of the forum shall determine the contingencies upon which the three months period may be interrupted or suspended (Article IV, 4.). In this frame, Contracting States shall not admit or recognise any right as taking priority over the rights the mutual recognition of is provided for according to Article I, 2. (Article IV, 5.).

316. In case of attachment or sale of an aircraft in execution, or of any right therein, the Contracting States shall not be obliged to recognise, as against the attaching or executing creditor or against the purchaser, any right the present Convention provides for the mutual recognition of, or the transfer of any such right, if constituted or effected with knowledge of the sale or execution proceedings by the person against whom the proceedings are directed (Article VI).

317. The proceedings of a sale of an aircraft in execution shall be determined by the law of the Contracting State where the sale takes place (Article VII, 1). It is submitted to specific procedural requirements as follows (Article VII, 2). The date and place of the sale shall be fixed at least six weeks in advance and the executing creditor shall supply to the Court or other competent authority a certified extract of the recordings concerning the aircraft. It shall give public notice of the sale at the place where the aircraft is registered as to nationality, in accordance with the law there applicable, at least one month before the day fixed, and shall concurrently notify by registered letter, if possible by air mail, the recorded owner and the holders of recorded rights in the aircraft and of rights noted on the record under Article IV, paragraph 3, according to their addresses as shown on the record.

318. The consequences of failure to observe such requirements (Article VII, 3) shall be as provided by the law of the Contracting State where the sale takes place. However, any sale taking place in contravention of these requirements may be annulled upon demand made within six months from the date of the sale by any person suffering damage as the result of such contravention.

319. No sale in execution can be effected unless all rights having priority over the claim of the executing creditor in accordance with this Convention which is established before the competent authority, are covered by the proceeds of sale or assumed by the purchaser (Article VII, 4).

320. When injury or damage is caused to persons or property(Article VII, 5) on the surface of the Contracting State where the execution sale takes place, by any aircraft subject to any right to be mutually recognised by the present Convention held as security for indebtedness unless adequate and effective insurance by a State or an insurance undertaking in any State has been provided by or on behalf of the operator to cover such injury or damage, the national law of such Contracting State may provide in case of the seizure of such aircraft or any other aircraft owned by the same person and encumbered with any similar right held by the same creditor:

- that the provisions of Article VII, 4. above shall have no effect with regard to the person suffering such injury or damage or his representative if he is an executing creditor;
- that any right to be mutually recognised pursuant to the present Convention held as security for an indebtedness encumbering the aircraft may not be set up against any person suffering such injury or damage or his representative in excess of an amount equal to 80% of the sale price. In the absence of other limits established by the law of the Contracting State where the execution sale takes place, the insurance shall be considered adequate within the meaning of the rule if the amount of the insurance corresponds to the value when new of the aircraft seized in execution.

321. Costs legally chargeable under the law of the Contracting State where the sale takes place, which are incurred in the common interest of creditors in the course of execution proceedings leading to sale shall be paid out of the proceeds of sale before any claims (Article VII, 6). Such sale of an aircraft in execution shall effect the transfer of the property in such aircraft free from all rights which are not assumed by the purchaser (Article VIII).

322. In other cases than this of the sale in execution in conformity with the provisions of Article VII, no transfer of an aircraft from the nationality register or the record of a Contracting State to that of another Contracting State shall be made, unless all holders of recorded rights have been satisfied or consent to the transfer (Article IX).

323. If a recorded right in an aircraft of the nature specified in Article I, and held as security for the payment of indebtedness, extends, in conformity with the law of the Contracting State where the aircraft is registered, to spare parts stored in a specified place or places, such right shall be recognised by all Contracting States, as long as the spare parts remain in the place or places specified, provided that an appropriate public notice, specifying the description of the right, the name and address of the holder of this right and the record in which such right is recorded, is exhibited at the place where the spare parts are located, so as to give due notification to third parties that such spare parts are encumbered (Article X, 1). Spare parts are parts of aircraft, engines, propellers, radio apparatus, instruments, appliances, furnishings, parts of any of the foregoing, and generally any other articles of whatever description maintained for installation in aircraft in substitution for parts or articles removed (Article X, 4). A statement indicating the character and the approximate number of such spare parts shall be annexed to or included in the recorded document and such parts may be replaced by similar parts without affecting the right of the creditor (Article X, 2).

324. According to Article X, 3, Article VII, 1 and 4, and Article VIII shall apply to a sale of spare parts in execution, but where the executing creditor is an unsecured creditor, paragraph 4 of Article VII in its application to such a sale shall be construed so as to permit the sale to take place if a bid is received in an amount not less than two-thirds of the value of the spare parts as determined by experts appointed by the authority responsible for the sale. Further, in the distribution of the proceeds of sale, the competent authority may, in order to provide for the claim of the executing creditor, limit the amount payable to holders of prior rights to two-thirds of such proceeds of sale after payment of the costs referred to in Article VII, paragraph 6.

325. The fact that both the Geneva Convention and the Cape Town Convention cover different types of international interests and rights has been qualified as a 'functional approach' (Giulia Mauri, *La Convenzione di Città del Capo e il protocollo aeronautico*. Contratta e Impresa, 2009, 509).

Chapter 5. The Convention Concerning International Carriage by Rail of 9 May 1980 in the Version of the Protocol of Modification of 3 June 1999

326. The COTIF 1999 has entered into force for forty-seven Contracting States as well as the EU.

327. According to Article 12, § 5 of the COTIF 1999, on the seizure of railway vehicles, the cases where such seizure is admitted are limited:

> Railway vehicles may only be seized on a territory other than that of the Member State in which the keeper has its registered office, under a judgment given by the judicial authority of that State. The term 'keeper' means the person who, being the owner or having the right to dispose of it, exploits the railway vehicle economically in a permanent manner as a means of transport.

328. This rule is different from Article 42 (Article 42 does not concern insolvency proceedings, pursuant to Article 45 of the Cape Town Convention) of the Cape Town Convention, which pays attention to the choice of jurisdiction (Benjamin B. von Bodungen, *Mobiliarsicherungsrecht an Luftfahrzeugen und Eisenbahnrollmaterial im nationalen und internationalen Rechtsverkehr, Zugleich ein Beitrag zur internationalen Vereinheitlichung des Rechtes nationaler Mobiliarsicherheiten durch das Kapstadt-Übereinkommen*. 2009, 385), and it is possible to incorporate the rule of Article 12, § 5. of the COTIF 1999 on the competence of the judicial authority of the State in which the keeper has its registered office as regarding the choice of the competent court.

329. Attention is to be paid to the position of the EU. According to Article 2 of the Agreement between the EU and the Intergovernmental Organization for International Carriage by Rail on the Accession of the EU to the Convention concerning International Carriage by Rail (COTIF) of 9 May 1980, as amended by the Vilnius Protocol of 3 June 1999, 'in their mutual relations, Parties to the Convention which are the Member States of the Union shall apply Union rules and shall therefore not apply the rules arising from that Convention except in so far as there is no Union rule governing the particular subject concerned'. It may concern the new Regulation (EU) No. 1215/2012 of the European Parliament and of the Council of 12 December 2012 on jurisdiction and the recognition and enforcement of judgments in civil and commercial matters, which modernises the Council Regulation (EC) No. 44/2001 of 22 December 2000 on jurisdiction and the recognition and enforcement of judgments in civil and commercial matters and also has been quoted in the 'Declaration to be made pursuant to Article XXII(2) concerning the competence of the European Union over matters governed by the Protocol to the Convention on International Interests in Mobile Equipment on Matters Specific to Railway Rolling Stock (the "Rail Protocol"), adopted in Luxembourg on 23 February 2007, in respect of which the Member States have transferred their competence to the

Union.' According to Article 6, 2 of this Regulation, which recalls Article 4, 2 of the Regulation 44/2001 exactly, as against a defendant not domiciled in a Member State, any person domiciled in a Member State may, whatever his nationality, avail himself in that State of the rules of jurisdiction there in force, and in particular those specified in Article 76, 1, (a), which refers to Annex I of the Regulation No. 44/2001, in the same way as the nationals of that State. The Cape Town Convention, which completes the Rail Protocol and thus constitutes the 'Convention on International Interests in Mobile Equipment as applied to railway rolling stock', applies only if the debtor is located in a Cape Town Contracting State at the time of the conclusion of the agreement creating or providing for the international interest, no matter the location of the creditor (Article 3 of the Cape Town Convention). As a matter of consequence, as for the defendant who is not located in an EU Member State and has not been, as a debtor, located in a Contracting State of the Cape Town Convention at the time of the conclusion of the agreement creating or providing for the international interest, such debtor may be, as for the seizure of the Railway vehicles it is the keeper of, subject to Article 6, 2 of the Regulation No. 1215/2012, for instance, concerning United Kingdom rules which enable a jurisdiction to be founded on the document instituting the proceedings having been served on the defendant during his temporary presence in the United Kingdom, or the presence within the United Kingdom of property belonging to the defendant, or the seizure by the plaintiff of property situated in the United Kingdom, according to the Annex I of the Regulation No. 44/2001 Article 76, 1, a) of the Regulation No. 1215/2012 refers to, provided that mutual relations between Member States are involved. This rule may be considered having common points with Article 12, § 5 of the COTIF 1999. Further developments are expected with the exit of the United Kingdom from the EU. Similarly, for this case, Irish law also enables jurisdiction to be founded on the document instituting the proceedings having been served on the defendant during his temporary presence in Ireland. At national level, jurisdiction may be based on the location of assets, for instance under German law (pursuant to Article § 23 of German Civil Procedure Code, Zivilprozessordnung) or under Austrian law (Article § 99 of Austrian Procedural Law, Jurisdiktionsnorm).

Part III. Method of the Cape Town Convention and Its Protocols

330. Numerous previous legal instruments inspire the Cape Town Convention and its Protocols. It results from the analysis of the methods used by the Cape Town Convention legal system, which has several common points with the other existing international legal instruments. The Cape Town Convention itself states in its preamble that it takes into consideration 'the objectives and principles enunciated in existing Conventions' relating to the mobile equipment it concerns.

Chapter 1. EBRD Model Law on Secured Transactions

331. The European Bank for Reconstruction and Development (EBRD) Model Law on secured transactions is a model for UNIDROIT. In 1994 (UNIDROIT 1994, Study LXXIIA, doc. 3, restricted working group responsible for determining the desirability and feasibility of the preparation by UNIDROIT of a model law in the general field of secured transactions, comments on the UNIDROIT project for drawing up a checklist of the issues to be addressed in a possible future model law in the general field of secured transactions, by John L. Simpson and Jan-Henrick M. Röver, EBRD), the restricted working group responsible for determining the desirability and feasibility of the preparation by UNIDROIT of a model law in the general field of secured transactions expressed the concepts underlying EBRD Model as follows:

1. The distinguished feature of a charge or security interest is that it is a right in rem. The right in rem under a charge is a limited entitlement to realise the charged property in order to satisfy a money obligation.
2. While recognising the attraction of a 'form over substance' approach, we did not consider it the best solution where there exists a wide diversity of legal traditions and varying levels of legal sophistication.
3. The limitation relating to business activity was only introduced because of the absence of adequate rules for consumer protection which were outside the scope of our brief.
4. A charge may secure all kinds of debt providing it is capable of expression in money terms.
5. A charge may cover all types of property, movable or immovable, things or rights, present or future.
6. Both the charged property and the secured debt may change during the life of the charge provided that they are properly identified (either specifically or generally) at the time the charge is granted. Thus a charge may be granted to secure a constantly changing pool of debt (e.g., all monies due under one of a number of bank facilities) over a constantly changing pool of assets (e.g., inventory).
7. There should be only one type of charge irrespective of the type of property charged, the type of debt secured, and the identity of the persons giving and receiving the charge (the unitary concept). This relates to the *substance* of a charge: the right in rem under a charge is always, in substance, the same. It does not prevent the *form* of a charge from being different according to the circumstances.
8. The creation of a charge necessitates an agreement between the parties and a means by which third parties may become aware of the charge (e.g., by registration or possession).
9. In the case of a non-possessory charge the charger remains free to use (and in some cases to sell) the charged property.

10. The charge must give flexible rights of enforcement which protect the charger and his other creditors from abuse but also recognise the fundamental purpose of a charge to give an effective alternative means of obtaining payment of a debt when the debtor defaults.

332. The EBRD Model Law insists on the importance of rights in rem in financing business activities and works as a toolbox for local legal systems, which have a broad sphere of appreciation while concretising the model law. Due to the numerous possibilities of reservations and declarations, the Cape Town Convention and its Protocol may be conceived as very similar to the system of Model Laws such as the EBRD one. Such a system is based on the willingness to avoid 'over-regulation' (Michel Nussbaumer & Frédérique Dahan, *Promoting Legal Reform in Eastern Europe: the EBRD Approach, in Private Law in the Eastern Europe*. 2010, 40).

Chapter 2. Model Inter-American Law on Secured Transactions

333. The Model Inter-American Law on Secured Transactions (*see* Herbert Kronke, 'Financial Leasing and Its Unification by UNIDROIT', *General Reports on the XVIIIth Congress of the International Academy of Comparative Law*, edited by Karen B. Brown & David V. Snyder, 332) also creates a legal frame for local legal orders on secured interests such as rights in rem. Its objective is to 'regulate security interest in movable property securing the performance of any obligations of any nature, present or future, determined or determinable' (Article 1, first paragraph). It specifies that a State may declare that it does not apply to the types of collateral expressly specified in its text (Article 1, paragraph 2), which is typical for a model law: in the frame of the implementation of the text, a sphere of freedom is let to the local law-makers.

334. Contrary to the EBRD Model Law, the Model Inter-American Law on Secured Transactions imposes the creation of a local registration system: a State adopting this Model Law shall create a unitary and uniform registration system applicable to all existing movable property security devices in the local legal framework, in order to give effect to this Model Law (Article 1, third paragraph).

335. At the international level, in particular, the present Model Law contains rules of conflicts of laws. According to its Article 69:

> In cases where a security interest has contacts with more than one State, the law of the State in which the collateral is located at the time the security interest is created shall govern issues relating to the validity, publicity and priority of:
>
> I. A security interest in corporeal movable property other than movable property of the kind referred to in the next Article; and
> II. A possessory security interest in incorporeal movable property.
>
> If the collateral is moved to a different State than that in which the security interest was previously publicized, the law of the State to which the collateral has been moved governs issues relating to the publicity and priority of the security interest as against unsecured creditors and third persons who acquire rights in the collateral after the relocation. However, the priority of the security interest acquired under the law of the previous location of the collateral is preserved if the security interest is publicized in accordance with the law of the State of the new location within ninety days after the relocation of the property.

Its Article 70 states that:

> In cases where a secured transaction has contacts with more than one State, the law of the State in which the secured debtor is located – According to Article 72, 'a secured debtor is considered located in the State where the secured

debtor maintains the central administration of its business and if the secured debtor does not operate a business or does not have a place of business, the secured debtor is considered located in the State of its habitual residence' – when the security interest is created governs issues relating to the validity, publicity and priority of:

I. A non-possessory security interest in incorporeal property; and
II. A security interest in movable corporeal property if the property is held by the secured debtor as equipment for use in the secured debtor's business, or as inventory for lease.

If the secured debtor changes its location to a different State than that in which the security interest was previously publicized, the law of the State of the secured debtor's new location governs issues relating to the publicity and priority of the security interest as against unsecured creditors and third persons who acquire rights in the collateral after the relocation. However, the priority of the security interest acquired under the law of the previous location of the secured debtor is preserved if the security interest is publicized in accordance with the law of the State of the secured debtor's new location within 90 days after the relocation of the debtor.

'The priority of a non-possessory security interest in negotiable incorporeal property as against third persons that acquire a possessory interest in the property is governed by the law of the State where the collateral is located when the possessory interest is acquired.' (Article 71).

336. This involvement of conflicts of law rules also appears in the Cape Town Convention ad its Protocols.

Chapter 3. UNCITRAL Model Law on Cross-Border Insolvency

337. The UNCITRAL Model Law on Cross-Border Insolvency 1997 is also a legal frame – partly – dedicated to rights in rem. It is considered a legal frame which could be suitable for a global legal harmonisation in this field of law: the General Assembly of the UN has recommended to the States Parties to the UN to follow this Model Law. This Model Law cares for insolvency cases where goods concerned are located in many States, concerning enterprises as well as individuals facing insolvency proceeds. One of the main principles of this Model Law is the concept of co-operation between Contracting States for their transnational litigations. Although this Model Law does not address very directly security interests over movable assets moved from one State to another, its principle of co-operation between foreign courts and foreign representatives (Articles 25–27) is recalled (Sara Isham, 'UNCITRAL's Model Law on Cross-Border Insolvency, a Workable Protection for Transnational Investment at Last', *Brooklyn Journal of International Law* Vol. 26 (2001): 1204) in the Cape Town Convention and its Protocols. In this context, one may say that the UNCITRAL Model Law on cross-border insolvency is concretely a 'first step' (André J. Berends, *The UNCITRAL Model Law on Cross-Border Insolvency*. 1998, 319) to international Conventions.

Chapter 4. OHADA Uniform Act on Securities

338. The Organisation for the Harmonization in Africa of Business Law (OHADA) Uniform Act on Securities from the 15 December 2010 (*see* Boubacar S. Diarrah, 'Les innovations introduites dans l'Acte uniforme portant organisation des sûretés', *Revue de droit uniforme africain* N°005, 2ème trimester 2011 (2011): 3–7; Crocq, Pierre, Le nouvel acte uniforme portant organisation de sûretés, La réforme du droit des sûretés de l'Ohada, 2012) is a uniform law on securities, including rights in rem. It pays attention to formalism (*see* Dalé Hélène Labitey, 'Quel droit des sûretés réelles pour l'Ohada?', *Revue congolaise de droit et des affaires* Vol. 6 (2011): 66) and sets up a specific legal order for the law of securities, first at national level. A specificity of the OHADA system is the Common Court of Justice and Arbitration (*see* Gaston Kenfack Douajni, 'L'expérience internationale de la Cour commune de justice et d'arbitrage (CCJA) de l'Organisation pour l'harmonisation en Afrique du droit des affaires (OHADA)', *Revue camerounaise de l'arbitrage* Vol. 39 (2007): 4 and 5; Assepo Assi Eugène, 'La Cour commune de justice et d'arbitrage de l'OHADA: un troisième degré de jurisdiction?', *Revue international de droit comparé* Vol. 57(4) (2005): 943–955), which is common to the seventeen States Parties to the OHADA and judges definitely, as a Supreme Court, as for judgments made, in the last instance, by the corresponding national Courts on the OHADA's uniform acts.

Chapter 5. European Union

339. At the level of the EU, the principle is the protection of the creditor's rights in rem in cases of insolvency proceedings. According to Article 8, point 1 of the European Insolvency Regulation, 'the opening of insolvency proceedings shall not affect the rights in rem of creditors or third parties in respect of tangible or intangible, moveable or immoveable assets, both specific assets and collections of indefinite assets as a whole which change from time to time, belonging to the debtor which are situated within the territory of another Member State at the time of the opening of proceedings', and according to its Article 10, point 1, 'the opening of insolvency proceedings against the purchaser of an asset shall not affect the seller's rights that are based on a reservation of title where at the time of the opening of proceedings the asset is situated within the territory of a Member State other than the State of opening of proceedings'. The Directive 2011/7/EU of 16 February 2011 on Combating Late Payment in Commercial Transactions states, in its Article 9, first paragraph, that 'Member States shall provide in conformity with the applicable national provisions designated by private international law that the seller retains title to goods until they are fully paid for if a retention of title clause has been expressly agreed between the buyer and the seller before the delivery of the goods.' In this frame, the European Union Court of Justice has judged, on 26 October 2006 (Case C-302/05, Commission of the European Communities against Italy), that that directive does not harmonise all the rules relating to late payments in commercial transactions (no. 23) and refers to a number of areas in which national law is to apply, in particular with regard to the various procedures of forced execution of an enforceable title as well as the conditions under which forced execution of such a title can be stopped (no. 24). In the frame of the entrance into force of the Cape Town Convention and its Aircraft Protocol at the level of the EU, and as regards to its approval of the Rail Protocol, the European Union Court of Justice is called to interpret the Cape Town Convention and its Protocol. In this frame, one may ask if the European Union Court of Justice will play a very similar role to this as the OHADA's Common Court of Justice and Arbitration.

Conclusion

340. To conclude, the Cape Town Convention on International Interests in Mobile Equipment and its Protocols seems to be a beginning ready for the future. Indeed, it now aims at harmonising diverse forms of security interests with a core legal instrument linked to protocols dedicated to special technical domains: aircraft, railway rolling stock, space assets and furthermore, agricultural, construction and mining equipment. As such, this new set of rules faces the challenge that it goes further than traditional transnational model laws: it adopts the role of coexisting with other international conventions, with private international law rules and contractual concepts such as contractual freedom, contractor's protection or the balance of the contracts. Simultaneously, this new legal system is only possible due to advances in modern technology, with which it is closely linked: international registers of security interests, which were denied by doctrine in the past legal history, are now trusted in order to fulfil legal harmonisation aspirations and are the base of this legal innovation. States are free to sovereignly adhere to any local or international legal norm: this rule is in force for competing agreements as well as for the Cape Town Convention and its Protocols. Even regional economic integration organisations, like the EU, are invited to adopt such adhesion, and the adhesion enshrined in the Cape Town Convention system is open to other such organisations which are able to make international relationships on security interests always more efficient in many decisive technical domains. One of the merits of the Cape Town Convention system for security interests is to bring transparency in a matter in which local legal barriers have been a concrete hindrance for transnational exchanges for a long time, through offering a unique set of normative texts which are open to States' adhesions and to the analysis of legal common sense. The Cape Town Convention Academic Project has understood this perspective and takes part in this legal harmonisation process. The limit of the methods used in order to spread legal rationality among the transnational management of security interests seems to be the contractual freedom itself, which is also duly encouraged, in a cooperative lawmaking process. The possible involvement of supranational justice entities such as the Court of Justice of the European Union as well as the OHADA Common Court of Justice and Arbitration, which care for security interests, seems to also pave the way for legal progress.

Part IV. Appendix: Documents

(These documents are reproduced with the permission of ICAO and UNIDROIT.)

Chapter 1. The Convention on International Interests in Mobile Equipment

CONVENTION ON INTERNATIONAL INTERESTS IN MOBILE EQUIPMENT
THE STATES PARTIES TO THIS CONVENTION,
AWARE of the need to acquire and use mobile equipment of high value or particular economic significance and to facilitate the financing of the acquisition and use of such equipment in an efficient manner,
RECOGNISING the advantages of asset-based financing and leasing for this purpose and desiring to facilitate these types of transaction by establishing clear rules to govern them,
MINDFUL of the need to ensure that interests in such equipment are recognised and protected universally,
DESIRING to provide broad and mutual economic benefits for all interested parties,
BELIEVING that such rules must reflect the principles underlying asset-based financing and leasing and promote the autonomy of the parties necessary in these transactions,
CONSCIOUS of the need to establish a legal framework for international interests in such equipment and for that purpose to create an international registration system for their protection,
TAKING INTO CONSIDERATION the objectives and principles enunciated in existing Conventions relating to such equipment,
HAVE AGREED upon the following provisions:

Chapter I – Sphere of application and general provisions

Article 1 – Definitions

In this Convention, except where the context otherwise requires, the following terms are employed with the meanings set out below:

(a) 'agreement' means a security agreement, a title reservation agreement or a leasing agreement;
(b) 'assignment' means a contract which, whether by way of security or otherwise, confers on the assignee associated rights with or without a transfer of the related international interest;
(c) 'associated rights' means all rights to payment or other performance by a debtor under an agreement which are secured by or associated with the object;
(d) 'commencement of the insolvency proceedings' means the time at which the insolvency proceedings are deemed to commence under the applicable insolvency law;
(e) 'conditional buyer' means a buyer under a title reservation agreement;
(f) 'conditional seller' means a seller under a title reservation agreement;
(g) 'contract of sale' means a contract for the sale of an object by a seller to a buyer which is not an agreement as defined in (a) above;

(h) 'court' means a court of law or an administrative or arbitral tribunal established by a Contracting State;
(i) 'creditor' means a chargee under a security agreement, a conditional seller under a title reservation agreement or a lessor under a leasing agreement;
(j) 'debtor' means a chargor under a security agreement, a conditional buyer under a title reservation agreement, a lessee under a leasing agreement or a person whose interest in an object is burdened by a registrable non-consensual right or interest;
(k) 'insolvency administrator' means a person authorised to administer the reorganisation or liquidation, including one authorised on an interim basis, and includes a debtor in possession if permitted by the applicable insolvency law;
(l) 'insolvency proceedings' means bankruptcy, liquidation or other collective judicial or administrative proceedings, including interim proceedings, in which the assets and affairs of the debtor are subject to control or supervision by a court for the purposes of reorganisation or liquidation;
(m) 'interested persons' means:
  (i) the debtor;
  (ii) any person who, for the purpose of assuring performance of any of the obligations in favour of the creditor, gives or issues a suretyship or demand guarantee or a standby letter of credit or any other form of credit insurance;
  (iii) any other person having rights in or over the object;
(n) 'internal transaction' means a transaction of a type listed in Article 2(2)(a) to (c) where the centre of the main interests of all parties to such transaction is situated, and the relevant object located (as specified in the Protocol), in the same Contracting State at the time of the conclusion of the contract and where the interest created by the transaction has been registered in a national registry in that Contracting State which has made a declaration under Article 50(1);
(o) 'international interest' means an interest held by a creditor to which Article 2 applies;
(p) 'International Registry' means the international registration facilities established for the purposes of this Convention or the Protocol;
(q) 'leasing agreement' means an agreement by which one person (the lessor) grants a right to possession or control of an object (with or without an option to purchase) to another person (the lessee) in return for a rental or other payment;
(r) 'national interest' means an interest held by a creditor in an object and created by an internal transaction covered by a declaration under Article 50(1);
(s) 'non-consensual right or interest' means a right or interest conferred under the law of a Contracting State which has made a declaration under Article 39 to secure the performance of an obligation, including an obligation to a State, State entity or an intergovernmental or private organisation;
(t) 'notice of a national interest' means notice registered or to be registered in the International Registry that a national interest has been created;
(u) 'object' means an object of a category to which Article 2 applies;

(v) 'pre-existing right or interest' means a right or interest of any kind in or over an object created or arising before the effective date of this Convention as defined by Article 60(2)(a);
(w) 'proceeds' means money or non-money proceeds of an object arising from the total or partial loss or physical destruction of the object or its total or partial confiscation, condemnation or requisition;
(x) 'prospective assignment' means an assignment that is intended to be made in the future, upon the occurrence of a stated event, whether or not the occurrence of the event is certain;
(y) 'prospective international interest' means an interest that is intended to be created or provided for in an object as an international interest in the future, upon the occurrence of a stated event (which may include the debtor's acquisition of an interest in the object), whether or not the occurrence of the event is certain;
(z) 'prospective sale' means a sale which is intended to be made in the future, upon the occurrence of a stated event, whether or not the occurrence of the event is certain;
(aa) 'Protocol' means, in respect of any category of object and associated rights to which this Convention applies, the Protocol in respect of that category of object and associated rights;
(bb) 'registered' means registered in the International Registry pursuant to Chapter V;
(cc) 'registered interest' means an international interest, a registrable non-consensual right or interest or a national interest specified in a notice of a national interest registered pursuant to Chapter V;
(dd) 'registrable non-consensual right or interest' means a non-consensual right or interest registrable pursuant to a declaration deposited under Article 40;
(ee) 'Registrar' means, in respect of the Protocol, the person or body designated by that Protocol or appointed under Article 17(2)(b);
(ff) 'regulations' means regulations made or approved by the Supervisory Authority pursuant to the Protocol;
(gg) 'sale' means a transfer of ownership of an object pursuant to a contract of sale;
(hh) 'secured obligation' means an obligation secured by a security interest;
(ii) 'security agreement' means an agreement by which a chargor grants or agrees to grant to a chargee an interest (including an ownership interest) in or over an object to secure the performance of any existing or future obligation of the chargor or a third person;
(jj) 'security interest' means an interest created by a security agreement;
(kk) 'Supervisory Authority' means, in respect of the Protocol, the Supervisory Authority referred to in Article 17(1);
(ll) 'title reservation agreement' means an agreement for the sale of an object on terms that ownership does not pass until fulfilment of the condition or conditions stated in the agreement;
(mm) 'unregistered interest' means a consensual interest or non-consensual right or interest (other than an interest to which Article 39 applies) which has not been registered, whether or not it is registrable under this Convention; and

(nn) 'writing' means a record of information (including information communicated by teletransmission) which is in tangible or other form and is capable of being reproduced in tangible form on a subsequent occasion and which indicates by reasonable means a person's approval of the record.

Article 2 – The international interest

1. This Convention provides for the constitution and effects of an international interest in certain categories of mobile equipment and associated rights.
2. For the purposes of this Convention, an international interest in mobile equipment is an interest, constituted under Article 7, in a uniquely identifiable object of a category of such objects listed in paragraph 3 and designated in the Protocol:
   (a) granted by the chargor under a security agreement;
   (b) vested in a person who is the conditional seller under a title reservation agreement; or
   (c) vested in a person who is the lessor under a leasing agreement.

   An interest falling within sub-paragraph (a) does not also fall within sub-paragraph (b) or (c).
3. The categories referred to in the preceding paragraphs are:
   (a) airframes, aircraft engines and helicopters;
   (b) railway rolling stock; and
   (c) space assets.
4. The applicable law determines whether an interest to which paragraph 2 applies falls within sub-paragraph (a), (b) or (c) of that paragraph.
5. An international interest in an object extends to proceeds of that object.

Article 3 – Sphere of application

1. This Convention applies when, at the time of the conclusion of the agreement creating or providing for the international interest, the debtor is situated in a Contracting State.
2. The fact that the creditor is situated in a non-Contracting State does not affect the applicability of this Convention.

Article 4 – Where debtor is situated

1. For the purposes of Article 3(1), the debtor is situated in any Contracting State:
   (a) under the law of which it is incorporated or formed;
   (b) where it has its registered office or statutory seat;
   (c) where it has its centre of administration; or
   (d) where it has its place of business.

2. A reference in sub-paragraph (d) of the preceding paragraph to the debtor's place of business shall, if it has more than one place of business, mean its principal place of business or, if it has no place of business, its habitual residence.

Article 5 – Interpretation and applicable law

1. In the interpretation of this Convention, regard is to be had to its purposes as set forth in the preamble, to its international character and to the need to promote uniformity and predictability in its application.
2. Questions concerning matters governed by this Convention which are not expressly settled in it are to be settled in conformity with the general principles on which it is based or, in the absence of such principles, in conformity with the applicable law.
3. References to the applicable law are to the domestic rules of the law applicable by virtue of the rules of private international law of the forum State.
4. Where a State comprises several territorial units, each of which has its own rules of law in respect of the matter to be decided, and where there is no indication of the relevant territorial unit, the law of that State decides which is the territorial unit whose rules shall govern. In the absence of any such rule, the law of the territorial unit with which the case is most closely connected shall apply.

Article 6 – Relationship between the Convention and the Protocol

1. This Convention and the Protocol shall be read and interpreted together as a single instrument.
2. To the extent of any inconsistency between this Convention and the Protocol, the Protocol shall prevail.

Chapter II – Constitution of an international interest

Article 7 – Formal requirements

An interest is constituted as an international interest under this Convention where the agreement creating or providing for the interest:

(a) is in writing;
(b) relates to an object of which the chargor, conditional seller or lessor has power to dispose;
(c) enables the object to be identified in conformity with the Protocol; and
(d) in the case of a security agreement, enables the secured obligations to be determined, but without the need to state a sum or maximum sum secured.

Chapter III – Default remedies

Article 8 – Remedies of chargee

1. In the event of default as provided in Article 11, the chargee may, to the extent that the chargor has at any time so agreed and subject to any declaration that may be made by a Contracting State under Article 54, exercise any one or more of the following remedies:
   (a) take possession or control of any object charged to it;
   (b) sell or grant a lease of any such object;
   (c) collect or receive any income or profits arising from the management or use of any such object.
2. The chargee may alternatively apply for a court order authorising or directing any of the acts referred to in the preceding paragraph.
3. Any remedy set out in sub-paragraph (a), (b) or (c) of paragraph 1 or by Article 13 shall be exercised in a commercially reasonable manner. A remedy shall be deemed to be exercised in a commercially reasonable manner where it is exercised in conformity with a provision of the security agreement except where such a provision is manifestly unreasonable.
4. A chargee proposing to sell or grant a lease of an object under paragraph 1 shall give reasonable prior notice in writing of the proposed sale or lease to:
   (a) interested persons specified in Article 1(m)(i) and (ii); and
   (b) interested persons specified in Article 1(m)(iii) who have given notice of their rights to the chargee within a reasonable time prior to the sale or lease.
5. Any sum collected or received by the chargee as a result of exercise of any of the remedies set out in paragraph 1 or 2 shall be applied towards discharge of the amount of the secured obligations.
6. Where the sums collected or received by the chargee as a result of the exercise of any remedy set out in paragraph 1 or 2 exceed the amount secured by the security interest and any reasonable costs incurred in the exercise of any such remedy, then unless otherwise ordered by the court the chargee shall distribute the surplus among holders of subsequently ranking interests which have been registered or of which the chargee has been given notice, in order of priority, and pay any remaining balance to the chargor.

Article 9 – Vesting of object in satisfaction; redemption

1. At any time after default as provided in Article 11, the chargee and all the interested persons may agree that ownership of (or any other interest of the chargor in) any object covered by the security interest shall vest in the chargee in or towards satisfaction of the secured obligations.
2. The court may on the application of the chargee order that ownership of (or any other interest of the chargor in) any object covered by the security interest shall vest in the chargee in or towards satisfaction of the secured obligations.

3. The court shall grant an application under the preceding paragraph only if the amount of the secured obligations to be satisfied by such vesting is commensurate with the value of the object after taking account of any payment to be made by the chargee to any of the interested persons.
4. At any time after default as provided in Article 11 and before sale of the charged object or the making of an order under paragraph 2, the chargor or any interested person may discharge the security interest by paying in full the amount secured, subject to any lease granted by the chargee under Article 8(1)(b) or ordered under Article 8(2). Where, after such default, the payment of the amount secured is made in full by an interested person other than the debtor, that person is subrogated to the rights of the chargee.
5. Ownership or any other interest of the chargor passing on a sale under Article 8(1)(b) or passing under paragraph 1 or 2 of this Article is free from any other interest over which the chargee's security interest has priority under the provisions of Article 29.

Article 10 – Remedies of conditional seller or lessor

In the event of default under a title reservation agreement or under a leasing agreement as provided in Article 11, the conditional seller or the lessor, as the case may be, may:

(a) subject to any declaration that may be made by a Contracting State under Article 54, terminate the agreement and take possession or control of any object to which the agreement relates; or
(b) apply for a court order authorising or directing either of these acts.

Article 11 – Meaning of default

1. The debtor and the creditor may at any time agree in writing as to the events that constitute a default or otherwise give rise to the rights and remedies specified in Articles 8 to 10 and 13.
2. Where the debtor and the creditor have not so agreed, 'default' for the purposes of Articles 8 to 10 and 13 means a default which substantially deprives the creditor of what it is entitled to expect under the agreement.

Article 12 – Additional remedies

Any additional remedies permitted by the applicable law, including any remedies agreed upon by the parties, may be exercised to the extent that they are not inconsistent with the mandatory provisions of this Chapter as set out in Article 15.

Article 13 – Relief pending final determination

1. Subject to any declaration that it may make under Article 55, a Contracting State shall ensure that a creditor who adduces evidence of default by the debtor may, pending final determination of its claim and to the extent that the debtor has at any time so agreed, obtain from a court speedy relief in the form of such one or more of the following orders as the creditor requests:
   (a) preservation of the object and its value;
   (b) possession, control or custody of the object;
   (c) immobilisation of the object; and
   (d) lease or, except where covered by sub-paragraphs (a) to (c), management of the object and the income therefrom.
2. In making any order under the preceding paragraph, the court may impose such terms as it considers necessary to protect the interested persons in the event that the creditor:
   (a) in implementing any order granting such relief, fails to perform any of its obligations to the debtor under this Convention or the Protocol; or
   (b) fails to establish its claim, wholly or in part, on the final determination of that claim.
3. Before making any order under paragraph 1, the court may require notice of the request to be given to any of the interested persons.
4. Nothing in this Article affects the application of Article 8(3) or limits the availability of forms of interim relief other than those set out in paragraph 1.

Article 14 – Procedural requirements

Subject to Article 54(2), any remedy provided by this Chapter shall be exercised in conformity with the procedure prescribed by the law of the place where the remedy is to be exercised.

Article 15 – Derogation

In their relations with each other, any two or more of the parties referred to in this Chapter may at any time, by agreement in writing, derogate from or vary the effect of any of the preceding provisions of this Chapter except Articles 8(3) to (6), 9(3) and (4), 13(2) and 14.

Chapter IV – The international registration system

Article 16 – The International Registry

1. An International Registry shall be established for registrations of:
   (a) international interests, prospective international interests and registrable non-consensual rights and interests;
   (b) assignments and prospective assignments of international interests;
   (c) acquisitions of international interests by legal or contractual subrogation under the applicable law;

(d) notices of national interests; and
(e) subordinations of interests referred to in any of the preceding sub-paragraphs.

2. Different international registries may be established for different categories of object and associated rights.
3. For the purposes of this Chapter and Chapter V, the term 'registration' includes, where appropriate, an amendment, extension or discharge of a registration.

Article 17 – The Supervisory Authority and the Registrar

1. There shall be a Supervisory Authority as provided by the Protocol.
2. The Supervisory Authority shall:
   (a) establish or provide for the establishment of the International Registry;
   (b) except as otherwise provided by the Protocol, appoint and dismiss the Registrar;
   (c) ensure that any rights required for the continued effective operation of the International Registry in the event of a change of Registrar will vest in or be assignable to the new Registrar;
   (d) after consultation with the Contracting States, make or approve and ensure the publication of regulations pursuant to the Protocol dealing with the operation of the International Registry;
   (e) establish administrative procedures through which complaints concerning the operation of the International Registry can be made to the Supervisory Authority;
   (f) supervise the Registrar and the operation of the International Registry;
   (g) at the request of the Registrar, provide such guidance to the Registrar as the Supervisory Authority thinks fit;
   (h) set and periodically review the structure of fees to be charged for the services and facilities of the International Registry;
   (i) do all things necessary to ensure that an efficient notice-based electronic registration system exists to implement the objectives of this Convention and the Protocol; and
   (j) report periodically to Contracting States concerning the discharge of its obligations under this Convention and the Protocol.
3. The Supervisory Authority may enter into any agreement requisite for the performance of its functions, including any agreement referred to in Article 27(3).
4. The Supervisory Authority shall own all proprietary rights in the data bases and archives of the International Registry.
5. The Registrar shall ensure the efficient operation of the International Registry and perform the functions assigned to it by this Convention, the Protocol and the regulations.

Chapter V – Other matters relating to registration

Article 18 – Registration requirements

1. The Protocol and regulations shall specify the requirements, including the criteria for the identification of the object:
   (a) for effecting a registration (which shall include provision for prior electronic transmission of any consent from any person whose consent is required under Article 20);
   (b) for making searches and issuing search certificates, and, subject thereto;
   (c) for ensuring the confidentiality of information and documents of the International Registry other than information and documents relating to a registration.
2. The Registrar shall not be under a duty to enquire whether a consent to registration under Article 20 has in fact been given or is valid.
3. Where an interest registered as a prospective international interest becomes an international interest, no further registration shall be required provided that the registration information is sufficient for a registration of an international interest.
4. The Registrar shall arrange for registrations to be entered into the International Registry data base and made searchable in chronological order of receipt, and the file shall record the date and time of receipt.
5. The Protocol may provide that a Contracting State may designate an entity or entities in its territory as the entry point or entry points through which the information required for registration shall or may be transmitted to the International Registry. A Contracting State making such a designation may specify the requirements, if any, to be satisfied before such information is transmitted to the International Registry.

Article 19 – Validity and time of registration

1. A registration shall be valid only if made in conformity with Article 20.
2. A registration, if valid, shall be complete upon entry of the required information into the International Registry data base so as to be searchable.
3. A registration shall be searchable for the purposes of the preceding paragraph at the time when:
   (a) the International Registry has assigned to it a sequentially ordered file number; and
   (b) the registration information, including the file number, is stored in durable form and may be accessed at the International Registry.
4. If an interest first registered as a prospective international interest becomes an international interest, that international interest shall be treated as registered from the time of registration of the prospective international interest provided that the registration was still current immediately before the international interest was constituted as provided by Article 7.

5. The preceding paragraph applies with necessary modifications to the registration of a prospective assignment of an international interest.
6. A registration shall be searchable in the International Registry data base according to the criteria prescribed by the Protocol.

Article 20 – Consent to registration

1. An international interest, a prospective international interest or an assignment or prospective assignment of an international interest may be registered, and any such registration amended or extended prior to its expiry, by either party with the consent in writing of the other.
2. The subordination of an international interest to another international interest may be registered by or with the consent in writing at any time of the person whose interest has been subordinated.
3. A registration may be discharged by or with the consent in writing of the party in whose favour it was made.
4. The acquisition of an international interest by legal or contractual subrogation may be registered by the subrogee.
5. A registrable non-consensual right or interest may be registered by the holder thereof.
6. A notice of a national interest may be registered by the holder thereof.

Article 21 – Duration of registration

Registration of an international interest remains effective until discharged or until expiry of the period specified in the registration.

Article 22 – Searches

1. Any person may, in the manner prescribed by the Protocol and regulations, make or request a search of the International Registry by electronic means concerning interests or prospective international interests registered therein.
2. Upon receipt of a request therefor, the Registrar, in the manner prescribed by the Protocol and regulations, shall issue a registry search certificate by electronic means with respect to any object:
   (a) stating all registered information relating thereto, together with a statement indicating the date and time of registration of such information; or
   (b) stating that there is no information in the International Registry relating thereto.
3. A search certificate issued under the preceding paragraph shall indicate that the creditor named in the registration information has acquired or intends to acquire an international interest in the object but shall not indicate whether what is registered is an international interest or a prospective international interest, even if this is ascertainable from the relevant registration information.

Article 23 – List of declarations and declared non-consensual rights or interests

The Registrar shall maintain a list of declarations, withdrawals of declaration and of the categories of nonconsensual right or interest communicated to the Registrar by the Depositary as having been declared by Contracting States in conformity with Articles 39 and 40 and the date of each such declaration or withdrawal of declaration. Such list shall be recorded and searchable in the name of the declaring State and shall be made available as provided in the Protocol and regulations to any person requesting it.

Article 24 – Evidentiary value of certificates

A document in the form prescribed by the regulations which purports to be a certificate issued by the International Registry is prima facie proof:

(a) that it has been so issued; and
(b) of the facts recited in it, including the date and time of a registration.

Article 25 – Discharge of registration

1. Where the obligations secured by a registered security interest or the obligations giving rise to a registered non-consensual right or interest have been discharged, or where the conditions of transfer of title under a registered title reservation agreement have been fulfilled, the holder of such interest shall, without undue delay, procure the discharge of the registration after written demand by the debtor delivered to or received at its address stated in the registration.
2. Where a prospective international interest or a prospective assignment of an international interest has been registered, the intending creditor or intending assignee shall, without undue delay, procure the discharge of the registration after written demand by the intending debtor or assignor which is delivered to or received at its address stated in the registration before the intending creditor or assignee has given value or incurred a commitment to give value.
3. Where the obligations secured by a national interest specified in a registered notice of a national interest have been discharged, the holder of such interest shall, without undue delay, procure the discharge of the registration after written demand by the debtor delivered to or received at its address stated in the registration.
4. Where a registration ought not to have been made or is incorrect, the person in whose favour the registration was made shall, without undue delay, procure its discharge or amendment after written demand by the debtor delivered to or received at its address stated in the registration.

Article 26 – Access to the international registration facilities

No person shall be denied access to the registration and search facilities of the International Registry on any ground other than its failure to comply with the procedures prescribed by this Chapter.

Chapter VI – Privileges and immunities of the Supervisory Authority and the Registrar

Article 27 – Legal personality; immunity

1. The Supervisory Authority shall have international legal personality where not already possessing such personality.
2. The Supervisory Authority and its officers and employees shall enjoy such immunity from legal or administrative process as is specified in the Protocol.
3. (a) The Supervisory Authority shall enjoy exemption from taxes and such other privileges as may be provided by agreement with the host State.
   (b) For the purposes of this paragraph, 'host State' means the State in which the Supervisory Authority is situated.
4. The assets, documents, data bases and archives of the International Registry shall be inviolable and immune from seizure or other legal or administrative process.
5. For the purposes of any claim against the Registrar under Article 28(1) or Article 44, the claimant shall be entitled to access to such information and documents as are necessary to enable the claimant to pursue its claim.
6. The Supervisory Authority may waive the inviolability and immunity conferred by paragraph 4.

Chapter VII – Liability of the Registrar

Article 28 – Liability and financial assurances

1. The Registrar shall be liable for compensatory damages for loss suffered by a person directly resulting from an error or omission of the Registrar and its officers and employees or from a malfunction of the international registration system except where the malfunction is caused by an event of an inevitable and irresistible nature, which could not be prevented by using the best practices in current use in the field of electronic registry design and operation, including those related to back-up and systems security and networking.
2. The Registrar shall not be liable under the preceding paragraph for factual inaccuracy of registration information received by the Registrar or transmitted by the Registrar in the form in which it received that information nor for acts or circumstances for which the Registrar and its officers and employees are not responsible and arising prior to receipt of registration information at the International Registry.
3. Compensation under paragraph 1 may be reduced to the extent that the person who suffered the damage caused or contributed to that damage.
4. The Registrar shall procure insurance or a financial guarantee covering the liability referred to in this Article to the extent determined by the Supervisory Authority, in accordance with the Protocol.

Chapter VIII – Effects of an international interest as against third parties

Article 29 – Priority of competing interests

1. A registered interest has priority over any other interest subsequently registered and over an unregistered interest.
2. The priority of the first-mentioned interest under the preceding paragraph applies:
   (a) even if the first-mentioned interest was acquired or registered with actual knowledge of the other interest; and
   (b) even as regards value given by the holder of the first-mentioned interest with such knowledge.
3. The buyer of an object acquires its interest in it:
   (a) subject to an interest registered at the time of its acquisition of that interest; and
   (b) free from an unregistered interest even if it has actual knowledge of such an interest.
4. The conditional buyer or lessee acquires its interest in or right over that object:
   (a) subject to an interest registered prior to the registration of the international interest held by its conditional seller or lessor; and
   (b) free from an interest not so registered at that time even if it has actual knowledge of that interest.
5. The priority of competing interests or rights under this Article may be varied by agreement between the holders of those interests, but an assignee of a subordinated interest is not bound by an agreement to subordinate that interest unless at the time of the assignment a subordination had been registered relating to that agreement.
6. Any priority given by this Article to an interest in an object extends to proceeds.
7. This Convention:
   (a) does not affect the rights of a person in an item, other than an object, held prior to its installation on an object if under the applicable law those rights continue to exist after the installation; and
   (b) does not prevent the creation of rights in an item, other than an object, which has previously been installed on an object where under the applicable law those rights are created.

Article 30 – Effects of insolvency

1. In insolvency proceedings against the debtor an international interest is effective if prior to the commencement of the insolvency proceedings that interest was registered in conformity with this Convention.
2. Nothing in this Article impairs the effectiveness of an international interest in the insolvency proceedings where that interest is effective under the applicable law.

3. Nothing in this Article affects:
   (a) any rules of law applicable in insolvency proceedings relating to the avoidance of a transaction as a preference or a transfer in fraud of creditors; or
   (b) any rules of procedure relating to the enforcement of rights to property which is under the control or supervision of the insolvency administrator.

Chapter IX – Assignments of associated rights and international interests; rights of subrogation

Article 31 – Effects of assignment

1. Except as otherwise agreed by the parties, an assignment of associated rights made in conformity with Article 32 also transfers to the assignee:
   (a) the related international interest; and
   (b) all the interests and priorities of the assignor under this Convention.
2. Nothing in this Convention prevents a partial assignment of the assignor's associated rights. In the case of such a partial assignment, the assignor and assignee may agree as to their respective rights concerning the related international interest assigned under the preceding paragraph but not so as adversely to affect the debtor without its consent.
3. Subject to paragraph 4, the applicable law shall determine the defences and rights of set-off available to the debtor against the assignee.
4. The debtor may at any time by agreement in writing waive all or any of the defences and rights of set-off referred to in the preceding paragraph other than defences arising from fraudulent acts on the part of the assignee.
5. In the case of an assignment by way of security, the assigned associated rights revest in the assignor, to the extent that they are still subsisting, when the obligations secured by the assignment have been discharged.

Article 32 – Formal requirements of assignment

1. An assignment of associated rights transfers the related international interest only if it:
   (a) is in writing;
   (b) enables the associated rights to be identified under the contract from which they arise; and
   (c) in the case of an assignment by way of security, enables the obligations secured by the assignment to be determined in accordance with the Protocol but without the need to state a sum or maximum sum secured.
2. An assignment of an international interest created or provided for by a security agreement is not valid unless some or all related associated rights also are assigned.

3. This Convention does not apply to an assignment of associated rights which is not effective to transfer the related international interest.

Article 33 – Debtor's duty to assignee

1. To the extent that associated rights and the related international interest have been transferred in accordance with Articles 31 and 32, the debtor in relation to those rights and that interest is bound by the assignment and has a duty to make payment or give other performance to the assignee, if but only if:
   (a) the debtor has been given notice of the assignment in writing by or with the authority of the assignor; and
   (b) the notice identifies the associated rights.
2. Irrespective of any other ground on which payment or performance by the debtor discharges the latter from liability, payment or performance shall be effective for this purpose if made in accordance with the preceding paragraph.
3. Nothing in this Article shall affect the priority of competing assignments.

Article 34 – Default remedies in respect of assignment by way of security

In the event of default by the assignor under the assignment of associated rights and the related international interest made by way of security, Articles 8, 9 and 11 to 14 apply in the relations between the assignor and the assignee (and, in relation to associated rights, apply in so far as those provisions are capable of application to intangible property) as if references:

(a) to the secured obligation and the security interest were references to the obligation secured by the assignment of the associated rights and the related international interest and the security interest created by that assignment;
(b) to the chargee or creditor and chargor or debtor were references to the assignee and assignor;
(c) to the holder of the international interest were references to the assignee; and
(d) to the object were references to the assigned associated rights and the related international interest.

Article 35 – Priority of competing assignments

1. Where there are competing assignments of associated rights and at least one of the assignments includes the related international interest and is registered, the provisions of Article 29 apply as if the references to a registered interest were references to an assignment of the associated rights and the related registered interest and as if references to a registered or unregistered interest were references to a registered or unregistered assignment.
2. Article 30 applies to an assignment of associated rights as if the references to an international interest were references to an assignment of the associated rights and the related international interest.

Article 36 – Assignee's priority with respect to associated rights

1. The assignee of associated rights and the related international interest whose assignment has been registered only has priority under Article 35(1) over another assignee of the associated rights:
   (a) if the contract under which the associated rights arise states that they are secured by or associated with the object; and
   (b) to the extent that the associated rights are related to an object.
2. For the purposes of sub-paragraph (b) of the preceding paragraph, associated rights are related to an object only to the extent that they consist of rights to payment or performance that relate to:
   (a) a sum advanced and utilised for the purchase of the object;
   (b) a sum advanced and utilised for the purchase of another object in which the assignor held another international interest if the assignor transferred that interest to the assignee and the assignment has been registered;
   (c) the price payable for the object;
   (d) the rentals payable in respect of the object; or
   (e) other obligations arising from a transaction referred to in any of the preceding sub-paragraphs.
3. In all other cases, the priority of the competing assignments of the associated rights shall be determined by the applicable law.

Article 37 – Effects of assignor's insolvency

The provisions of Article 30 apply to insolvency proceedings against the assignor as if references to the debtor were references to the assignor.

Article 38 – Subrogation

1. Subject to paragraph 2, nothing in this Convention affects the acquisition of associated rights and the related international interest by legal or contractual subrogation under the applicable law.
2. The priority between any interest within the preceding paragraph and a competing interest may be varied by agreement in writing between the holders of the respective interests but an assignee of a subordinated interest is not bound by an agreement to subordinate that interest unless at the time of the assignment a subordination had been registered relating to that agreement.

Chapter X – Rights or interests subject to declarations by Contracting States

Article 39 – Rights having priority without registration

1. A Contracting State may at any time, in a declaration deposited with the Depositary of the Protocol declare, generally or specifically:

(a) those categories of non-consensual right or interest (other than a right or interest to which Article 40 applies) which under that State's law have priority over an interest in an object equivalent to that of the holder of a registered international interest and which shall have priority over a registered international interest, whether in or outside insolvency proceedings; and
(b) that nothing in this Convention shall affect the right of a State or State entity, intergovernmental organisation or other private provider of public services to arrest or detain an object under the laws of that State for payment of amounts owed to such entity, organisation or provider directly relating to those services in respect of that object or another object.

2. A declaration made under the preceding paragraph may be expressed to cover categories that are created after the deposit of that declaration.
3. A non-consensual right or interest has priority over an international interest if and only if the former is of a category covered by a declaration deposited prior to the registration of the international interest.
4. Notwithstanding the preceding paragraph, a Contracting State may, at the time of ratification, acceptance, approval of, or accession to the Protocol, declare that a right or interest of a category covered by a declaration made under subparagraph (a) of paragraph 1 shall have priority over an international interest registered prior to the date of such ratification, acceptance, approval or accession.

Article 40 – Registrable non-consensual rights or interests

A Contracting State may at any time in a declaration deposited with the Depositary of the Protocol list the categories of non-consensual right or interest which shall be registrable under this Convention as regards any category of object as if the right or interest were an international interest and shall be regulated accordingly. Such a declaration may be modified from time to time.

Chapter XI – Application of the Convention to sales

Article 41 – Sale and prospective sale

This Convention shall apply to the sale or prospective sale of an object as provided for in the Protocol with any modifications therein.

Chapter XII – Jurisdiction

Article 42 – Choice of forum

1. Subject to Articles 43 and 44, the courts of a Contracting State chosen by the parties to a transaction have jurisdiction in respect of any claim brought under this Convention, whether or not the chosen forum has a connection with the parties or the transaction. Such jurisdiction shall be exclusive unless otherwise agreed between the parties.

2. Any such agreement shall be in writing or otherwise concluded in accordance with the formal requirements of the law of the chosen forum.

Article 43 – Jurisdiction under Article 13

1. The courts of a Contracting State chosen by the parties and the courts of the Contracting State on the territory of which the object is situated have jurisdiction to grant relief under Article 13(1)(a), (b), (c) and Article 13(4) in respect of that object.
2. Jurisdiction to grant relief under Article 13(1)(d) or other interim relief by virtue of Article 13(4) may be exercised either:
   (a) by the courts chosen by the parties; or
   (b) by the courts of a Contracting State on the territory of which the debtor is situated, being relief which, by the terms of the order granting it, is enforceable only in the territory of that Contracting State.
3. A court has jurisdiction under the preceding paragraphs even if the final determination of the claim referred to in Article 13(1) will or may take place in a court of another Contracting State or by arbitration.

Article 44 – Jurisdiction to make orders against the Registrar

1. The courts of the place in which the Registrar has its centre of administration shall have exclusive jurisdiction to award damages or make orders against the Registrar.
2. Where a person fails to respond to a demand made under Article 25 and that person has ceased to exist or cannot be found for the purpose of enabling an order to be made against it requiring it to procure discharge of the registration, the courts referred to in the preceding paragraph shall have exclusive jurisdiction, on the application of the debtor or intending debtor, to make an order directed to the Registrar requiring the Registrar to discharge the registration.
3. Where a person fails to comply with an order of a court having jurisdiction under this Convention or, in the case of a national interest, an order of a court of competent jurisdiction requiring that person to procure the amendment or discharge of a registration, the courts referred to in paragraph 1 may direct the Registrar to take such steps as will give effect to that order.
4. Except as otherwise provided by the preceding paragraphs, no court may make orders or give judgments or rulings against or purporting to bind the Registrar.

Article 45 – Jurisdiction in respect of insolvency proceedings

The provisions of this Chapter are not applicable to insolvency proceedings.

Chapter XIII – Relationship with other Conventions

Article 45 bis – Relationship with the United Nations Convention on the Assignment of Receivables in International Trade

This Convention shall prevail over the United Nations Convention on the Assignment of Receivables in International Trade, opened for signature in New York on 12 December 2001, as it relates to the assignment of receivables which are associated rights related to international interests in aircraft objects, railway rolling stock and space assets.

Article 46 – Relationship with the UNIDROIT Convention on International Financial Leasing

The Protocol may determine the relationship between this Convention and the UNIDROIT Convention on International Financial Leasing, signed at Ottawa on 28 May 1988.

Chapter XIV – Final provisions

Article 47 – Signature, ratification, acceptance, approval or accession

1. This Convention shall be open for signature in Cape Town on 16 November 2001 by States participating in the Diplomatic Conference to Adopt a Mobile Equipment Convention and an Aircraft Protocol held at Cape Town from 29 October to 16 November 2001. After 16 November 2001, the Convention shall be open to all States for signature at the Headquarters of the International Institute for the Unification of Private Law (UNIDROIT) in Rome until it enters into force in accordance with Article 49.
2. This Convention shall be subject to ratification, acceptance or approval by States which have signed it.
3. Any State which does not sign this Convention may accede to it at any time.
4. Ratification, acceptance, approval or accession is effected by the deposit of a formal instrument to that effect with the Depositary.

Article 48 – Regional Economic Integration Organisations

1. A Regional Economic Integration Organisation which is constituted by sovereign States and has competence over certain matters governed by this Convention may similarly sign, accept, approve or accede to this Convention. The Regional Economic Integration Organisation shall in that case have the rights and obligations of a Contracting State, to the extent that that Organisation has competence over matters governed by this Convention. Where the number of Contracting States is relevant in this Convention, the Regional Economic Integration Organisation shall not count as a Contracting State in addition to its Member States which are Contracting States.

2. The Regional Economic Integration Organisation shall, at the time of signature, acceptance, approval or accession, make a declaration to the Depositary specifying the matters governed by this Convention in respect of which competence has been transferred to that Organisation by its Member States. The Regional Economic Integration Organisation shall promptly notify the Depositary of any changes to the distribution of competence, including new transfers of competence, specified in the declaration under this paragraph.
3. Any reference to a 'Contracting State' or 'Contracting States' or 'State Party' or 'States Parties' in this Convention applies equally to a Regional Economic Integration Organisation where the context so requires.

Article 49 – Entry into force

1. This Convention enters into force on the first day of the month following the expiration of three months after the date of the deposit of the third instrument of ratification, acceptance, approval or accession but only as regards a category of objects to which a Protocol applies:
   (a) as from the time of entry into force of that Protocol;
   (b) subject to the terms of that Protocol; and
   (c) as between States Parties to this Convention and that Protocol.
2. For other States, this Convention enters into force on the first day of the month following the expiration of three months after the date of the deposit of their instrument of ratification, acceptance, approval or accession but only as regards a category of objects to which a Protocol applies and subject, in relation to such Protocol, to the requirements of sub-paragraphs (a), (b) and (c) of the preceding paragraph.

Article 50 – Internal transactions

1. A Contracting State may, at the time of ratification, acceptance, approval of, or accession to the Protocol, declare that this Convention shall not apply to a transaction which is an internal transaction in relation to that State with regard to all types of objects or some of them.
2. Notwithstanding the preceding paragraph, the provisions of Articles 8(4), 9(1), 16, Chapter V, Article 29, and any provisions of this Convention relating to registered interests shall apply to an internal transaction.
3. Where notice of a national interest has been registered in the International Registry, the priority of the holder of that interest under Article 29 shall not be affected by the fact that such interest has become vested in another person by assignment or subrogation under the applicable law.

Article 51 – Future Protocols

1. The Depositary may create working groups, in co-operation with such relevant non-governmental organisations as the Depositary considers appropriate, to assess the feasibility of extending the application of this Convention, through one or more Protocols, to objects of any category of high-value mobile equipment, other than a category referred to in Article 2(3), each member of which is uniquely identifiable, and associated rights relating to such objects.
2. The Depositary shall communicate the text of any preliminary draft Protocol relating to a category of objects prepared by such a working group to all States Parties to this Convention, all Member States of the Depositary, member States of the United Nations which are not members of the Depositary and the relevant intergovernmental organisations, and shall invite such States and organisations to participate in intergovernmental negotiations for the completion of a draft Protocol on the basis of such a preliminary draft Protocol.
3. The Depositary shall also communicate the text of any preliminary draft Protocol prepared by such a working group to such relevant non-governmental organisations as the Depositary considers appropriate. Such non-governmental organisations shall be invited promptly to submit comments on the text of the preliminary draft Protocol to the Depositary and to participate as observers in the preparation of a draft Protocol.
4. When the competent bodies of the Depositary adjudge such a draft Protocol ripe for adoption, the Depositary shall convene a diplomatic conference for its adoption.
5. Once such a Protocol has been adopted, subject to paragraph 6, this Convention shall apply to the category of objects covered thereby.
6. Article 45 bis of this Convention applies to such a Protocol only if specifically provided for in that Protocol.

Article 52 – Territorial units

1. If a Contracting State has territorial units in which different systems of law are applicable in relation to the matters dealt with in this Convention, it may, at the time of ratification, acceptance, approval or accession, declare that this Convention is to extend to all its territorial units or only to one or more of them and may modify its declaration by submitting another declaration at any time.
2. Any such declaration shall state expressly the territorial units to which this Convention applies.
3. If a Contracting State has not made any declaration under paragraph 1, this Convention shall apply to all territorial units of that State.
4. Where a Contracting State extends this Convention to one or more of its territorial units, declarations permitted under this Convention may be made in

respect of each such territorial unit, and the declarations made in respect of one territorial unit may be different from those made in respect of another territorial unit.

5. If by virtue of a declaration under paragraph 1, this Convention extends to one or more territorial units of a Contracting State:
   (a) the debtor is considered to be situated in a Contracting State only if it is incorporated or formed under a law in force in a territorial unit to which this Convention applies or if it has its registered office or statutory seat, centre of administration, place of business or habitual residence in a territorial unit to which this Convention applies;
   (b) any reference to the location of the object in a Contracting State refers to the location of the object in a territorial unit to which this Convention applies; and
   (c) any reference to the administrative authorities in that Contracting State shall be construed as referring to the administrative authorities having jurisdiction in a territorial unit to which this Convention applies.

Article 53 – Determination of courts

A Contracting State may, at the time of ratification, acceptance, approval of, or accession to the Protocol, declare the relevant 'court' or 'courts' for the purposes of Article 1 and Chapter XII of this Convention.

Article 54 – Declarations regarding remedies

1. A Contracting State may, at the time of ratification, acceptance, approval of, or accession to the Protocol, declare that while the charged object is situated within, or controlled from its territory the chargee shall not grant a lease of the object in that territory.
2. A Contracting State shall, at the time of ratification, acceptance, approval of, or accession to the Protocol, declare whether or not any remedy available to the creditor under any provision of this Convention which is not there expressed to require application to the court may be exercised only with leave of the court.

Article 55 – Declarations regarding relief pending final determination

A Contracting State may, at the time of ratification, acceptance, approval of, or accession to the Protocol, declare that it will not apply the provisions of Article 13 or Article 43, or both, wholly or in part. The declaration shall specify under which conditions the relevant Article will be applied, in case it will be applied partly, or otherwise which other forms of interim relief will be applied.

Article 56 – Reservations and declarations

1. No reservations may be made to this Convention but declarations authorised by Articles 39, 40, 50, 52, 53, 54, 55, 57, 58 and 60 may be made in accordance with these provisions.
2. Any declaration or subsequent declaration or any withdrawal of a declaration made under this Convention shall be notified in writing to the Depositary.

Article 57 – Subsequent declarations

1. A State Party may make a subsequent declaration, other than a declaration authorised under Article 60, at any time after the date on which this Convention has entered into force for it, by notifying the Depositary to that effect.
2. Any such subsequent declaration shall take effect on the first day of the month following the expiration of six months after the date of receipt of the notification by the Depositary. Where a longer period for that declaration to take effect is specified in the notification, it shall take effect upon the expiration of such longer period after receipt of the notification by the Depositary.
3. Notwithstanding the previous paragraphs, this Convention shall continue to apply, as if no such subsequent declarations had been made, in respect of all rights and interests arising prior to the effective date of any such subsequent declaration.

Article 58 – Withdrawal of declarations

1. Any State Party having made a declaration under this Convention, other than a declaration authorised under Article 60, may withdraw it at any time by notifying the Depositary. Such withdrawal is to take effect on the first day of the month following the expiration of six months after the date of receipt of the notification by the Depositary.
2. Notwithstanding the previous paragraph, this Convention shall continue to apply, as if no such withdrawal of declaration had been made, in respect of all rights and interests arising prior to the effective date of any such withdrawal.

Article 59 – Denunciations

1. Any State Party may denounce this Convention by notification in writing to the Depositary.
2. Any such denunciation shall take effect on the first day of the month following the expiration of twelve months after the date on which notification is received by the Depositary.
3. Notwithstanding the previous paragraphs, this Convention shall continue to apply, as if no such denunciation had been made, in respect of all rights and interests arising prior to the effective date of any such denunciation.

Article 60 – Transitional provisions

1. Unless otherwise declared by a Contracting State at any time, the Convention does not apply to a pre-existing right or interest, which retains the priority it enjoyed under the applicable law before the effective date of this Convention.
2. For the purposes of Article 1(v) and of determining priority under this Convention:
   (a) 'effective date of this Convention' means in relation to a debtor the time when this Convention enters into force or the time when the State in which the debtor is situated becomes a Contracting State, whichever is the later; and
   (b) the debtor is situated in a State where it has its centre of administration or, if it has no centre of administration, its place of business or, if it has more than one place of business, its principal place of business or, if it has no place of business, its habitual residence.
3. A Contracting State may in its declaration under paragraph 1 specify a date, not earlier than three years after the date on which the declaration becomes effective, when this Convention and the Protocol will become applicable, for the purpose of determining priority, including the protection of any existing priority, to pre-existing rights or interests arising under an agreement made at a time when the debtor was situated in a State referred to in sub-paragraph (b) of the preceding paragraph but only to the extent and in the manner specified in its declaration.

Article 61 – Review Conferences, amendments and related matters

1. The Depositary shall prepare reports yearly or at such other time as the circumstances may require for the States Parties as to the manner in which the international regimen established in this Convention has operated in practice. In preparing such reports, the Depositary shall take into account the reports of the Supervisory Authority concerning the functioning of the international registration system.
2. At the request of not less than twenty-five per cent of the States Parties, Review Conferences of States Parties shall be convened from time to time by the Depositary, in consultation with the Supervisory Authority, to consider:
   (a) the practical operation of this Convention and its effectiveness in facilitating the asset-based financing and leasing of the objects covered by its terms;
   (b) the judicial interpretation given to, and the application made of the terms of this Convention and the regulations;
   (c) the functioning of the international registration system, the performance of the Registrar and its oversight by the Supervisory Authority, taking into account the reports of the Supervisory Authority; and
   (d) whether any modifications to this Convention or the arrangements relating to the International Registry are desirable.

3. Subject to paragraph 4, any amendment to this Convention shall be approved by at least a two-thirds majority of States Parties participating in the Conference referred to in the preceding paragraph and shall then enter into force in respect of States which have ratified, accepted or approved such amendment when ratified, accepted, or approved by three States in accordance with the provisions of Article 49 relating to its entry into force.
4. Where the proposed amendment to this Convention is intended to apply to more than one category of equipment, such amendment shall also be approved by at least a two-thirds majority of States Parties to each Protocol that are participating in the Conference referred to in paragraph 2.

Article 62 – Depositary and its functions

1. Instruments of ratification, acceptance, approval or accession shall be deposited with the International Institute for the Unification of Private Law (UNIDROIT), which is hereby designated the Depositary.
2. The Depositary shall:
   (a) inform all Contracting States of:
      (i) each new signature or deposit of an instrument of ratification, acceptance, approval or accession, together with the date thereof;
      (ii) the date of entry into force of this Convention;
      (iii) each declaration made in accordance with this Convention, together with the date thereof;
      (iv) the withdrawal or amendment of any declaration, together with the date thereof; and
      (v) the notification of any denunciation of this Convention together with the date thereof and the date on which it takes effect;
   (b) transmit certified true copies of this Convention to all Contracting States;
   (c) provide the Supervisory Authority and the Registrar with a copy of each instrument of ratification, acceptance, approval or accession, together with the date of deposit thereof, of each declaration or withdrawal or amendment of a declaration and of each notification of denunciation, together with the date of notification thereof, so that the information contained therein is easily and fully available; and
   (d) perform such other functions customary for depositaries.

IN WITNESS WHEREOF the undersigned Plenipotentiaries, having been duly authorised, have signed this Convention.
DONE at Cape Town, this sixteenth day of November, two thousand and one, in a single original in the English, Arabic, Chinese, French, Russian and Spanish languages, all texts being equally authentic, such authenticity to take effect upon verification by the Joint Secretariat of the Conference under the authority of the President of the Conference within ninety days hereof as to the conformity of the texts with one another.

Chapter 2. The Protocol to the Convention on International Interests in Mobile Equipment on Matters Specific to Aircraft Equipment

PROTOCOL TO THE CONVENTION ON INTERNATIONAL INTERESTS IN MOBILE EQUIPMENT ON MATTERS SPECIFIC TO AIRCRAFT EQUIPMENT THE STATES PARTIES TO THIS PROTOCOL,

CONSIDERING it necessary to implement the Convention on International Interests in Mobile Equipment (hereinafter referred to as 'the Convention') as it relates to aircraft equipment, in the light of the purposes set out in the preamble to the Convention,

MINDFUL of the need to adapt the Convention to meet the particular requirements of aircraft finance and to extend the sphere of application of the Convention to include contracts of sale of aircraft equipment,

MINDFUL of the principles and objectives of the Convention on International Civil Aviation, signed at Chicago on 7 December 1944,

HAVE AGREED upon the following provisions relating to aircraft equipment:

Chapter I – Sphere of application and general provisions

Article I – Defined terms

1. In this Protocol, except where the context otherwise requires, terms used in it have the meanings set out in the Convention.
2. In this Protocol the following terms are employed with the meanings set out below:
   (a) 'aircraft' means aircraft as defined for the purposes of the Chicago Convention which are either airframes with aircraft engines installed thereon or helicopters;
   (b) 'aircraft engines' means aircraft engines (other than those used in military, customs or police services) powered by jet propulsion or turbine or piston technology and:
      (i) in the case of jet propulsion aircraft engines, have at least 1750 lb of thrust or its equivalent; and
      (ii) in the case of turbine-powered or piston-powered aircraft engines, have at least 550 rated take-off shaft horsepower or its equivalent,

   together with all modules and other installed, incorporated or attached accessories, parts and equipment and all data, manuals and records relating thereto;
   (c) 'aircraft objects' means airframes, aircraft engines and helicopters;
   (d) 'aircraft register' means a register maintained by a State or a common mark registering authority for the purposes of the Chicago Convention;
   (e) 'airframes' means airframes (other than those used in military, customs or police services) that, when appropriate aircraft engines are installed thereon, are type certified by the competent aviation authority to transport:
      (i) at least eight (8) persons including crew; or
      (ii) goods in excess of 2750 kilograms,

together with all installed, incorporated or attached accessories, parts and equipment (other than aircraft engines), and all data, manuals and records relating thereto;

(f) 'authorised party' means the party referred to in Article XIII(3);

(g) 'Chicago Convention' means the Convention on International Civil Aviation, signed at Chicago on 7 December 1944, as amended, and its Annexes;

(h) 'common mark registering authority' means the authority maintaining a register in accordance with Article 77 of the Chicago Convention as implemented by the Resolution adopted on 14 December 1967 by the Council of the International Civil Aviation Organization on nationality and registration of aircraft operated by international operating agencies;

(i) 'de-registration of the aircraft' means deletion or removal of the registration of the aircraft from its aircraft register in accordance with the Chicago Convention;

(j) 'guarantee contract' means a contract entered into by a person as guarantor;

(k) 'guarantor' means a person who, for the purpose of assuring performance of any obligations in favour of a creditor secured by a security agreement or under an agreement, gives or issues a suretyship or demand guarantee or a standby letter of credit or any other form of credit insurance;

(l) 'helicopters' means heavier-than-air machines (other than those used in military, customs or police services) supported in flight chiefly by the reactions of the air on one or more power-driven rotors on substantially vertical axes and which are type certified by the competent aviation authority to transport:

(i) at least five (5) persons including crew; or

(ii) goods in excess of 450 kilograms,

together with all installed, incorporated or attached accessories, parts and equipment (including rotors), and all data, manuals and records relating thereto;

(m) 'insolvency-related event' means:

(i) the commencement of the insolvency proceedings; or

(ii) the declared intention to suspend or actual suspension of payments by the debtor where the creditor's right to institute insolvency proceedings against the debtor or to exercise remedies under the Convention is prevented or suspended by law or State action;

(n) 'primary insolvency jurisdiction' means the Contracting State in which the centre of the debtor's main interests is situated, which for this purpose shall be deemed to be the place of the debtor's statutory seat or, if there is none, the place where the debtor is incorporated or formed, unless proved otherwise;

(o) 'registry authority' means the national authority or the common mark registering authority, maintaining an aircraft register in a Contracting State and responsible for the registration and de-registration of an aircraft in accordance with the Chicago Convention; and

(p) 'State of registry' means, in respect of an aircraft, the State on the national register of which an aircraft is entered or the State of location of the common mark registering authority maintaining the aircraft register.

Article II – Application of Convention as regards aircraft objects

1. The Convention shall apply in relation to aircraft objects as provided by the terms of this Protocol.
2. The Convention and this Protocol shall be known as the Convention on International Interests in Mobile Equipment as applied to aircraft objects.

Article III – Application of Convention to sales

The following provisions of the Convention apply as if references to an agreement creating or providing for an international interest were references to a contract of sale and as if references to an international interest, a prospective international interest, the debtor and the creditor were references to a sale, a prospective sale, the seller and the buyer respectively:

Articles 3 and 4;
Article 16(1)(a);
Article 19(4);
Article 20(1) (as regards registration of a contract of sale or a prospective sale);
Article 25(2) (as regards a prospective sale); and
Article 30.

In addition, the general provisions of Article 1, Article 5, Chapters IV to VII, Article 29 (other than Article 29(3) which is replaced by Article XIV(1) and (2)), Chapter X, Chapter XII (other than Article 43), Chapter XIII and Chapter XIV (other than Article 60) shall apply to contracts of sale and prospective sales.

Article IV – Sphere of application

1. Without prejudice to Article 3(1) of the Convention, the Convention shall also apply in relation to a helicopter, or to an airframe pertaining to an aircraft, registered in an aircraft register of a Contracting State which is the State of registry, and where such registration is made pursuant to an agreement for registration of the aircraft it is deemed to have been effected at the time of the agreement.
2. For the purposes of the definition of 'internal transaction' in Article 1 of the Convention:
   (a) an airframe is located in the State of registry of the aircraft of which it is a part;

(b) an aircraft engine is located in the State of registry of the aircraft on which it is installed or, if it is not installed on an aircraft, where it is physically located; and

(c) a helicopter is located in its State of registry,

at the time of the conclusion of the agreement creating or providing for the interest.

3. The parties may, by agreement in writing, exclude the application of Article XI and, in their relations with each other, derogate from or vary the effect of any of the provisions of this Protocol except Article IX (2)–(4).

Article V – Formalities, effects and registration of contracts of sale

1. For the purposes of this Protocol, a contract of sale is one which:
   (a) is in writing;
   (b) relates to an aircraft object of which the seller has power to dispose; and
   (c) enables the aircraft object to be identified in conformity with this Protocol.
2. A contract of sale transfers the interest of the seller in the aircraft object to the buyer according to its terms.
3. Registration of a contract of sale remains effective indefinitely. Registration of a prospective sale remains effective unless discharged or until expiry of the period, if any, specified in the registration.

Article VI – Representative capacities

A person may enter into an agreement or a sale, and register an international interest in, or a sale of, an aircraft object, in an agency, trust or other representative capacity. In such case, that person is entitled to assert rights and interests under the Convention.

Article VII – Description of aircraft objects

A description of an aircraft object that contains its manufacturer's serial number, the name of the manufacturer and its model designation is necessary and sufficient to identify the object for the purposes of Article 7(c) of the Convention and Article V(1)(c) of this Protocol.

Article VIII – Choice of law

1. This Article applies only where a Contracting State has made a declaration pursuant to Article XXX(1).
2. The parties to an agreement, or a contract of sale, or a related guarantee contract or subordination agreement may agree on the law which is to govern their contractual rights and obligations, wholly or in part.

3. Unless otherwise agreed, the reference in the preceding paragraph to the law chosen by the parties is to the domestic rules of law of the designated State or, where that State comprises several territorial units, to the domestic law of the designated territorial unit.

Chapter II – Default remedies, priorities and assignments

Article IX – Modification of default remedies provisions

1. In addition to the remedies specified in Chapter III of the Convention, the creditor may, to the extent that the debtor has at any time so agreed and in the circumstances specified in that Chapter:
   (a) procure the de-registration of the aircraft; and
   (b) procure the export and physical transfer of the aircraft object from the territory in which it is situated.
2. The creditor shall not exercise the remedies specified in the preceding paragraph without the prior consent in writing of the holder of any registered interest ranking in priority to that of the creditor.
3. Article 8(3) of the Convention shall not apply to aircraft objects. Any remedy given by the Convention in relation to an aircraft object shall be exercised in a commercially reasonable manner. A remedy shall be deemed to be exercised in a commercially reasonable manner where it is exercised in conformity with a provision of the agreement except where such a provision is manifestly unreasonable.
4. A chargee giving ten or more working days' prior written notice of a proposed sale or lease to interested persons shall be deemed to satisfy the requirement of providing 'reasonable prior notice' specified in Article 8(4) of the Convention. The foregoing shall not prevent a chargee and a chargor or a guarantor from agreeing to a longer period of prior notice.
5. The registry authority in a Contracting State shall, subject to any applicable safety laws and regulations, honour a request for de-registration and export if:
   (a) the request is properly submitted by the authorised party under a recorded irrevocable deregistration and export request authorisation; and
   (b) the authorised party certifies to the registry authority, if required by that authority, that all registered interests ranking in priority to that of the creditor in whose favour the authorisation has been issued have been discharged or that the holders of such interests have consented to the de-registration and export.
6. A chargee proposing to procure the de-registration and export of an aircraft under paragraph 1 otherwise than pursuant to a court order shall give reasonable prior notice in writing of the proposed deregistration and export to:
   (a) interested persons specified in Article 1(m)(i) and (ii) of the Convention; and

(b) interested persons specified in Article 1(m)(iii) of the Convention who have given notice of their rights to the chargee within a reasonable time prior to the de-registration and export.

Article X – Modification of provisions regarding relief pending final determination

1. This Article applies only where a Contracting State has made a declaration under Article XXX(2) and to the extent stated in such declaration.
2. For the purposes of Article 13(1) of the Convention, 'speedy' in the context of obtaining relief means within such number of working days from the date of filing of the application for relief as is specified in a declaration made by the Contracting State in which the application is made.
3. Article 13(1) of the Convention applies with the following being added immediately after sub-paragraph (d):

'(e) if at any time the debtor and the creditor specifically agree, sale and application of proceeds therefrom',
and Article 43(2) applies with the insertion after the words 'Article 13(1)(d)' of the words 'and (e)'.

4. Ownership or any other interest of the debtor passing on a sale under the preceding paragraph is free from any other interest over which the creditor's international interest has priority under the provisions of Article 29 of the Convention.
5. The creditor and the debtor or any other interested person may agree in writing to exclude the application of Article 13(2) of the Convention.
6. With regard to the remedies in Article IX(1):
   (a) they shall be made available by the registry authority and other administrative authorities, as applicable, in a Contracting State no later than five working days after the creditor notifies such authorities that the relief specified in Article IX(1) is granted or, in the case of relief granted by a foreign court, recognised by a court of that Contracting State, and that the creditor is entitled to procure those remedies in accordance with the Convention; and
   (b) the applicable authorities shall expeditiously co-operate with and assist the creditor in the exercise of such remedies in conformity with the applicable aviation safety laws and regulations.
7. Paragraphs 2 and 6 shall not affect any applicable aviation safety laws and regulations.

Article XI – Remedies on insolvency

1. This Article applies only where a Contracting State that is the primary insolvency jurisdiction has made a declaration pursuant to Article XXX(3).

Alternative A

2. Upon the occurrence of an insolvency-related event, the insolvency administrator or the debtor, as applicable, shall, subject to paragraph 7, give possession of the aircraft object to the creditor no later than the earlier of:
   (a) the end of the waiting period; and
   (b) the date on which the creditor would be entitled to possession of the aircraft object if this Article did not apply.
3. For the purposes of this Article, the 'waiting period' shall be the period specified in a declaration of the Contracting State which is the primary insolvency jurisdiction.
4. References in this Article to the 'insolvency administrator' shall be to that person in its official, not in its personal, capacity.
5. Unless and until the creditor is given the opportunity to take possession under paragraph 2:
   (a) the insolvency administrator or the debtor, as applicable, shall preserve the aircraft object and maintain it and its value in accordance with the agreement; and
   (b) the creditor shall be entitled to apply for any other forms of interim relief available under the applicable law.
6. Sub-paragraph (a) of the preceding paragraph shall not preclude the use of the aircraft object under arrangements designed to preserve the aircraft object and maintain it and its value.
7. The insolvency administrator or the debtor, as applicable, may retain possession of the aircraft object where, by the time specified in paragraph 2, it has cured all defaults other than a default constituted by the opening of insolvency proceedings and has agreed to perform all future obligations under the agreement. A second waiting period shall not apply in respect of a default in the performance of such future obligations.
8. With regard to the remedies in Article IX(1):
   (a) they shall be made available by the registry authority and the administrative authorities in a Contracting State, as applicable, no later than five working days after the date on which the creditor notifies such authorities that it is entitled to procure those remedies in accordance with the Convention; and
   (b) the applicable authorities shall expeditiously co-operate with and assist the creditor in the exercise of such remedies in conformity with the applicable aviation safety laws and regulations.
9. No exercise of remedies permitted by the Convention or this Protocol may be prevented or delayed after the date specified in paragraph 2.

10. No obligations of the debtor under the agreement may be modified without the consent of the creditor.
11. Nothing in the preceding paragraph shall be construed to affect the authority, if any, of the insolvency administrator under the applicable law to terminate the agreement.
12. No rights or interests, except for non-consensual rights or interests of a category covered by a declaration pursuant to Article 39(1), shall have priority in insolvency proceedings over registered interests.
13. The Convention as modified by Article IX of this Protocol shall apply to the exercise of any remedies under this Article.

Alternative B

2. Upon the occurrence of an insolvency-related event, the insolvency administrator or the debtor, as applicable, upon the request of the creditor, shall give notice to the creditor within the time specified in a declaration of a Contracting State pursuant to Article XXX(3) whether it will:
   (a) cure all defaults other than a default constituted by the opening of insolvency proceedings and agree to perform all future obligations, under the agreement and related transaction documents; or
   (b) give the creditor the opportunity to take possession of the aircraft object, in accordance with the applicable law.
3. The applicable law referred to in sub-paragraph (b) of the preceding paragraph may permit the court to require the taking of any additional step or the provision of any additional guarantee.
4. The creditor shall provide evidence of its claims and proof that its international interest has been registered.
5. If the insolvency administrator or the debtor, as applicable, does not give notice in conformity with paragraph 2, or when the insolvency administrator or the debtor has declared that it will give the creditor the opportunity to take possession of the aircraft object but fails to do so, the court may permit the creditor to take possession of the aircraft object upon such terms as the court may order and may require the taking of any additional step or the provision of any additional guarantee.
6. The aircraft object shall not be sold pending a decision by a court regarding the claim and the international interest.

Article XII – Insolvency assistance

1. This Article applies only where a Contracting State has made a declaration pursuant to Article XXX(1).
2. The courts of a Contracting State in which an aircraft object is situated shall, in accordance with the law of the Contracting State, co-operate to the maximum extent possible with foreign courts and foreign insolvency administrators in carrying out the provisions of Article XI.

Article XIII – De-registration and export request authorisation

1. This Article applies only where a Contracting State has made a declaration pursuant to Article XXX(1).
2. Where the debtor has issued an irrevocable de-registration and export request authorisation substantially in the form annexed to this Protocol and has submitted such authorisation for recordation to the registry authority, that authorisation shall be so recorded.
3. The person in whose favour the authorisation has been issued (the 'authorised party') or its certified designee shall be the sole person entitled to exercise the remedies specified in Article IX(1) and may do so only in accordance with the authorisation and applicable aviation safety laws and regulations. Such authorisation may not be revoked by the debtor without the consent in writing of the authorised party. The registry authority shall remove an authorisation from the registry at the request of the authorised party.
4. The registry authority and other administrative authorities in Contracting States shall expeditiously co-operate with and assist the authorised party in the exercise of the remedies specified in Article IX.

Article XIV – Modification of priority provisions

1. A buyer of an aircraft object under a registered sale acquires its interest in that object free from an interest subsequently registered and from an unregistered interest, even if the buyer has actual knowledge of the unregistered interest.
2. A buyer of an aircraft object acquires its interest in that object subject to an interest registered at the time of its acquisition.
3. Ownership of or another right or interest in an aircraft engine shall not be affected by its installation on or removal from an aircraft.
4. Article 29(7) of the Convention applies to an item, other than an object, installed on an airframe, aircraft engine or helicopter.

Article XV – Modification of assignment provisions

Article 33(1) of the Convention applies as if the following were added immediately after sub-paragraph (b):

> and (c) the debtor has consented in writing, whether or not the consent is given in advance of the assignment or identifies the assignee.

Article XVI – Debtor provisions

1. In the absence of a default within the meaning of Article 11 of the Convention, the debtor shall be entitled to the quiet possession and use of the object in accordance with the agreement as against:

(a) its creditor and the holder of any interest from which the debtor takes free pursuant to Article 29(4) of the Convention or, in the capacity of buyer, Article XIV(1) of this Protocol, unless and to the extent that the debtor has otherwise agreed; and
(b) the holder of any interest to which the debtor's right or interest is subject pursuant to Article 29(4) of the Convention or, in the capacity of buyer, Article XIV(2) of this Protocol, but only to the extent, if any, that such holder has agreed.

2. Nothing in the Convention or this Protocol affects the liability of a creditor for any breach of the agreement under the applicable law in so far as that agreement relates to an aircraft object.

Chapter III – Registry provisions relating to international interests in aircraft objects

Article XVII – The Supervisory Authority and the Registrar

1. The Supervisory Authority shall be the international entity designated by a Resolution adopted by the Diplomatic Conference to Adopt a Mobile Equipment Convention and an Aircraft Protocol.
2. Where the international entity referred to in the preceding paragraph is not able and willing to act as Supervisory Authority, a Conference of Signatory and Contracting States shall be convened to designate another Supervisory Authority.
3. The Supervisory Authority and its officers and employees shall enjoy such immunity from legal and administrative process as is provided under the rules applicable to them as an international entity or otherwise.
4. The Supervisory Authority may establish a commission of experts, from among persons nominated by Signatory and Contracting States and having the necessary qualifications and experience, and entrust it with the task of assisting the Supervisory Authority in the discharge of its functions.
5. The first Registrar shall operate the International Registry for a period of five years from the date of entry into force of this Protocol. Thereafter, the Registrar shall be appointed or reappointed at regular five-yearly intervals by the Supervisory Authority.

Article XVIII – First regulations

The first regulations shall be made by the Supervisory Authority so as to take effect upon the entry into force of this Protocol.

Article XIX – Designated entry points

1. Subject to paragraph 2, a Contracting State may at any time designate an entity or entities in its territory as the entry point or entry points through which there

shall or may be transmitted to the International Registry information required for registration other than registration of a notice of a national interest or a right or interest under Article 40 in either case arising under the laws of another State.

2. A designation made under the preceding paragraph may permit, but not compel, use of a designated entry point or entry points for information required for registrations in respect of aircraft engines.

Article XX – Additional modifications to Registry provisions

1. For the purposes of Article 19(6) of the Convention, the search criteria for an aircraft object shall be the name of its manufacturer, its manufacturer's serial number and its model designation, supplemented as necessary to ensure uniqueness. Such supplementary information shall be specified in the regulations.
2. For the purposes of Article 25(2) of the Convention and in the circumstances there described, the holder of a registered prospective international interest or a registered prospective assignment of an international interest or the person in whose favour a prospective sale has been registered shall take such steps as are within its power to procure the discharge of the registration no later than five working days after the receipt of the demand described in such paragraph.
3. The fees referred to in Article 17(2)(h) of the Convention shall be determined so as to recover the reasonable costs of establishing, operating and regulating the International Registry and the reasonable costs of the Supervisory Authority associated with the performance of the functions, exercise of the powers, and discharge of the duties contemplated by Article 17(2) of the Convention.
4. The centralised functions of the International Registry shall be operated and administered by the Registrar on a twenty-four hour basis. The various entry points shall be operated at least during working hours in their respective territories.
5. The amount of the insurance or financial guarantee referred to in Article 28(4) of the Convention shall, in respect of each event, not be less than the maximum value of an aircraft object as determined by the Supervisory Authority.
6. Nothing in the Convention shall preclude the Registrar from procuring insurance or a financial guarantee covering events for which the Registrar is not liable under Article 28 of the Convention.

Chapter IV – Jurisdiction

Article XXI – Modification of jurisdiction provisions

For the purposes of Article 43 of the Convention and subject to Article 42 of the Convention, a court of a Contracting State also has jurisdiction where the object is a helicopter, or an airframe pertaining to an aircraft, for which that State is the State of registry.

Article XXII – Waivers of sovereign immunity

1. Subject to paragraph 2, a waiver of sovereign immunity from jurisdiction of the courts specified in Article 42 or Article 43 of the Convention or relating to enforcement of rights and interests relating to an aircraft object under the Convention shall be binding and, if the other conditions to such jurisdiction or enforcement have been satisfied, shall be effective to confer jurisdiction and permit enforcement, as the case may be.
2. A waiver under the preceding paragraph must be in writing and contain a description of the aircraft object.

Chapter V – Relationship with other conventions

Article XXIII – Relationship with the Convention on the International Recognition of Rights in Aircraft

The Convention shall, for a Contracting State that is a party to the Convention on the International Recognition of Rights in Aircraft, signed at Geneva on 19 June 1948, supersede that Convention as it relates to aircraft, as defined in this Protocol, and to aircraft objects. However, with respect to rights or interests not covered or affected by the present Convention, the Geneva Convention shall not be superseded.
Article XXIV – Relationship with the Convention for the Unification of Certain Rules Relating to the Precautionary Attachment of Aircraft

1. The Convention shall, for a Contracting State that is a Party to the *Convention for the Unification of Certain Rules Relating to the Precautionary Attachment of Aircraft*, signed at Rome on 29 May 1933, supersede that Convention as it relates to aircraft, as defined in this Protocol.
2. A Contracting State Party to the above Convention may declare, at the time of ratification, acceptance, approval of, or accession to this Protocol, that it will not apply this Article.

Article XXV – Relationship with the UNIDROIT Convention on International Financial Leasing

The Convention shall supersede the UNIDROIT Convention on International Financial Leasing, signed at Ottawa on 28 May 1988, as it relates to aircraft objects.

Chapter VI – Final provisions

Article XXVI – Signature, ratification, acceptance, approval or accession

1. This Protocol shall be open for signature in Cape Town on 16 November 2001 by States participating in the Diplomatic Conference to Adopt a Mobile Equipment Convention and an Aircraft Protocol held at Cape Town from 29

October to 16 November 2001. After 16 November 2001, this Protocol shall be open to all States for signature at the Headquarters of the International Institute for the Unification of Private Law (UNIDROIT) in Rome until it enters into force in accordance with Article XXVIII.

2. This Protocol shall be subject to ratification, acceptance or approval by States which have signed it.
3. Any State which does not sign this Protocol may accede to it at any time.
4. Ratification, acceptance, approval or accession is effected by the deposit of a formal instrument to that effect with the Depositary.
5. A State may not become a Party to this Protocol unless it is or becomes also a Party to the Convention.

Article XXVII – Regional Economic Integration Organisations

1. A Regional Economic Integration Organisation which is constituted by sovereign States and has competence over certain matters governed by this Protocol may similarly sign, accept, approve or accede to this Protocol. The Regional Economic Integration Organisation shall in that case have the rights and obligations of a Contracting State, to the extent that that Organisation has competence over matters governed by this Protocol. Where the number of Contracting States is relevant in this Protocol, the Regional Economic Integration Organisation shall not count as a Contracting State in addition to its Member States which are Contracting States.
2. The Regional Economic Integration Organisation shall, at the time of signature, acceptance, approval or accession, make a declaration to the Depositary specifying the matters governed by this Protocol in respect of which competence has been transferred to that Organisation by its Member States. The Regional Economic Integration Organisation shall promptly notify the Depositary of any changes to the distribution of competence, including new transfers of competence, specified in the declaration under this paragraph.
3. Any reference to a 'Contracting State' or 'Contracting States' or 'State Party' or 'States Parties' in this Protocol applies equally to a Regional Economic Integration Organisation where the context so requires.

Article XXVIII – Entry into force

1. This Protocol enters into force on the first day of the month following the expiration of three months after the date of the deposit of the eighth instrument of ratification, acceptance, approval or accession, between the States which have deposited such instruments.
2. For other States this Protocol enters into force on the first day of the month following the expiration of three months after the date of the deposit of its instrument of ratification, acceptance, approval or accession.

Article XXIX – Territorial units

1. If a Contracting State has territorial units in which different systems of law are applicable in relation to the matters dealt with in this Protocol, it may, at the time of ratification, acceptance, approval or accession, declare that this Protocol is to extend to all its territorial units or only to one or more of them and may modify its declaration by submitting another declaration at any time.
2. Any such declaration shall state expressly the territorial units to which this Protocol applies.
3. If a Contracting State has not made any declaration under paragraph 1, this Protocol shall apply to all territorial units of that State.
4. Where a Contracting State extends this Protocol to one or more of its territorial units, declarations permitted under this Protocol may be made in respect of each such territorial unit, and the declarations made in respect of one territorial unit may be different from those made in respect of another territorial unit.
5. If by virtue of a declaration under paragraph 1, this Protocol extends to one or more territorial units of a Contracting State:
   (a) the debtor is considered to be situated in a Contracting State only if it is incorporated or formed under a law in force in a territorial unit to which the Convention and this Protocol apply or if it has its registered office or statutory seat, centre of administration, place of business or habitual residence in a territorial unit to which the Convention and this Protocol apply;
   (b) any reference to the location of the object in a Contracting State refers to the location of the object in a territorial unit to which the Convention and this Protocol apply; and
   (c) any reference to the administrative authorities in that Contracting State shall be construed as referring to the administrative authorities having jurisdiction in a territorial unit to which the Convention and this Protocol apply and any reference to the national register or to the registry authority in that Contracting State shall be construed as referring to the aircraft register in force or to the registry authority having jurisdiction in the territorial unit or units to which the Convention and this Protocol apply.

Article XXX – Declarations relating to certain provisions

1. A Contracting State may, at the time of ratification, acceptance, approval of, or accession to this Protocol, declare that it will apply any one or more of Articles VIII, XII and XIII of this Protocol.
2. A Contracting State may, at the time of ratification, acceptance, approval of, or accession to this Protocol, declare that it will apply Article X of this Protocol, wholly or in part. If it so declares with respect to Article X(2), it shall specify the time-period required thereby.
3. A Contracting State may, at the time of ratification, acceptance, approval of, or accession to this Protocol, declare that it will apply the entirety of Alternative A, or the entirety of Alternative B of Article XI and, if so, shall specify

the types of insolvency proceeding, if any, to which it will apply Alternative A and the types of insolvency proceeding, if any, to which it will apply Alternative B. A Contracting State making a declaration pursuant to this paragraph shall specify the time-period required by Article XI.

4. The courts of Contracting States shall apply Article XI in conformity with the declaration made by the Contracting State which is the primary insolvency jurisdiction.
5. A Contracting State may, at the time of ratification, acceptance, approval of, or accession to this Protocol, declare that it will not apply the provisions of Article XXI, wholly or in part. The declaration shall specify under which conditions the relevant Article will be applied, in case it will be applied partly, or otherwise which other forms of interim relief will be applied.

Article XXXI – Declarations under the Convention

Declarations made under the Convention, including those made under Articles 39, 40, 50, 53, 54, 55, 57, 58 and 60 of the Convention, shall be deemed to have also been made under this Protocol unless stated otherwise.

Article XXXII – Reservations and declarations

1. No reservations may be made to this Protocol but declarations authorised by Articles XXIV, XXIX, XXX, XXXI, XXXIII and XXXIV may be made in accordance with these provisions.
2. Any declaration or subsequent declaration or any withdrawal of a declaration made under this Protocol shall be notified in writing to the Depositary.

Article XXXIII – Subsequent declarations

1. A State Party may make a subsequent declaration, other than a declaration made in accordance with Article XXXI under Article 60 of the Convention, at any time after the date on which this Protocol has entered into force for it, by notifying the Depositary to that effect.
2. Any such subsequent declaration shall take effect on the first day of the month following the expiration of six months after the date of receipt of the notification by the Depositary. Where a longer period for that declaration to take effect is specified in the notification, it shall take effect upon the expiration of such longer period after receipt of the notification by the Depositary.
3. Notwithstanding the previous paragraphs, this Protocol shall continue to apply, as if no such subsequent declarations had been made, in respect of all rights and interests arising prior to the effective date of any such subsequent declaration.

Article XXXIV – Withdrawal of declarations

1. Any State Party having made a declaration under this Protocol, other than a declaration made in accordance with Article XXXI under Article 60 of the Convention, may withdraw it at any time by notifying the Depositary. Such withdrawal is to take effect on the first day of the month following the expiration of six months after the date of receipt of the notification by the Depositary.
2. Notwithstanding the previous paragraph, this Protocol shall continue to apply, as if no such withdrawal of declaration had been made, in respect of all rights and interests arising prior to the effective date of any such withdrawal.

Article XXXV – Denunciations

1. Any State Party may denounce this Protocol by notification in writing to the Depositary.
2. Any such denunciation shall take effect on the first day of the month following the expiration of twelve months after the date of receipt of the notification by the Depositary.
3. Notwithstanding the previous paragraphs, this Protocol shall continue to apply, as if no such denunciation had been made, in respect of all rights and interests arising prior to the effective date of any such denunciation.

Article XXXVI – Review Conferences, amendments and related matters

1. The Depositary, in consultation with the Supervisory Authority, shall prepare reports yearly, or at such other time as the circumstances may require, for the States Parties as to the manner in which the international regime established in the Convention as amended by this Protocol has operated in practice. In preparing such reports, the Depositary shall take into account the reports of the Supervisory Authority concerning the functioning of the international registration system.
2. At the request of not less than twenty-five per cent of the States Parties, Review Conferences of the States Parties shall be convened from time to time by the Depositary, in consultation with the Supervisory Authority, to consider:
   (a) the practical operation of the Convention as amended by this Protocol and its effectiveness in facilitating the asset-based financing and leasing of the objects covered by its terms;
   (b) the judicial interpretation given to, and the application made of the terms of this Protocol and the regulations;
   (c) the functioning of the international registration system, the performance of the Registrar and its oversight by the Supervisory Authority, taking into account the reports of the Supervisory Authority; and
   (d) whether any modifications to this Protocol or the arrangements relating to the International Registry are desirable.

3. Any amendment to this Protocol shall be approved by at least a two-thirds majority of States Parties participating in the Conference referred to in the preceding paragraph and shall then enter into force in respect of States which have ratified, accepted or approved such amendment when it has been ratified, accepted or approved by eight States in accordance with the provisions of Article XXVIII relating to its entry into force.

Article XXXVII – Depositary and its functions

1. Instruments of ratification, acceptance, approval or accession shall be deposited with the International Institute for the Unification of Private Law (UNIDROIT), which is hereby designated the Depositary.
2. The Depositary shall:
   (a) inform all Contracting States of:
      (i) each new signature or deposit of an instrument of ratification, acceptance, approval or accession, together with the date thereof;
      (ii) the date of entry into force of this Protocol;
      (iii) each declaration made in accordance with this Protocol, together with the date thereof;
      (iv) the withdrawal or amendment of any declaration, together with the date thereof; and
      (v) the notification of any denunciation of this Protocol together with the date thereof and the date on which it takes effect;
   (b) transmit certified true copies of this Protocol to all Contracting States;
   (c) provide the Supervisory Authority and the Registrar with a copy of each instrument of ratification, acceptance, approval or accession, together with the date of deposit thereof, of each declaration or withdrawal or amendment of a declaration and of each notification of denunciation, together with the date of notification thereof, so that the information contained therein is easily and fully available; and
   (d) perform such other functions customary for depositaries.

IN WITNESS WHEREOF the undersigned Plenipotentiaries, having been duly authorised, have signed this Protocol.
DONE at Cape Town, this sixteenth day of November, two thousand and one, in a single original in the English, Arabic, Chinese, French, Russian and Spanish languages, all texts being equally authentic, such authenticity to take effect upon verification by the Joint Secretariat of the Conference under the authority of the President of the Conference within ninety days hereof as to the conformity of the texts with one another.

Chapter 3. The Luxembourg Protocol to the Convention on International Interests in Mobile Equipment on Matters Specific to Railway Rolling Stock

LUXEMBOURG PROTOCOL TO THE CONVENTION ON INTERNATIONAL INTERESTS IN MOBILE EQUIPMENT ON MATTERS SPECIFIC TO RAILWAY ROLLING STOCK

THE STATES PARTIES TO THIS PROTOCOL
CONSIDERING it necessary to implement the Convention on International Interests in Mobile Equipment (the 'Convention') as it relates to railway rolling stock, in the light of the purposes set out in the preamble to the Convention,
MINDFUL of the need to adapt the Convention to meet the particular requirements of railway rolling stock and their finance,
HAVE AGREED upon the following provisions relating to railway rolling stock:

Chapter I – Sphere of application and general provisions

Article I – Defined terms

1. In this Protocol, except where the context otherwise requires, terms used in it have the meanings set out in the Convention.
2. In this Protocol the following terms are employed with the meanings set out below:
   (a) 'guarantee contract' means a contract entered into by a person as guarantor;
   (b) 'guarantor' means a person who, for the purpose of assuring performance of any obligations in favour of a creditor secured by a security agreement or under an agreement, gives or issues a suretyship or demand guarantee or a standby letter of credit or any other form of credit insurance;
   (c) 'insolvency-related event' means:
      (i) the commencement of the insolvency proceedings; or
      (ii) the declared intention to suspend or actual suspension of payments by the debtor where the creditor's right to institute insolvency proceedings against the debtor or to exercise remedies under the Convention is prevented or suspended by law or State action;
   (d) 'primary insolvency jurisdiction' means the Contracting State in which the centre of the debtor's main interests is situated, which for this purpose shall be deemed to be the place of the debtor's statutory seat or, if there is none, the place where the debtor is incorporated or formed, unless proved otherwise;
   (e) 'railway rolling stock' means vehicles movable on a fixed railway track or directly on, above or below a guideway, together with traction systems, engines, brakes, axles, bogies, pantographs, accessories and other

components, equipment and parts, in each case installed on or incorporated in the vehicles, and together with all data, manuals and records relating thereto.

Article II – Application of Convention as regards railway rolling stock

1. The Convention shall apply in relation to railway rolling stock as provided by the terms of this Protocol.
2. The Convention and this Protocol shall be known as the Convention on International Interests in Mobile Equipment as applied to railway rolling stock.

Article III – Derogation

The parties may, by agreement in writing, exclude the application of Article IX and, in their relations with each other, derogate from or vary the effect of any of the provisions of this Protocol except Article VII(3) and (4).

Article IV – Representative capacities

A person may, in relation to railway rolling stock, enter into an agreement, effect a registration as defined by Article 16(3) of the Convention and assert rights and interests under the Convention, in an agency, trust or representative capacity.

Article V – Identification of railway rolling stock in the agreement

1. For the purposes of Article 7(c) of the Convention and Article XVIII(2) of this Protocol, a description of railway rolling stock is sufficient to identify the railway rolling stock if it contains:
   (a) a description of the railway rolling stock by item;
   (b) a description of the railway rolling stock by type;
   (c) a statement that the agreement covers all present and future railway rolling stock; or
   (d) a statement that the agreement covers all present and future railway rolling stock except for specified items or types.
2. For the purposes of Article 7 of the Convention, an interest in future railway rolling stock identified in accordance with the preceding paragraph shall be constituted as an international interest as soon as the chargor, conditional seller or lessor acquires the power to dispose of the railway rolling stock, without the need for any new act of transfer.

Article VI – Choice of law

1. This Article applies only where a Contracting State has made a declaration pursuant to Article XXVII.

2. The parties to an agreement or a related guarantee contract or subordination agreement may agree on the law which is to govern their contractual rights and obligations, wholly or in part.
3. Unless otherwise agreed, the reference in the preceding paragraph to the law chosen by the parties is to the domestic rules of law of the designated State or, where that State comprises several territorial units, to the domestic law of the designated territorial unit.

Chapter II – Default remedies, priorities and assignments

Article VII – Modification of default remedies provisions

1. In addition to the remedies specified in Chapter III of the Convention, the creditor may, to the extent that the debtor has at any time so agreed and in the circumstances specified in that Chapter, procure the export and physical transfer of railway rolling stock from the territory in which it is situated.
2. The creditor shall not exercise the remedies specified in the preceding paragraph without the prior consent in writing of the holder of any registered interest ranking in priority to that of the creditor.
3. Article 8(3) of the Convention shall not apply to railway rolling stock. Any remedy given by the Convention in relation to railway rolling stock shall be exercised in a commercially reasonable manner. A remedy shall be deemed to be exercised in a commercially reasonable manner where it is exercised in conformity with a provision of the agreement except where such a provision is manifestly unreasonable.
4. A chargee giving fourteen or more calendar days' prior written notice of a proposed sale or lease to interested persons as provided by Article 8(4) of the Convention shall be deemed to satisfy the requirement of giving the 'reasonable prior notice' specified therein. The foregoing shall not prevent a chargee and a chargor or a guarantor from agreeing to a longer period of prior notice.
5. Subject to any applicable safety laws and regulations, a Contracting State shall ensure that the relevant administrative authorities expeditiously co-operate with and assist the creditor to the extent necessary for the exercise of the remedies specified in paragraph 1.
6. A chargee proposing to procure the export of railway rolling stock under paragraph 1 otherwise than pursuant to a court order shall give reasonable prior notice in writing of the proposed export to:
   (a) interested persons specified in Article 1(m)(i) and (ii) of the Convention; and
   (b) interested persons specified in Article 1(m)(iii) of the Convention who have given notice of their rights to the chargee within a reasonable time prior to the export.

Article VIII – Modification of provisions regarding relief pending final determination

1. This Article applies only in a Contracting State which has made a declaration pursuant to Article XXVII and to the extent stated in such declaration.
2. For the purposes of Article 13(1) of the Convention, 'speedy' in the context of obtaining relief means within such number of calendar days from the date of filing of the application for relief as is specified in a declaration made by the Contracting State in which the application is made.
3. Article 13(1) of the Convention applies with the following being added immediately after sub-paragraph (d):

'(e) if at any time the debtor and the creditor specifically agree, sale of the object and application of proceeds therefrom',

and Article 43(2) applies with the insertion after the words 'Article 13(1)(d)' of the words 'and (e)'.

4. Ownership or any other interest of the debtor passing on a sale under the preceding paragraph is free from any other interest over which the creditor's international interest has priority under the provisions of Article 29 of the Convention.
5. The creditor and the debtor or any other interested person may agree in writing to exclude the application of Article 13(2) of the Convention.
6. With regard to the remedies in Article VII(1):
   (a) they shall be made available by the administrative authorities in a Contracting State no later than seven calendar days after the creditor notifies such authorities that the relief specified in Article VII(1) is granted or, in the case of relief granted by a foreign court, recognised by a court of that Contracting State, and that the creditor is entitled to procure those remedies in accordance with the Convention; and
   (b) the applicable authorities shall expeditiously co-operate with and assist the creditor in the exercise of such remedies in conformity with the applicable safety laws and regulations.
7. Paragraphs 2 and 6 shall not affect any applicable safety laws and regulations.

Article IX – Remedies on insolvency

1. This Article applies only where a Contracting State that is the primary insolvency jurisdiction has made a declaration pursuant to Article XXVII.
2. References in this Article to the 'insolvency administrator' shall be to that person in its official, not in its personal, capacity.

Alternative A

3. Upon the occurrence of an insolvency-related event, the insolvency administrator or the debtor, as applicable, shall, subject to paragraph 7, give possession of the railway rolling stock to the creditor no later than the earlier of:
   (a) the end of the waiting period; and
   (b) the date on which the creditor would be entitled to possession of the railway rolling stock if this Article did not apply.
4. For the purposes of this Article, the 'waiting period' shall be the period specified in a declaration of the Contracting State which is the primary insolvency jurisdiction.
5. Unless and until the creditor is given the opportunity to take possession under paragraph 3:
   (a) the insolvency administrator or the debtor, as applicable, shall preserve the railway rolling stock and maintain it and its value in accordance with the agreement; and
   (b) the creditor shall be entitled to apply for any other forms of interim relief available under the applicable law.
6. Sub-paragraph (a) of the preceding paragraph shall not preclude the use of the railway rolling stock under arrangements designed to preserve the railway rolling stock and maintain it and its value.
7. The insolvency administrator or the debtor, as applicable, may retain possession of the railway rolling stock where, by the time specified in paragraph 3, it has cured all defaults other than a default constituted by the opening of insolvency proceedings and has agreed to perform all future obligations under the agreement and related transaction documents. A second waiting period shall not apply in respect of a default in the performance of such future obligations.
8. With regard to the remedies in Article VII(1):
   (a) they shall be made available by the administrative authorities in a Contracting State no later than seven calendar days after the date on which the creditor notifies such authorities that it is entitled to procure those remedies in accordance with the Convention; and
   (b) the applicable authorities shall expeditiously co-operate with and assist the creditor in the exercise of such remedies in conformity with the applicable safety laws and regulations.
9. No exercise of remedies permitted by the Convention or this Protocol may be prevented or delayed after the date specified in paragraph 3.
10. No obligations of the debtor under the agreement may be modified without the consent of the creditor.
11. Nothing in the preceding paragraph shall be construed to affect the authority, if any, of the insolvency administrator under the applicable law to terminate the agreement.
12. No rights or interests, except for non-consensual rights or interests of a category covered by a declaration pursuant to Article 39(1) of the Convention, shall have priority in insolvency proceedings over registered interests.
13. The Convention as modified by Articles VII and XXV of this Protocol shall apply to the exercise of any remedies under this Article.

Alternative B

3. Upon the occurrence of an insolvency-related event, the insolvency administrator or the debtor, as applicable, upon the request of the creditor, shall give notice to the creditor within the time specified in a declaration of a Contracting State pursuant to Article XXVII whether it will:
   (a) cure all defaults other than a default constituted by the opening of insolvency proceedings and agree to perform all future obligations, under the agreement and related transaction documents; or
   (b) give the creditor the opportunity to take possession of the railway rolling stock, in accordance with the applicable law.
4. The applicable law referred to in sub-paragraph (b) of the preceding paragraph may permit the court to require the taking of any additional step or the provision of any additional guarantee.
5. The creditor shall provide evidence of its claims and proof that its international interest has been registered.
6. If the insolvency administrator or the debtor, as applicable, does not give notice in conformity with paragraph 3, or when the insolvency administrator or the debtor has declared that it will give the creditor the opportunity to take possession of the railway rolling stock but fails to do so, the court may permit the creditor to take possession of the railway rolling stock upon such terms as the court may order and may require the taking of any additional step or the provision of any additional guarantee.
7. The railway rolling stock shall not be sold pending a decision by a court regarding the claim and the international interest.

Alternative C

3. Upon the occurrence of an insolvency-related event, the insolvency administrator or the debtor, as applicable, shall within the cure period:
   (a) cure all defaults other than a default constituted by the opening of insolvency proceedings and agree to perform all future obligations, under the agreement and related transaction documents; or
   (b) give the creditor the opportunity to take possession of the railway rolling stock in accordance with the applicable law.
4. Before the end of the cure period, the insolvency administrator or the debtor, as applicable, may apply to the court for an order suspending its obligation under sub-paragraph (b) of the preceding paragraph for a period commencing from the end of the cure period and ending no later than the expiration of the agreement or any renewal thereof, and on such terms as the court considers just (the 'suspension period'). Any such order shall require that all sums accruing to the creditor during the suspension period be paid from the insolvency estate or by the debtor as they become due and that the insolvency administrator or the debtor, as applicable, perform all other obligations arising during the suspension period.

5. If an application is made to the court under the preceding paragraph, the creditor shall not take possession of the railway rolling stock pending an order of the court. If the application is not granted within such number of calendar days from the date of filing of the application for relief as is specified in a declaration made by the Contracting State in which the application is made, the application will be deemed withdrawn unless the creditor and the insolvency administrator or the debtor, as applicable, otherwise agree.
6. Unless and until the creditor is given the opportunity to take possession under paragraph 3:
   (a) the insolvency administrator or the debtor, as applicable, shall preserve the railway rolling stock and maintain it and its value in accordance with the agreement; and
   (b) the creditor shall be entitled to apply for any other forms of interim relief available under the applicable law.
7. Sub-paragraph (a) of the preceding paragraph shall not preclude the use of the railway rolling stock under arrangements designed to preserve and maintain it and its value.
8. Where during the cure period or any suspension period the insolvency administrator or the debtor, as applicable, cures all defaults other than a default constituted by the opening of insolvency proceedings and agrees to perform all future obligations under the agreement and related transaction documents, the insolvency administrator or debtor may retain possession of the railway rolling stock and any order made by the court under paragraph 4 shall cease to have effect. A second cure period shall not apply in respect of a default in the performance of such future obligations.
9. With regard to the remedies in Article VII(1):
   (a) they shall be made available by the administrative authorities in a Contracting State no later than seven calendar days after the date on which the creditor notifies such authorities that it is entitled to procure those remedies in accordance with the Convention; and
   (b) the applicable authorities shall expeditiously co-operate with and assist the creditor in the exercise of such remedies in conformity with the applicable safety laws and regulations.
10. Subject to paragraphs 4, 5 and 8, no exercise of remedies permitted by the Convention may be prevented or delayed after the cure period.
11. Subject to paragraphs 4, 5 and 8, no obligations of the debtor under the agreement and related transactions may be modified in insolvency proceedings without the consent of the creditor.
12. Nothing in the preceding paragraph shall be construed to affect the authority, if any, of the insolvency administrator under the applicable law to terminate the agreement.
13. No rights or interests, except for non-consensual rights or interests of a category covered by a declaration pursuant to Article 39(1) of the Convention, shall have priority in insolvency proceedings over registered interests.
14. The Convention as modified by Articles VII and XXV of this Protocol shall apply to the exercise of any remedies under this Article.

15. For the purposes of this Article, the 'cure period' shall be the period, commencing with the date of the insolvency-related event, specified in a declaration of the Contracting State which is the primary insolvency jurisdiction.

Article X – Insolvency assistance

1. This Article applies only in a Contracting State which has made a declaration pursuant to Article XXVII(1).
2. The courts of a Contracting State in which railway rolling stock is situated shall, in accordance with the law of the Contracting State, co-operate to the maximum extent possible with foreign courts and foreign insolvency administrators in carrying out the provisions of Article IX.

Article XI – Debtor provisions

1. In the absence of a default within the meaning of Article 11 of the Convention, the debtor shall be entitled to the quiet possession and use of the railway rolling stock in accordance with the agreement as against:
   (a) its creditor and the holder of any interest from which the debtor takes free pursuant to Article 29(4)(b) of the Convention unless and to the extent that the debtor has otherwise agreed; and
   (b) the holder of any interest to which the debtor's right or interest is subject pursuant to Article 29(4)(a) of the Convention, but only to the extent, if any, that such holder has agreed.
2. Nothing in the Convention or this Protocol affects the liability of a creditor for any breach of the agreement under the applicable law in so far as that agreement relates to railway rolling stock.

Chapter III – Registry provisions relating to international interests in railway rolling stock

Article XII – The Supervisory Authority and the Registrar

1. The Supervisory Authority shall be a body established by representatives, one representative to be appointed:
   (a) by each State Party;
   (b) by each of a maximum of three other States to be designated by the International Institute for the Unification of Private Law (UNIDROIT); and
   (c) by each of a maximum of three other States to be designated by the Intergovernmental Organisation for International Carriage by Rail (OTIF).
2. In the designation of the States referred to in sub-paragraphs (b) and (c) of the preceding paragraph regard shall be had to the need to ensure broad geographical representation.

3. The term of appointment of the representatives appointed pursuant to sub-paragraphs (b) and (c) of paragraph 1 shall be that specified by the designating Organisations. The terms of those representatives serving on the date when this Protocol enters into force for the tenth State Party shall expire no later than two years after that date.
4. The representatives referred to in paragraph 1 shall adopt the initial rules of procedure for the Supervisory Authority. Adoption shall require agreement of:
   (a) a majority of all the representatives; and
   (b) a majority of the representatives appointed pursuant to sub-paragraph (a) of paragraph 1.
5. The Supervisory Authority may establish a commission of experts consisting of:
   (a) persons nominated by Signatory and Contracting States and having the necessary qualifications and experience; and
   (b) other experts as necessary

   and entrust the commission with the task of assisting the Supervisory Authority in the discharge of its functions.
6. A secretariat (the Secretariat) shall assist the Supervisory Authority in the discharge of its functions, as directed by the Supervisory Authority. The Secretariat shall be OTIF.
7. In the event that the Secretariat becomes unable or unwilling to discharge its functions, the Supervisory Authority shall designate another Secretariat.
8. The Secretariat shall, on being satisfied that the International Registry is fully operational, forthwith deposit a certificate to that effect with the Depositary.
9. The Secretariat shall have legal personality where not already possessing such personality, and shall enjoy, in relation to its functions under the Convention and this Protocol, the same exemptions and immunities as are provided to the Supervisory Authority under Article 27(3) of the Convention and to the International Registry under Article 27(4) of the Convention.
10. A measure taken by the Supervisory Authority that affects only the interests of a State Party or a group of States Parties shall be taken if such State Party or the majority of the group of States Parties also approve of the measure. A measure that could adversely affect the interests of a State Party or a group of States Parties shall have effect in such State Party or group of States Parties if such State Party or the majority of the group of States Parties also approve of the measure.
11. The first Registrar shall be appointed for a period of not less than five or more than ten years. Thereafter, the Registrar shall be appointed or re-appointed for successive periods each not exceeding ten years.

Article XIII – Designated entry points

1. A Contracting State may at any time designate, by declaration, an entity or entities as the entry point or entry points through which there shall or may be transmitted to the International Registry information required for registration other than registration of a notice of a national interest or of a right or interest

under Article 40 of the Convention in either case arising under the laws of another State. The various entry points shall be operated at least during working hours in their respective territories.

2. A designation made under the preceding paragraph may permit, but not compel, use of a designated entry point or entry points for information required for registrations in respect of notices of sale.

Article XIV – Identification of railway rolling stock for registration purposes

1. For the purposes of Article 18(1)(a) of the Convention, the regulations shall prescribe a system for the allocation of identification numbers by the Registrar which enable the unique identification of items of railway rolling stock. The identification number shall be:
   (a) affixed to the item of railway rolling stock;
   (b) associated in the International Registry with the manufacturer's name and the manufacturer's identification number for the item so affixed; or
   (c) associated in the International Registry with a national or regional identification number so affixed.
2. For the purposes of the preceding paragraph, a Contracting State may, by declaration, state the system of national or regional identification numbers that shall be used with respect to items of railway rolling stock subject to an international interest that is created or provided for, or is intended to be created or provided for, by an agreement entered into by a debtor situated in that Contracting State at the time of the conclusion of that agreement. Such a national or regional identification system shall, subject to agreement between the Supervisory Authority and the Contracting State making the declaration, ensure the unique identification of each item of railway rolling stock to which the system applies.
3. A declaration by a Contracting State according to the preceding paragraph shall include detailed information on the operation of the national or regional identification system.
4. A registration in respect of an item of railway rolling stock for which a declaration pursuant to paragraph 2 has been made shall, in order for the registration to be valid, specify all the national or regional identification numbers to which the item has been subject since the entry into force of this Protocol under Article XXIII(1) and the time during which each number has applied to the item.

Article XV – Additional modifications to Registry provisions

1. For the purposes of Article 19(6) of the Convention, the search criteria at the International Registry shall be established by the regulations.
2. For the purposes of Article 25(2) of the Convention, and in the circumstances there described, the holder of a registered prospective international interest or a registered prospective assignment of an international interest shall take such

steps as are within its power to procure the discharge of the registration no later than ten calendar days after the receipt of the demand described in such paragraph.

3. Where a subordination has been registered and the obligations of the debtor to the beneficiary of the subordination have been discharged, the beneficiary shall procure the discharge of the registration no later than ten calendar days after written demand by the subordinated party delivered to or received at the beneficiary's address stated in the registration.
4. The centralised functions of the International Registry shall be operated and administered by the Registrar on a twenty-four hour basis.
5. The Registrar shall be liable under Article 28 (1) of the Convention for loss caused up to an amount not exceeding the value of the railway rolling stock to which the loss relates. Notwithstanding the preceding sentence, the liability of the Registrar shall not exceed 5 million Special Drawing Rights in any calendar year, or such greater amount, computed in such manner, as the Supervisory Authority may from time to time determine by regulations.
6. The preceding paragraph shall not limit the Registrar's liability for damages for loss caused by gross negligence or intentional misconduct of the Registrar and its officers and employees.
7. The amount of the insurance or financial guarantee referred to in Article 28(4) of the Convention shall be not less than the amount determined by the Supervisory Authority to be appropriate, having regard to the prospective liability of the Registrar.
8. Nothing in the Convention shall preclude the Registrar from procuring insurance or a financial guarantee covering events for which the Registrar is not liable under Article 28 of the Convention.

Article XVI – International Registry fees

1. The Supervisory Authority shall set and may from time to time amend the fees to be paid in connection with registrations, filings, searches and other services the International Registry may provide, in accordance with its regulations.
2. The fees referred to in the preceding paragraph shall be determined so as to recover, to the extent necessary, the reasonable costs of establishing, implementing and operating the International Registry, as well as the reasonable costs of the Secretariat associated with the performance of its functions. Nothing in this paragraph shall preclude the Registrar from operating for a reasonable profit.

Article XVII – Notices of sale

The regulations shall authorise the registration in the International Registry of notices of sale of railway rolling stock. The provisions of this Chapter and of Chapter V of the Convention shall, in so far as relevant, apply to these registrations. However, any such registration and any search made or certificate issued in respect of a notice of sale shall be for the purposes of information only and shall not affect the rights of any person, or have any other effect, under the Convention or this Protocol.

Chapter IV – Jurisdiction

Article XVIII – Waivers of sovereign immunity

1. Subject to paragraph 2, a waiver of sovereign immunity from jurisdiction of the courts specified in Article 42 or Article 43 of the Convention or relating to enforcement of rights and interests relating to railway rolling stock under the Convention shall be binding and, if the other conditions to such jurisdiction or enforcement have been satisfied, shall be effective to confer jurisdiction and permit enforcement, as the case may be.
2. A waiver under the preceding paragraph must be in writing and contain a description of the railway rolling stock as specified in Article V(1) of this Protocol.

Chapter V – Relationship with other Conventions

Article XIX – Relationship with the UNIDROIT Convention on International Financial Leasing

The Convention shall, to the extent of any inconsistency, prevail over the UNIDROIT Convention on International Financial Leasing, signed in Ottawa on 28 May 1988.

Article XX – Relationship with the Convention concerning International Carriage by Rail (COTIF)

The Convention shall, to the extent of any inconsistency, prevail over the Convention concerning International Carriage by Rail (COTIF) of 9 May 1980 in the version of the Protocol of Modification of 3 June 1999.

Chapter VI – Final provisions

Article XXI – Signature, ratification, acceptance, approval or accession

1. This Protocol shall be open for signature in Luxembourg on 23 February 2007 by States participating in the diplomatic Conference to adopt a Rail Protocol to the Convention on International Interests in Mobile Equipment held at Luxembourg from 12 to 23 February 2007. After 23 February 2007 this Protocol shall be open to all States for signature at the Headquarters of UNIDROIT in Rome until it enters into force in accordance with Article XXIII.
2. This Protocol shall be subject to ratification, acceptance or approval by States which have signed it.

3. Any State which does not sign this Protocol may accede to it at any time.
4. Ratification, acceptance, approval or accession is effected by the deposit of a formal instrument to that effect with the Depositary.
5. A State may not become a Party to this Protocol unless it is or becomes also a Party to the Convention.

Article XXII – Regional Economic Integration Organisations

1. A Regional Economic Integration Organisation which is constituted by sovereign States and has competence over certain matters governed by this Protocol may similarly sign, accept, approve or accede to this Protocol. The Regional Economic Integration Organisation shall in that case have the rights and obligations of a Contracting State, to the extent that that Organisation has competence over matters governed by this Protocol. Where the number of Contracting States is relevant in this Protocol, the Regional Economic Integration Organisation shall not count as a Contracting State in addition to its Member States which are Contracting States.
2. The Regional Economic Integration Organisation shall, at the time of signature, acceptance, approval or accession, make a declaration to the Depositary specifying the matters governed by this Protocol in respect of which competence has been transferred to that Organisation by its Member States. The Regional Economic Integration Organisation shall promptly notify the Depositary of any changes to the distribution of competence, including new transfers of competence, specified in the declaration under this paragraph.
3. Any reference to a 'Contracting State' or 'Contracting States' or 'State Party' or 'States Parties' in this Protocol applies equally to a Regional Economic Integration Organisation where the context so requires.

Article XXIII – Entry into force

1. This Protocol enters into force between the States which have deposited instruments referred to in sub-paragraph (a) on the later of:
   (a) the first day of the month following the expiration of three months after the date of the deposit of the fourth instrument of ratification, acceptance, approval or accession, and
   (b) the date of the deposit by the Secretariat with the Depositary of a certificate confirming that the International Registry is fully operational.
2. For other States this Protocol enters into force on the first day of the month following the later of:
   (a) the expiration of three months after the date of the deposit of its instrument of ratification, acceptance, approval or accession; and
   (b) the date referred to in sub-paragraph (b) of the preceding paragraph.

Article XXIV – Territorial units

1. If a Contracting State has territorial units in which different systems of law are applicable in relation to the matters dealt with in this Protocol, it may, at the time of ratification, acceptance, approval or accession, declare that this Protocol is to extend to all its territorial units or only to one or more of them, and may modify its declaration by submitting another declaration at any time.
2. Any such declarations are to be notified to the Depositary and shall state expressly the territorial units to which this Protocol applies.
3. If a Contracting State has not made any declaration under paragraph 1, this Protocol shall apply to all territorial units of that State.
4. Where a Contracting State extends this Protocol to one or more of its territorial units, declarations permitted under this Protocol may be made in respect of each such territorial unit, and the declarations made in respect of one territorial unit may be different from those made in respect of another territorial unit.
5. If by virtue of a declaration under paragraph 1, this Protocol extends to one or more territorial units of a Contracting State:
   (a) the debtor is considered to be situated in a Contracting State only if it is incorporated or formed under a law in force in a territorial unit to which the Convention and this Protocol apply or if it has its registered office or statutory seat, centre of administration, place of business or habitual residence in a territorial unit to which the Convention and this Protocol apply;
   (b) any reference to the location of the railway rolling stock in a Contracting State refers to the location of the railway rolling stock in a territorial unit to which the Convention and this Protocol apply; and
   (c) any reference to the administrative authorities in that Contracting State shall be construed as referring to the administrative authorities having jurisdiction in a territorial unit to which the Convention and this Protocol apply.

Article XXV – Public service railway rolling stock

1. A Contracting State may, at any time, declare that it will continue to apply, to the extent specified in its declaration, rules of its law in force at that time which preclude, suspend or govern the exercise within its territory of any of the remedies specified in Chapter III of the Convention and Articles VII to IX of this Protocol in relation to railway rolling stock habitually used for the purpose of providing a service of public importance ('public service railway rolling stock') as specified in that declaration notified to the Depositary.
2. Any person, including a governmental or other public authority, that, under rules of law of a Contracting State making a declaration under the preceding paragraph, exercises a power to take or procure possession, use or control of any public service railway rolling stock, shall preserve and maintain such railway rolling stock from the time of exercise of such power until possession, use or control is restored to the creditor.

3. During the period of time specified in the preceding paragraph, the person referred to in that paragraph shall also make or procure payment to the creditor of an amount equal to the greater of:
   (a) such amount as that person shall be required to pay under the rules of law of the Contracting State making the declaration; and
   (b) the market lease rental in respect of such railway rolling stock.

   The first such payment shall be made within ten calendar days of the date on which such power is exercised, and subsequent payments shall be made on the first day of each successive month thereafter. In the event that in any month the amount payable exceeds the amount due to the creditor from the debtor, the surplus shall be paid to any other creditors to the extent of their claims in the order of their priority and thereafter to the debtor.
4. A Contracting State whose rules of law do not provide for the obligations specified in paragraphs 2 and 3 may, to the extent specified in a separate declaration notified to the Depositary, declare that it will not apply those paragraphs with regard to railway rolling stock specified in that declaration. Nothing in this paragraph shall preclude a person from agreeing with the creditor to perform the obligations specified in paragraphs 2 or 3 or affect the enforceability of any agreement so concluded.
5. Any initial or subsequent declaration made under this Article by a Contracting State shall not adversely affect rights and interests of creditors arising under an agreement entered into prior to the date on which that declaration is received by the Depositary.
6. A Contracting State making a declaration under this Article shall take into consideration the protection of the interests of creditors and the effect of the declaration on the availability of credit.

Article XXVI – Transitional provisions

In relation to railway rolling stock Article 60 of the Convention shall be modified as follows:

(a) in paragraph 2(a), after 'situated' insert 'at the time the right or interest is created or arises';
(b) replace paragraph 3 with the following:

> 3. A Contracting State may in its declaration under paragraph 1 specify a date, not earlier than three years and not later than ten years after the date on which the declaration becomes effective, when Articles 29, 35 and 36 of this Convention as modified or supplemented by the Protocol will become applicable, to the extent and in the manner specified in the declaration, to pre-existing rights or interests arising under an agreement made at a time when the debtor was situated in that State. Any priority of the right or interest under the law of that State, so far as applicable, shall continue if the right or interest is registered in

the International Registry before the expiration of the period specified in the declaration, whether or not any other right or interest has previously been registered.

Article XXVII – Declarations relating to certain provisions

1. A Contracting State may, at the time of ratification, acceptance, approval of, or accession to this Protocol, declare that it will apply either or both of Articles VI and X.
2. A Contracting State may, at the time of ratification, acceptance, approval of, or accession to this Protocol, declare that it will apply Article VIII, wholly or in part. If it so declares, it shall specify the time-period required by Article VIII(2).
3. A Contracting State may, at the time of ratification, acceptance, approval of, or accession to this Protocol, declare that it will apply the entirety of one of Alternatives A, B and C of Article IX and, if it so declares, it shall specify the type of insolvency proceeding, if any, to which it will apply such Alternative. A Contracting State making a declaration pursuant to this paragraph shall specify the time-period required by Article IX under paragraph 4 of Alternative A, paragraph 3 of Alternative B or paragraphs 5 and 15 of Alternative C, as applicable.
4. The courts of Contracting States shall apply Article IX in conformity with the declaration made by the Contracting State which is the primary insolvency jurisdiction.

Article XXVIII – Reservations and declarations

1. No reservations may be made to this Protocol but declarations authorised by Articles XIII, XIV, XXIV, XXV, XXVII, XXIX and XXX may be made in accordance with these provisions.
2. Any declaration or subsequent declaration or any withdrawal of a declaration made under this Protocol shall be notified in writing to the Depositary.

Article XXIX – Declarations under the Convention

1. Declarations made under the Convention, including those made under Articles 39, 40, 50, 53, 54, 55, 57, 58 and 60, shall be deemed to have also been made under this Protocol unless stated otherwise.
2. For the purposes of Article 50(1) of the Convention, an ‘internal transaction’ shall also mean, in relation to railway rolling stock, a transaction of a type listed in Article 2(2)(a) to (c) of the Convention where the relevant railway rolling stock is only capable, in its normal course of use, of being operated on a single railway system within the Contracting State concerned, because of track gauge or other elements of the design of such railway rolling stock.

Article XXX – Subsequent declarations

1. A State Party may make a subsequent declaration, other than a declaration made in accordance with Article XXIX under Article 60 of the Convention, at any time after the date on which this Protocol has entered into force for it, by notifying the Depositary to that effect.
2. Any such subsequent declaration shall take effect on the first day of the month following the expiration of six months after the date of receipt of the notification by the Depositary. Where a longer period for that declaration to take effect is specified in the notification, it shall take effect upon the expiration of such longer period after receipt of the notification by the Depositary.
3. Notwithstanding the previous paragraphs, this Protocol shall continue to apply, as if no such subsequent declarations had been made, in respect of all rights and interests arising prior to the effective date of any such subsequent declaration.

Article XXXI – Withdrawal of declarations

1. Any State Party having made a declaration under this Protocol, other than a declaration made in accordance with Article XXIX under Article 60 of the Convention, may withdraw it at any time by notifying the Depositary. Such withdrawal is to take effect on the first day of the month following the expiration of six months after the date of receipt of the notification by the Depositary.
2. Notwithstanding the preceding paragraph, this Protocol shall continue to apply, as if no such withdrawal had been made, in respect of all rights and interests arising prior to the effective date of any such withdrawal.

Article XXXII – Denunciations

1. Any State Party may denounce this Protocol by notification in writing to the Depositary.
2. Any such denunciation shall take effect on the first day of the month following the expiration of twelve months after the date of receipt of the notification by the Depositary.
3. Notwithstanding the previous paragraphs, this Protocol shall continue to apply, as if no such denunciation had been made, in respect of all rights and interests arising prior to the effective date of any such denunciation.

Article XXXIII – Review Conferences, amendments and related matters

1. The Depositary, in consultation with the Supervisory Authority, shall prepare reports yearly, or at such other time as the circumstances may require, for the States Parties as to the manner in which the international regime established

in the Convention as amended by the Protocol has operated in practice. In preparing such reports, the Depositary shall take into account the reports of the Supervisory Authority concerning the functioning of the international registration system.

2. At the request of not less than twenty-five per cent of the States Parties, Review Conferences of the States Parties shall be convened from time to time by the Depositary, in consultation with the Supervisory Authority, to consider:
   (a) the practical operation of the Convention as amended by this Protocol and its effectiveness in facilitating the asset-based financing and leasing of the objects covered by its terms;
   (b) the judicial interpretation given to, and the application made of the terms of this Protocol and the regulations;
   (c) the functioning of the international registration system, the performance of the Registrar and its oversight by the Supervisory Authority, taking into account the reports of the Supervisory Authority; and
   (d) whether any modifications to this Protocol or the arrangements relating to the International Registry are desirable.
3. Any amendment to this Protocol shall be approved by at least a two-thirds majority of States Parties participating in the Conference referred to in the preceding paragraph and shall then enter into force in respect of States which have ratified, accepted or approved such amendment when it has been ratified, accepted or approved by four States in accordance with the provisions of Article XXIII relating to its entry into force.

Article XXXIV – Depositary and its functions

1. Instruments of ratification, acceptance, approval or accession shall be deposited with UNIDROIT, which is hereby designated the Depositary.
2. The Depositary shall:
   (a) inform all Contracting States of:
      (i) each new signature or deposit of an instrument of ratification, acceptance, approval or accession, together with the date thereof;
      (ii) the date of the deposit of the certificate referred to in Article XXIII(1)(b);
      (iii) the date of entry into force of this Protocol;
      (iv) each declaration made in accordance with this Protocol, together with the date thereof;
      (v) the withdrawal or amendment of any declaration, together with the date thereof; and
      (vi) the notification of any denunciation of this Protocol together with the date thereof and the date on which it takes effect;
   (b) transmit certified true copies of this Protocol to all Contracting States;
   (c) provide the Supervisory Authority and the Registrar with a copy of each instrument of ratification, acceptance, approval or accession, together with the date of deposit thereof, of each declaration or withdrawal or amendment of a declaration and of each notification of denunciation, together

with the date of notification thereof, so that the information contained therein is easily and fully available; and

(d) perform such other functions customary for depositaries.

IN WITNESS WHEREOF the undersigned Plenipotentiaries, having been duly authorised, have signed this Protocol.

DONE at Luxembourg, this twenty-third day of February, two thousand and seven, in a single original in the English, French and German languages, all texts being equally authentic, such authenticity to take effect upon verification by the Secretariat of the Conference under the authority of the President of the Conference within ninety days hereof as to the consistency of the texts with one another.

Chapter 4. The Protocol to the Convention on International Interests in Mobile Equipment on Matters Specific to Space Assets

PROTOCOL TO THE CONVENTION ON INTERNATIONAL INTERESTS IN MOBILE EQUIPMENT ON MATTERS SPECIFIC TO SPACE ASSETS

THE STATES PARTIES TO THIS PROTOCOL,

CONSIDERING it desirable to implement the Convention on International Interests in Mobile Equipment (hereinafter referred to as the Convention) as it relates to space assets, in the light of the purposes set out in the preamble to the Convention,
CONSCIOUS of the need to adapt the Convention to meet the particular demand for and the utility of space assets and the need to finance their acquisition and use,
TAKING INTO CONSIDERATION the benefits to all States from expanded space-based services and financing which the Convention and this Protocol may yield,
MINDFUL of the principles of space law, including those contained in the international space treaties of the United Nations and the instruments of the International Telecommunication Union,
RECALLING, for the carrying out of the transfers contemplated by this Protocol, the pre-eminence of State Party rights and obligations under the international space treaties of the United Nations by which the States Parties concerned are bound,
RECOGNISING the continuing development of the international commercial space industry and contemplating the expected benefits of a uniform and predictable regimen governing interests in space assets and in related rights and facilitating asset-based financing of the same,
HAVE AGREED upon the following provisions relating to space assets:

Chapter I – Sphere of application and general provisions

Article I – Defined terms

1. – In this Protocol, except where the context otherwise requires, terms used in it have the meanings set out in the Convention.
2. – In this Protocol the following terms are employed with the meanings set out below:
   (a) 'debtor's rights' means rights to payment or other performance due or to become due to a debtor by any person with respect to a space asset;
   (b) 'guarantee contract' means a contract entered into by a person as a guarantor;
   (c) 'guarantor' means a person who, for the purpose of assuring performance of any obligations in favour of a creditor secured by a security agreement or under an agreement, gives or issues a suretyship or demand guarantee or standby letter of credit or other form of credit insurance;
   (d) 'insolvency-related event' means:
      (i) the commencement of the insolvency proceedings; or

(ii) the declared intention to suspend or actual suspension of payments by the debtor where the creditor's right to institute insolvency proceedings against the debtor or to exercise remedies under the Convention is prevented or suspended by law or State action;

(e) 'licence' means any permit, authorisation, concession or equivalent instrument that is granted or issued by, or pursuant to the authority of, a national or intergovernmental or other international body or authority, when acting in a regulatory capacity, to manufacture, launch, control, use or operate a space asset, or relating to the use of orbital positions or the transmission, emission or reception of electromagnetic signals to and from a space asset;

(f) 'obligor' means a person from whom payment or other performance of debtor's rights is due or to become due;

(g) 'primary insolvency jurisdiction' means the Contracting State in which the centre of the debtor's main interests is situated, which for this purpose shall be deemed to be the place of the debtor's statutory seat, or, if there is none, the place where the debtor is incorporated or formed, unless proved otherwise;

(h) 'rights assignment' means a contract by which the debtor confers on the creditor an interest (including an ownership interest) in or over the whole or part of existing or future debtor's rights to secure the performance of, or in reduction or discharge of, any existing or future obligation of the debtor to the creditor which under the agreement creating or providing for the international interest is secured by or associated with the space asset to which the agreement relates;

(i) 'rights reassignment' means:
   (i) a contract by which the creditor transfers to the assignee, or an assignee transfers to a subsequent assignee, the whole or part of its rights and interest under a rights assignment; or
   (ii) a transfer of debtor's rights under Article XII(4)(a) of this Protocol;

(j) 'space' means outer space, including the Moon and other celestial bodies; and

(k) 'space asset' means any man-made uniquely identifiable asset in space or designed to be launched into space, and comprising
   (i) a spacecraft, such as a satellite, space station, space module, space capsule, space vehicle or reusable launch vehicle, whether or not including a space asset falling within (ii) or (iii) below;
   (ii) a payload (whether telecommunications, navigation, observation, scientific or otherwise) in respect of which a separate registration may be effected in accordance with the regulations; or
   (iii) a part of a spacecraft or payload such as a transponder, in respect of which a separate registration may be effected in accordance with the regulations,

   together with all installed, incorporated or attached accessories, parts and equipment and all data, manuals and records relating thereto.

3. – For the purposes of the definition of 'internal transaction' in Article 1(n) of the Convention, a space asset, when not on Earth, is deemed located in the

Contracting State which registers the space asset, or on the registry of which the space asset is carried, as a space object under one of the following:

(a) the Treaty on Principles Governing the Activities of States in the Exploration and Use of Outer Space, Including the Moon and Other Celestial Bodies, signed at London, Moscow and Washington, D.C. on 27 January 1967;

(b) the Convention on Registration of Objects Launched into Outer Space, signed at New York on 14 January 1975; or

(c) United Nations General Assembly Resolution 1721 (XVI) B of 20 December 1961.

4. – In Article 43(1) of the Convention and Article XXII of this Protocol, references to a Contracting State on the territory of which an object or space asset is situated shall, as regards a space asset when not on Earth, be treated as references to any of the following:

(a) the Contracting State referred to in the preceding paragraph;

(b) a Contracting State which has issued a licence to operate the space asset; or

(c) a Contracting State on the territory of which a mission control centre for the space asset is located.

Article II – Application of the Convention as regards space assets, debtor's rights and aircraft objects

1. – The Convention shall apply in relation to space assets, rights assignments and rights reassignments as provided by the terms of this Protocol.
2. – The Convention and this Protocol shall be known as the Convention on International Interests in Mobile Equipment as applied to space assets.
3. – This Protocol does not apply to objects falling within the definition of 'aircraft objects' under the Protocol to the Convention on International Interests in Mobile Equipment on Matters specific to Aircraft Equipment except where such objects are primarily designed for use in space, in which case this Protocol applies even while such objects are not in space.
4. – This Protocol does not apply to an aircraft object merely because it is designed to be temporarily in space.

Article III – Preservation of rights and interests in a space asset

Ownership of or another right or interest in a space asset shall not be affected by:

(a) the docking of the space asset with another space asset in space;

(b) the installation of the space asset on or the removal of the space asset from another space asset; or

(c) the return of the space asset from space.

Article IV – Application of the Convention to sales; salvage

1. – Article XL of this Protocol and the following provisions of the Convention apply as if references to an agreement creating or providing for an international interest were references to a contract of sale and as if references to an international interest, a prospective international interest, the debtor and the creditor were references to a sale, a prospective sale, the seller and the buyer respectively:
   Articles 3 and 4;
   Article 16(1)(a);
   Article 19(4);
   Article 20(1) (as regards registration of a contract of sale or a prospective sale);
   Article 25(2) (as regards a prospective sale); and
   Article 30.

   In addition, the general provisions of Article 1, Article 5, Chapters IV to VII, Article 29 (other than Article 29(3) which is replaced by Article XXIII of this Protocol), Chapter X, Chapter XII (other than Article 43), Chapter XIII and Chapter XIV (other than Article 60) of the Convention shall apply to contracts of sale and prospective sales.
2. – The provisions of this Protocol applicable to rights assignments also apply to a transfer to the buyer of a space asset of rights to payment or other performance due or to become due to the seller by any person with respect to the space asset as if references to the debtor and the creditor were references to the seller and the buyer respectively.
3. – Nothing in the Convention or this Protocol affects any legal or contractual rights of an insurer to salvage recognised by the applicable law. 'Salvage' means a legal or contractual right or interest in, relating to or derived from a space asset that vests in the insurer upon the payment of a loss relating to the space asset.

Article V – Formalities, effects and registration of contracts of sale

1. – For the purposes of this Protocol, a contract of sale is one which:
   (a) is in writing;
   (b) relates to a space asset of which the seller has power to dispose; and
   (c) enables the space asset to be identified in conformity with this Protocol.
2. – A contract of sale transfers the interest of the seller in the space asset to the buyer according to its terms.
3. – Registration of a contract of sale remains effective indefinitely. Registration of a prospective sale remains effective unless discharged or until expiry of the period, if any, specified in the registration.

Article VI – Representative capacities

A person may, in relation to a space asset, enter into an agreement or a contract of sale, effect a registration as defined by Article 16(3) of the Convention and assert rights and interests under the Convention in an agency, trust or representative capacity.

Article VII – Identification of space assets

1. – For the purposes of Article 7(c) of the Convention and Articles V and IX of this Protocol, a description of a space asset is sufficient to identify the space asset if it contains:
   (a) a description of the space asset by item;
   (b) a description of the space asset by type;
   (c) a statement that the agreement covers all present and future space assets; or
   (d) a statement that the agreement covers all present and future space assets except for specified items or types.
2. – For the purposes of Article 7 of the Convention, an interest in a future space asset identified in accordance with the preceding paragraph shall be constituted as an international interest as soon as the chargor, conditional seller or lessor acquires the power to dispose of the space asset, without the need for any new act of transfer.

Article VIII – Choice of law

1. – This Article applies unless a Contracting State has made a declaration pursuant to Article XLI(2)(a) of this Protocol.
2. – The parties to an agreement, a contract of sale, a rights assignment or rights reassignment or a related guarantee contract or subordination agreement may agree on the law which is to govern their contractual rights and obligations, wholly or in part.
3. – Unless otherwise agreed, the reference in the preceding paragraph to the law chosen by the parties is to the domestic rules of law of the designated State or, where that State comprises several territorial units, to the domestic law of the designated territorial unit.

Article IX – Formal requirements for rights assignment

A transfer of debtor's rights is constituted as a rights assignment where it is in writing and enables:

(a) the debtor's rights the subject of the rights assignment to be identified;
(b) the space asset to which those rights relate to be identified; and

(c) in the case of a rights assignment by way of security, the obligations secured by the agreement to be determined, but without the need to state a sum or maximum sum secured.

Article X – Effects of rights assignment

1. – A rights assignment made in conformity with Article IX of this Protocol transfers to the creditor the debtor's rights the subject of the rights assignment to the extent permitted by the applicable law.
2. – Subject to paragraph 3, the applicable law shall determine the defences and rights of set-off available to the obligor against the creditor.
3. – The obligor may at any time by agreement in writing waive all or any of the defences and rights of set-off referred to in the preceding paragraph other than defences arising from fraudulent acts on the part of the creditor.

Article XI – Assignment of future rights

A provision in a rights assignment by which future debtor's rights are assigned operates to confer on the creditor an interest in the assigned rights when they come into existence, without the need for any new act of transfer.

Article XII – Recording of rights assignment or acquisition by subrogation as part of registration of international interest

1. – The holder of an international interest or prospective international interest in a space asset who has acquired an interest in or over debtor's rights under a rights assignment or by subrogation may, when registering the international interest or prospective international interest or subsequently by amendment to such registration, record the rights assignment or acquisition by subrogation as part of the registration. Such recording may identify the rights so assigned or acquired either specifically or by a statement that the debtor has assigned, or the holder of the international interest or prospective international interest has acquired, all or some of the debtor's rights, without further specification.
2. – Articles 18, 19, 20(1)–(4), 25(1), (2) and (4) and 30 of the Convention apply in relation to a recording made in accordance with the preceding paragraph as if:
   (a) references to an international interest were references to a rights assignment;
   (b) references to registration were references to the recording of the rights assignment; and
   (c) references to the debtor were references to the obligor.
3. – A search certificate issued under Article 22 of the Convention shall include the particulars recorded under paragraph 1.

4. – Where a rights assignment has been recorded as part of the registration of an international interest which is subsequently transferred in accordance with Articles 31 and 32 of the Convention, the transferee of the international interest acquires:
   (a) all the rights of the creditor under the rights assignment; and
   (b) the right to be shown in the record as assignee under the rights assignment.
5. – Discharge of the registration of an international interest also discharges any recording forming part of that registration under paragraph 1.

Article XIII – Priority of recorded rights assignment

1. – Subject to Article 29(6) of the Convention and paragraph 2 of the present Article, a recorded rights assignment has priority over any other transfer of debtor's rights (whether or not a rights assignment) except a rights assignment previously recorded.
2. – Where a rights assignment is recorded in the registration of a prospective international interest, it shall be treated as unrecorded unless and until the prospective international interest becomes an international interest, in which event the rights assignment has priority as from the time it was recorded provided that the registration was still current immediately before the international interest was constituted as provided by Article 7 of the Convention.

Article XIV – Obligor's duty to creditor

1. – To the extent that the debtor's rights have been assigned to the creditor under a rights assignment, the obligor is bound by the rights assignment, and has a duty to make payment or give other performance to the creditor, if and only if:
   (a) the obligor has been given notice of the rights assignment in writing by or with the authority of the debtor; and
   (b) the notice identifies the debtor's rights.
2. – For the purposes of the preceding paragraph, a notice given by the creditor after the debtor defaults in performance of any obligation secured by a rights assignment is deemed given with the authority of the debtor.
3. – Irrespective of any other ground on which payment or performance by the obligor discharges the obligor from liability, payment or performance shall be effective for this purpose if made in accordance with paragraph 1.
4. – Nothing in this Article shall affect the priority of competing rights assignments.

Article XV – Rights reassignment

1. – Articles IX to XIV of this Protocol apply to a rights reassignment by the creditor or a subsequent assignee. Where those Articles so apply, any references made to the creditor or holder are references to the assignee or subsequent assignee.
2. – A rights reassignment relating to an international interest in a space asset may be recorded only as part of the registration of the assignment of the international interest to the person to whom the rights reassignment was made.

Article XVI – Derogation

The parties may, by agreement in writing, exclude the application of Article XXI of this Protocol and, in their relations with each other, derogate from or vary the effect of any of the provisions of this Protocol except Article XVII(1) and (2).

Chapter II – Default remedies, priorities and assignments

Article XVII – Modification of default remedies provisions as regards space assets

1. – Article 8(3) of the Convention shall not apply to space assets. Any remedy given by the Convention in relation to a space asset shall be exercised in a commercially reasonable manner. A remedy shall be deemed to be exercised in a commercially reasonable manner where it is exercised in conformity with a provision of the agreement except where such a provision is manifestly unreasonable.
2. – A chargee giving fourteen or more calendar days' prior written notice of a proposed sale or lease to interested persons shall be deemed to satisfy the requirement of providing 'reasonable prior notice' specified in Article 8(4) of the Convention. The foregoing shall not prevent a chargee and a chargor or a guarantor from agreeing to a longer period of prior notice.
3. – Unless otherwise agreed, a creditor may not enforce an international interest in a space asset that is physically linked with another space asset so as to impair or interfere with the operation of the other space asset if an international interest or sale has been registered with respect to the other space asset prior to the registration of the international interest being enforced. For the purposes of this paragraph, a sale or an interest equivalent to an international interest made or arising before the effective date of the Convention, as defined in Article XL of this Protocol, which is registered within three years from that date is deemed to be an international interest or a sale registered at the time of the constitution of the international interest or the sale, as the case may be.

Article XVIII – Default remedies as regards rights assignments and rights reassignments

1. – In the event of default by the debtor under a rights assignment by way of security, Articles 8, 9 and 11 to 14 of the Convention apply in the relations between the debtor and the creditor (and in relation to debtor's rights apply in so far as those provisions are capable of application to intangible property) as if:
   (a) references to the secured obligations and to the security interest were references to the obligations secured by the rights assignment and to the security interest created by that assignment;
   (b) references to the object were references to the debtor's rights.
2. – In the event of default by the assignor under a rights reassignment by way of security, the preceding paragraph applies as if references to the assignment were references to the reassignment.

Article XIX – Placement of data and materials

Subject to Article XXVI of this Protocol, the parties to an agreement may specifically agree for the placement of command codes and related data and materials with another person in order to afford the creditor an opportunity to take possession of, establish control over or operate the space asset.

Article XX – Modification of provisions regarding relief pending final determination

1. – This Article applies only where a Contracting State has made a declaration to that effect under Article XLI(3) of this Protocol and to the extent stated in such declaration.
2. – For the purposes of Article 13(1) of the Convention, 'speedy' in the context of obtaining relief means within such number of calendar days from the date of filing of the application for relief as is specified in a declaration made by the Contracting State in which the application is made.
3. – Article 13(1) of the Convention applies with the following being added immediately after sub-paragraph (d):

   'and (e) if at any time the debtor and the creditor specifically agree, sale and application of proceeds therefrom',

   and Article 43(2) of the Convention applies with the substitution of 'Article 13' for the words 'Article 13(1)(d) or other interim relief by virtue of Article 13(4)'.

4. – Ownership or any other interest of the debtor passing on a sale under the preceding paragraph is free from any other interest over which the creditor's international interest has priority under the provisions of Article 29 of the Convention.

5. – The creditor and the debtor or any other interested person may agree in writing to exclude the application of Article 13(2) of the Convention.

Article XXI – Remedies on insolvency

1. – This Article applies only where a Contracting State that is the primary insolvency jurisdiction has made a declaration pursuant to Article XLI(4) of this Protocol.

Alternative A

2. – Upon the occurrence of an insolvency-related event, the insolvency administrator or the debtor, as applicable, shall, subject to paragraph 8 and to Article XXVI(2) of this Protocol, give possession of or control over the space asset to the creditor no later than the earlier of:
   (a) the end of the waiting period; and
   (b) the date on which the creditor would be entitled to possession of or control over the space asset if this Article did not apply.
3. – Upon the occurrence of an insolvency-related event, the insolvency administrator or the debtor, as applicable, shall, subject to paragraph 8 and to Article XXVI(2) of this Protocol, give possession of or control over the debtor's rights covered by a rights assignment to the creditor, no later than the earlier of:
   (a) the end of the waiting period; and
   (b) the date on which the creditor would be entitled to possession of or control over the debtor's rights covered by the rights assignment.
4. – For the purposes of this Article, the 'waiting period' shall be the period specified in a declaration of the Contracting State which is the primary insolvency jurisdiction.
5. – References in this Article to the 'insolvency administrator' shall be to that person in its official, not its personal, capacity.
6. – Unless and until the creditor is given possession of or control over the space asset under paragraph 2 or the debtor's rights under paragraph 3:
   (a) the insolvency administrator or the debtor, as applicable, shall preserve the space asset and maintain it and its value in accordance with the agreement; and
   (b) the creditor shall be entitled to apply for any other forms of interim relief available under the applicable law.
7. – Sub-paragraph (a) of the preceding paragraph shall not preclude the use of the space asset under arrangements designed to preserve the space asset and maintain it and its value.
8. – The insolvency administrator or the debtor, as applicable, may retain possession of and control over the space asset and the debtor's rights covered by a rights assignment where by the time specified in paragraph 2 or paragraph 3 it has cured all defaults other than a default constituted by the opening of insolvency proceedings and has agreed to perform all future obligations under the

agreement. A second waiting period shall not apply in respect of a default in the performance of such future obligations.

9. – No exercise of remedies permitted by the Convention or this Protocol may be prevented or delayed after the date specified in paragraph 2 or paragraph 3.
10. – No obligations of the debtor under the agreement may be modified without the consent of the creditor.
11. – Nothing in the preceding paragraph shall be construed to affect the authority, if any, of the insolvency administrator under the applicable law to terminate the agreement.
12. – No rights or interests, except for non-consensual rights or interests of a category covered by a declaration pursuant to Article 39(1) of the Convention, shall have priority in insolvency proceedings over registered interests. This provision shall not derogate from the provisions of Article XXVI(2) of this Protocol.
13. – The Convention as modified by Article XVII of this Protocol shall apply to the exercise of any remedies under this Article.

Alternative B

2. – Upon the occurrence of an insolvency-related event, the insolvency administrator or the debtor, as applicable, upon the request of the creditor, shall give notice to the creditor within the time specified in a declaration of a Contracting State pursuant to Article XLI(4) of this Protocol whether it will:
   (a) cure all defaults other than a default constituted by the opening of insolvency proceedings and agree to perform all future obligations, under the agreement and related transaction documents; or
   (b) give the creditor the opportunity to take possession of or control and operation over the space asset, in accordance with the applicable law.
3. – The applicable law referred to in sub-paragraph (b) of the preceding paragraph may permit the court to require the taking of any additional step or the provision of any additional guarantee.
4. – The creditor shall provide evidence of its claims and proof that its international interest has been registered.
5. – If the insolvency administrator or the debtor, as applicable, does not give notice in conformity with paragraph 2, or when it has declared that it will give the creditor the opportunity to take possession of or control and operation over the space asset but fails to do so, the court may permit the creditor to take possession of or control and operation over the space asset upon such terms as the court may order and may require the taking of any additional step or the provision of any additional guarantee.
6. – The space asset shall not be sold pending a decision by a court regarding the claim and the international interest.

Article XXII – Insolvency assistance

1. – This Article applies only where a Contracting State has made a declaration pursuant to Article XLI(2)(b) of this Protocol.
2. – The courts of a Contracting State: (i) in the territory of which the space asset is situated; (ii) from the territory of which the space asset may be controlled; (iii) in the territory of which the debtor is located; (iv) in the territory of which the space asset is registered; (v) which has issued a licence in respect of the space asset; or (vi) otherwise having a close connection with the space asset, shall, in accordance with the law of the Contracting State, co-operate to the maximum extent possible with foreign courts and foreign insolvency administrators in carrying out the provisions of Article XXI of this Protocol.

Article XXIII – Modification of priority provisions

1. – The buyer of a space asset under a registered sale acquires its interest in that asset free from an interest subsequently registered and from an unregistered interest, even if the buyer has actual knowledge of the unregistered interest.
2. – The buyer of a space asset under a registered sale acquires its interest in that asset subject to an interest previously registered.

Article XXIV – Modification of assignment provisions

Article 33(1) of the Convention applies with the following being added immediately after sub-paragraph (b):

> 'and (c) the debtor has consented in writing, whether or not the consent is given in advance of the assignment or identifies the assignee.'

Article XXV – Debtor provisions

1. – In the absence of a default within the meaning of Article 11 of the Convention, the debtor shall be entitled to the quiet possession and use of the space asset in accordance with the agreement as against:
   (a) its creditor and the holder of any interest from which the debtor takes free pursuant to Article 29(4)(b) of the Convention or, in the capacity of buyer, Article XXIII(1) of this Protocol, unless and to the extent that the debtor has otherwise agreed; and
   (b) the holder of any interest to which the debtor's right or interest is subject pursuant to Article 29(4)(a) of the Convention or, in the capacity of buyer, Article XXIII(2) of this Protocol, but only to the extent, if any, that such holder has agreed.

2. – Nothing in the Convention or this Protocol affects the liability of a creditor for any breach of the agreement under the applicable law in so far as that agreement relates to space assets.

Article XXVI – Preservation of powers of Contracting States

1. – This Protocol does not affect the exercise by a Contracting State of its authority to issue licences, approvals, permits or authorisations for the launch or operation of space assets or the provision of any service through the use or with the support of space assets.
2. – This Protocol further does not:
   (a) render transferable or assignable any licences, approvals, permits or authorisations which, in accordance with the laws and regulations of the granting Contracting State or the contractual or administrative provisions under which they are granted, may not be transferred or assigned;
   (b) limit the right of a Contracting State to authorise the use of orbital positions and frequencies in relation to space assets; or
   (c) affect the ability of a Contracting State in accordance with its laws and regulations to prohibit, restrict or attach conditions to the placement of command codes and related data and materials pursuant to Article XIX of this Protocol.
3. – Nothing in this Protocol shall be construed so as to require a Contracting State to recognise or enforce an international interest in a space asset when the recognition or enforcement of such interest would conflict with its laws or regulations concerning:
   (a) the export of controlled goods, technology, data and services; or
   (b) national security.

Article XXVII – Limitations on remedies in respect of public service

1. – Where the debtor or an entity controlled by the debtor and a public services provider enter into a contract that provides for the use of a space asset to provide services that are needed for the provision of a public service in a Contracting State, the parties and the Contracting State may agree that the public services provider or the Contracting State may register a public service notice.
2. – For the purposes of this Article:
   (a) 'public service notice' means a notice in the International Registry describing, in accordance with the regulations, the services which under the contract are intended to support the provision of a public service recognised as such under the laws of the relevant Contracting State at the time of registration; and
   (b) 'public services provider' means an entity of a Contracting State, another entity situated in that Contracting State and designated by the Contracting State as a provider of a public service or an entity recognised as a provider of a public service under the laws of a Contracting State.

3. – Subject to paragraph 9, a creditor holding an international interest in a space asset that is the subject of a public service notice may not, in the event of default, exercise any of the remedies provided in Chapter III of the Convention or Chapter II of this Protocol that would make the space asset unavailable for the provision of the relevant public service prior to the expiration of the period specified in a declaration by a Contracting State as provided by paragraph 4.
4. – A Contracting State shall at the time of ratification, acceptance, approval of, or accession to this Protocol specify by a declaration under Article XLI(1) a period for the purposes of the preceding paragraph not less than three months nor more than six months from the date of registration by the creditor of a notice in the International Registry that the creditor may exercise any such remedies if the debtor does not cure its default within that period.
5. – Paragraph 3 does not affect the ability of a creditor, if so authorised by the relevant authorities, temporarily to operate or ensure the continued operation of a space asset during the period referred to in that paragraph where the debtor is not able to do so.
6. – The creditor shall promptly notify the debtor and the public services provider of the date of registration of its notice under paragraph 3 and of the date of expiry of the period referred to therein.
7. – During the period referred to in paragraph 3:
   (a) the creditor, the debtor and the public services provider shall co-operate in good faith with a view to finding a commercially reasonable solution permitting the continuation of the public service;
   (b) the regulatory authority of a Contracting State that issued a licence required by the debtor to operate the space asset that is the subject of a public service notice shall, as appropriate, give the public services provider the opportunity to participate in any proceedings in which the debtor may participate in that Contracting State, with a view to the appointment of another operator under a new licence to be issued by that regulatory authority; and
   (c) the creditor is not precluded from initiating proceedings with a view to the replacement of the debtor by another person as operator of the space asset concerned in accordance with the rules of the licensing authorities.
8. – Notwithstanding paragraphs 3 and 7, the creditor is free to exercise any of the remedies provided in Chapter III of the Convention or Chapter II of this Protocol if, at any time during the period referred to in paragraph 3, the public services provider fails to perform its duties under the contract referred to in paragraph 1.
9. – Unless otherwise agreed, the limitation on the remedies of the creditor provided for in paragraph 3 shall not apply in respect of an international interest registered by a creditor prior to the registration of a public service notice pursuant to paragraph 1, where:
   (a) the international interest was created pursuant to an agreement made before the conclusion of the contract with the public services provider referred to in paragraph 1; and

(b) at the time the international interest was registered in the International Registry, the creditor had no knowledge that such a public services contract had been entered into.

10. – The preceding paragraph does not apply if such public service notice is registered no later than six months after the initial launch of the space asset.

Chapter III – Registry Provisions Relating to International Interests in Space Assets

Article XXVIII – The Supervisory Authority

1. – The Supervisory Authority shall be designated at, or pursuant to a resolution of, the diplomatic Conference for the adoption of the draft Protocol to the Convention on International Interests in Mobile Equipment on Matters specific to Space Assets, provided that such Supervisory Authority is able and willing to act in such capacity.
2. – The Supervisory Authority and its officers and employees shall enjoy such immunity from legal and administrative process as is provided under the rules applicable to them as an international entity or otherwise.
3. – The Supervisory Authority shall establish a commission of experts, from among persons nominated by the negotiating States and having the necessary qualifications and experience, and entrust it with the task of assisting the Supervisory Authority in the discharge of its functions.

Article XXIX – First regulations

The first regulations shall be made by the Supervisory Authority so as to take effect on the entry into force of this Protocol.

Article XXX – Identification of space assets for registration purposes

A description of a space asset in accordance with the criteria for identification provided by the regulations is necessary and sufficient to identify the space asset for the purposes of registration in the International Registry.

Article XXXI – Designated entry points

A Contracting State may at any time designate an entity or entities in its territory as the entry point or entry points through which there shall or may be transmitted to the International Registry information required for registration other than registration of a notice of a national interest or a right or interest under Article 40 of the Convention in either case arising under the laws of another State.

Article XXXII – Additional modifications to Registry provisions

1. – Article 16 of the Convention applies with the following being added immediately after paragraph 1:

   '1 bis The International Registry shall also provide for:
   (a) the recording of rights assignments and rights reassignments;
   (b) the recording of acquisitions of debtor's rights by subrogation;
   (c) the registration of public service notices under Article XXVII(1) of the Protocol to the Convention on International Interests in Mobile Equipment on Matters specific to Space Assets; and
   (d) the registration of creditors' notices under Article XXVII(4) of the Protocol to the Convention on International Interests in Mobile Equipment on Matters specific to Space Assets.'

2. – For the purposes of Article 19(6) of the Convention, the search criteria for space assets shall be the criteria specified in Article XXX of this Protocol.
3. – For the purposes of Article 25(2) of the Convention, and in the circumstances there described, the holder of a registered prospective international interest or a registered prospective assignment of an international interest or the person in whose favour a prospective sale has been registered shall take such steps as are within its power to procure the discharge of the registration no later than ten calendar days after the receipt of the demand described in such paragraph.
4. – The fees referred to in Article 17(2)(h) of the Convention shall be determined so as to recover the reasonable costs of establishing, operating and regulating the International Registry and the reasonable costs of the Supervisory Authority associated with the performance of the functions, exercise of the powers and discharge of the duties contemplated by Article 17(2) of the Convention.
5. – The centralised functions of the International Registry shall be operated and administered by the Registrar on a twenty-four hour basis.
6. – The insurance or financial guarantee referred to in Article 28(4) of the Convention shall cover the liability of the Registrar under the Convention to the extent provided by the regulations.
7. – Nothing in the Convention shall preclude the Registrar from procuring insurance or a financial guarantee covering events for which the Registrar is not liable under Article 28 of the Convention.

Chapter IV – Jurisdiction

Article XXXIII – Waiver of sovereign immunity

1. – Subject to paragraph 2, a waiver of sovereign immunity from jurisdiction of the courts specified in Article 42 or Article 43 of the Convention or relating to enforcement of rights and interests relating to a space asset under the Convention shall be binding and, if the other conditions to such jurisdiction or enforcement have been satisfied, shall be effective to confer jurisdiction and permit enforcement, as the case may be.
2. – A waiver under the preceding paragraph must be in writing and contain a description of the space asset in accordance with Article VII of this Protocol.

Chapter V – Relationship with Other Conventions

Article XXXIV – Relationship with the UNIDROIT Convention on International Financial Leasing

The Convention as applied to space assets shall supersede the UNIDROIT Convention on International Financial Leasing in respect of the subject matter of this Protocol, as between States Parties to both Conventions.

Article XXXV – Relationship with the United Nations outer space treaties and instruments of the International Telecommunication Union

The Convention as applied to space assets shall not affect State Party rights and obligations under the existing United Nations outer space treaties or instruments of the International Telecommunication Union.

Chapter VI – Final Provisions

Article XXXVI – Signature, ratification, acceptance, approval or accession

1. – This Protocol shall be open for signature in Berlin on 9 March 2012 by States participating in the diplomatic Conference for the adoption of the draft Protocol to the Convention on International Interests in Mobile Equipment on Matters specific to Space Assets held in Berlin from 27 February to 9 March 2012. After 9 March 2012 this Protocol shall be open to all States for signature at Rome until it enters into force in accordance with Article XXXVIII.
2. – This Protocol shall be subject to ratification, acceptance or approval by States which have signed it.
3. – Any State which does not sign this Protocol may accede to it at any time.
4. – Ratification, acceptance, approval or accession is effected by the deposit of a formal instrument to that effect with the Depositary.
5. – A State may not become a Party to this Protocol unless it is or becomes also a Party to the Convention.

Article XXXVII – Regional Economic Integration Organisations

1. – A Regional Economic Integration Organisation which is constituted by sovereign States and has competence over certain matters governed by this Protocol may similarly sign, accept, approve or accede to this Protocol. The Regional Economic Integration Organisation shall in that case have the rights and obligations of a Contracting State, to the extent that that Organisation has competence over matters governed by this Protocol. Where the number of Contracting States is relevant in this Protocol, the Regional Economic Integration Organisation shall not count as a Contracting State in addition to its Member States which are Contracting States.
2. – The Regional Economic Integration Organisation shall, at the time of signature, acceptance, approval or accession, make a declaration to the Depositary specifying the matters governed by this Protocol in respect of which competence has been transferred to that Organisation by its Member States. The Regional Economic Integration Organisation shall promptly notify the Depositary in writing of any changes to the distribution of competence, including new transfers of competence, specified in the declaration under this paragraph.
3. – Any reference to a 'Contracting State', 'Contracting States', 'State Party' or 'States Parties' in this Protocol applies equally to a Regional Economic Integration Organisation where the context so requires.

Article XXXVIII – Entry into force

1. – This Protocol enters into force between the States which have deposited instruments referred to in sub-paragraph (a) on the later of:
   (a) the first day of the month following the expiration of three months after the date of the deposit of the tenth instrument of ratification, acceptance, approval or accession; and
   (b) the date of the deposit by the Supervisory Authority with the Depositary of a certificate confirming that the International Registry is fully operational.
2. – For other States this Protocol enters into force on the first day of the month following the later of:
   (a) the expiration of three months after the date of the deposit of their instrument of ratification, acceptance, approval or accession; and
   (b) the date referred to in sub-paragraph (b) of the preceding paragraph.

Article XXXIX – Territorial units

1. – If a Contracting State has two or more territorial units in which different systems of law are applicable in relation to the matters dealt with in this Protocol, it may, at the time of signature, ratification, acceptance, approval or accession, make an initial declaration that this Protocol is to extend to all its territorial

units or only to one or more of them and may modify its declaration by submitting another declaration at any time.

2. – Any such declaration shall state expressly the territorial units to which this Protocol applies.
3. – If a Contracting State has not made any declaration under paragraph 1, this Protocol shall apply to all territorial units of that State.
4. – Where a Contracting State extends this Protocol to one or more of its territorial units, declarations permitted under this Protocol may be made in respect of each such territorial unit, and the declarations made in respect of one territorial unit may be different from those made in respect of another territorial unit.
5. – In relation to a Contracting State with two or more territorial units in which different systems of law are applicable in relation to the matters dealt with in this Protocol, any reference to the law in force in a Contracting State or to the law of a Contracting State shall be construed as referring to the law in force in the relevant territorial unit.
6. – If a Contracting State has a federal system where the federal legislative power has competence over matters governed by this Protocol, that Contracting State shall have the same rights and obligations over those matters as those Contracting States which do not have a federal system.

Article XL – Transitional provisions

1. – Article 60 of the Convention shall not apply in relation to space assets.
2. – Subject to the second sentence of Article XVII(3) of this Protocol, the Convention does not apply to a right or interest of any kind in or over a space asset created or arising before the effective date of the Convention, which retains the priority it enjoyed under the applicable law before the effective date of the Convention.
3. – For the purposes of this Protocol:
   (a) 'effective date of the Convention' means in relation to a debtor the time when the Convention enters into force or the time when the State in which the debtor is situated at the time the right or interest is created or arises becomes a Contracting State, whichever is the later; and
   (b) the debtor is situated in a State where it has its centre of administration or, if it has no centre of administration, its place of business or, if it has more than one place of business, its principal place of business or, if it has no place of business, its habitual residence.

Article XLI – Declarations relating to certain provisions

1. – A Contracting State shall, at the time of ratification, acceptance, approval of, or accession to this Protocol, make a declaration pursuant to Article XXVII(4) of this Protocol.

2. – A Contracting State may, at the time of ratification, acceptance, approval of, or accession to this Protocol, declare:
   (a) that it will not apply Article VIII;
   (b) that it will apply Article XXII.
3. – A Contracting State may, at the time of ratification, acceptance, approval of, or accession to this Protocol, declare that it will apply Article XX wholly or in part. If it so declares with respect to Article XX(2), it shall specify the time-period required thereby.
4. – A Contracting State may, at the time of ratification, acceptance, approval of, or accession to this Protocol, declare that it will apply the entirety of Alternative A, or the entirety of Alternative B of Article XXI and, if so, shall specify the types of insolvency proceeding, if any, to which it will apply Alternative A and the types of insolvency proceeding, if any, to which it will apply Alternative B. A Contracting State making a declaration pursuant to this paragraph shall specify the time-period required by Article XXI.
5. – The courts of Contracting States shall apply Article XXI in conformity with the declaration made by the Contracting State that is the primary insolvency jurisdiction.

Article XLII – Declarations under the Convention

Declarations made under the Convention, including those made under Articles 39, 40, 53, 54, 55, 57 and 58 of the Convention, shall be deemed to have also been made under this Protocol unless stated otherwise.

Article XLIII – Reservations and declarations

1. – No reservations may be made to this Protocol but declarations authorised by Articles XXXIX, XLI, XLII and XLIV may be made in accordance with these provisions.
2. – Any declaration, subsequent declaration or any withdrawal of a declaration made under this Protocol shall be notified in writing to the Depositary.

Article XLIV – Subsequent declarations

1. – A State Party may make a subsequent declaration at any time after the date on which this Protocol has entered into force for it, by notifying the Depositary to that effect.
2. – Any such subsequent declaration shall take effect on the first day of the month following the expiration of six months after the date of receipt of the notification by the Depositary. Where a longer period for that declaration to take effect is specified in the notification, it shall take effect upon the expiration of such longer period after receipt of the notification by the Depositary.

3. – Notwithstanding the previous paragraphs, this Protocol shall continue to apply, as if no such subsequent declaration had been made, in respect of all rights and interests arising prior to the effective date of any such subsequent declaration.

Article XLV – Withdrawal of declarations

1. – Any State Party having made a declaration under this Protocol may withdraw it at any time by notifying the Depositary. Such withdrawal is to take effect on the first day of the month following the expiration of six months after the date of receipt of the notification by the Depositary.
2. – Notwithstanding the previous paragraph, this Protocol shall continue to apply, as if no such withdrawal of declaration had been made, in respect of all rights and interests arising prior to the effective date of any such withdrawal of declaration.

Article XLVI – Denunciations

1. – Any State Party may denounce this Protocol by notification in writing to the Depositary.
2. – Any such denunciation shall take effect on the first day of the month following the expiration of twelve months after the date of receipt of the notification by the Depositary.
3. – Notwithstanding the previous paragraphs, this Protocol shall continue to apply, as if no such denunciation had been made, in respect of all rights and interests arising prior to the effective date of any such denunciation.

Article XLVII – Review Conferences, amendments and related matters

1. – The Depositary, in consultation with the Supervisory Authority, shall prepare reports yearly, or at such other time as the circumstances may require, for the States Parties as to the manner in which the international regimen established in the Convention as amended by this Protocol has operated in practice. In preparing such reports, the Depositary shall take into account the reports of the Supervisory Authority concerning the functioning of the international registration system.
2. – At the request of not less than twenty-five per cent of the States Parties, Review Conferences of the States Parties shall be convened from time to time by the Depositary, in consultation with the Supervisory Authority, to consider:
   (a) the practical operation of the Convention as amended by this Protocol and its effectiveness in facilitating the asset-based financing and leasing of the assets covered by its terms;
   (b) the judicial interpretation given to, and the application made of the terms of this Protocol and the regulations;

(c) the functioning of the international registration system, the performance of the Registrar and its oversight by the Supervisory Authority, taking into account the reports of the Supervisory Authority; and
(d) whether any modifications to this Protocol or the arrangements relating to the International Registry are desirable.

3. – Any amendment to this Protocol shall be approved by at least a two-thirds majority of States Parties participating in the Conference referred to in the preceding paragraph and shall then enter into force in respect of States Parties which have ratified, accepted or approved such amendment when it has been ratified, accepted or approved by ten States Parties in accordance with the provisions of Article XXXVIII relating to its entry into force.

Article XLVIII – Depositary and its functions

1. – Instruments of ratification, acceptance, approval or accession shall be deposited with the International Institute for the Unification of Private Law (UNIDROIT), which is hereby designated the Depositary.
2. – The Depositary shall:
(a) inform all Contracting States of:
  (i) each new signature or deposit of an instrument of ratification, acceptance, approval or accession, together with the date thereof;
  (ii) the date of entry into force of this Protocol;
  (iii) each declaration made in accordance with this Protocol, together with the date thereof;
  (iv) the withdrawal or amendment of any declaration, together with the date thereof; and
  (v) the notification of any denunciation of this Protocol together with the date thereof and the date on which it takes effect;
(b) transmit certified true copies of this Protocol to all Contracting States;
(c) provide the Supervisory Authority and the Registrar with a copy of each instrument of ratification, acceptance, approval or accession, together with the date of deposit thereof, of each declaration or withdrawal or amendment of a declaration and of each notification of denunciation, together with the date of notification thereof, so that the information contained therein is easily and fully available; and
(d) perform such other functions customary for depositaries.

IN WITNESS WHEREOF the undersigned Plenipotentiaries, having been duly authorised, have signed this Protocol.
DONE at Berlin, this ninth day of March, two thousand and twelve, in a single original in the English and French languages, both texts being equally authentic, such authenticity to take effect upon verification by the Secretariat of the Conference under the authority of the President of the Conference within ninety days hereof as to the consistency of the texts with one another.

Chapter 5. The Protocol to the Convention on International Interests in Mobile Equipment on Matters Specific to Mining, Agricultural and Construction Equipment

PROTOCOL TO THE CONVENTION ON INTERNATIONAL INTERESTS IN MOBILE EQUIPMENT ON MATTERS SPECIFIC TO MINING, AGRICULTURAL AND CONSTRUCTION EQUIPMENT

THE STATES PARTIES TO THIS PROTOCOL,
CONSIDERING the significant benefits of the Convention on International Interests in Mobile Equipment (hereinafter referred to as the "Convention"), as facilitating the financing and leasing of uniquely identifiable high-value mobile equipment,
RECOGNISING the important role that mining, agricultural and construction equipment play in the global economy,
AWARE of the benefits of extending the Convention to mining, agricultural and construction equipment,
MINDFUL of the need to adapt the Convention to the particular requirements of the mining, agricultural and construction sectors and of their finance,
NOTING that the World Customs Organization's Harmonized System governed by the International Convention on the Harmonized Commodity Description and Coding System allows the determination of the categories of mining, agricultural and construction equipment to which the extension of the Convention is warranted,
HAVE AGREED upon the following provisions relating to mining, agricultural and construction equipment:

CHAPTER I – SPHERE OF APPLICATION AND GENERAL PROVISIONS

Article I – Defined terms

1. In this Protocol, except where the context otherwise requires, terms used in it have the meanings set out in the Convention.
2. In this Protocol the following terms are employed with the meanings set out below:
   (a) "agricultural equipment" means an object that falls under a Harmonized System code listed in Annex 2 to the Protocol, including all installed, incorporated or attached accessories, components and parts which do not fall within a separate Harmonized System code listed in that Annex, and all data, manuals and records relating thereto;
   (b) "construction equipment" means an object that falls under a Harmonized System code listed in Annex 3 to the Protocol, including all installed, incorporated or attached accessories, components and parts which do not fall within a separate Harmonized System code listed in that Annex, and all data, manuals and records relating thereto;
   (c) "Contracting State proposal" means a proposal for modification of the Annexes made by at least two Contracting States;

(d) "dealer" means a person (including a manufacturer) that sells or leases equipment in the ordinary course of its business;
(e) "Depositary proposal" means a notification from the Depositary pursuant to Article XXXV(2) relating to the Harmonized System codes in the Annexes affected by a Harmonized System revision and containing a proposal of adjustments to those codes in the Annexes;
(f) "equipment" means mining equipment, agricultural equipment or construction equipment;
(g) "guarantee contract" means a contract entered into by a person as guarantor;
(h) "guarantor" means a person, who, for the purpose of assuring performance of any obligations in favour of a creditor secured by a security agreement or under an agreement, gives or issues a suretyship or demand guarantee or a standby letter of credit or any other form of credit insurance;
(i) "Harmonized System" means the Harmonized Commodity Description and Coding System governed by the International Convention on the Harmonized Commodity Description and Coding System, as amended by the Protocol of Amendment of 24 June 1986;
(j) "Harmonized System revision" means a revision of the Harmonized System codes as accepted by the World Customs Organization (established as the Customs Co-operation Council) according to its procedures;
(k) "immovable-associated equipment" means equipment that is so associated with immovable property that an interest in the immovable property extends to the equipment under the law of the State in which the immovable property is situated;
(l) "implementation period" means:
   (i) for the purposes of Article XXXV, the initial period commencing on the date the Depositary sends a notification to Contracting States under Article XXXV(6) and ending on the date on which adjustments would enter into force as specified in that paragraph; and
   (ii) for the purposes of Article XXXVI, the initial period commencing on the date the Depositary sends a notification to Contracting States under Article XXXVI(8) and ending on the date on which modifications would enter into force as specified in that paragraph.
(m) "insolvency-related event" means:
   (i) the commencement of the insolvency proceedings; or
   (ii) the declared intention to suspend or actual suspension of payments by the debtor where the creditor's right to institute insolvency proceedings against the debtor or to exercise remedies under the Convention is prevented or suspended by law or State action;
(n) "inventory" means equipment held by a dealer for sale or lease in the ordinary course of its business;
(o) "mining equipment" means an object that falls under a Harmonized System code listed in Annex 1 to the Protocol, including all installed, incorporated or attached accessories, components and parts which do not fall

within a separate Harmonized System code listed in that Annex, and all data, manuals and records relating thereto;

(p) "new Contracting State" means a State that becomes a Contracting State after the date the Depositary sends to Contracting States a Depositary proposal or a notification of a Contracting State proposal, as applicable; and

(q) "primary insolvency jurisdiction" means the Contracting State in which the centre of the debtor's main interests is situated, which for this purpose shall be deemed to be the place of the debtor's statutory seat or, if there is none, the place where the debtor is incorporated or formed, unless proved otherwise.

Article II – Application of the Convention as regards equipment

1. The Convention shall apply in relation to mining equipment, agricultural equipment and construction equipment as provided by the terms of this Protocol and Annexes 1, 2 and 3 irrespective of any intended or actual use of the equipment.
2. A Contracting State may, at the time of ratification, acceptance, approval of, or accession to this Protocol, declare that it will limit the application of this Protocol to the entirety of the equipment comprised in one or two of the Annexes.
3. This Protocol does not apply to objects falling within the definition of "aircraft objects" under the Protocol to the Convention on International Interests in Mobile Equipment on Matters Specific to Aircraft Equipment, "railway rolling stock" under the Luxembourg Protocol to the Convention on International Interests in Mobile Equipment on Matters Specific to Railway Rolling Stock or "space assets" under the Protocol to the Convention on International Interests in Mobile Equipment on Matters Specific to Space Assets.
4. The Convention and this Protocol shall be known as the Convention on International Interests in Mobile Equipment as applied to mining equipment, agricultural equipment and construction equipment.

Article III – Derogation

The parties may, by agreement in writing, exclude the application of Article X and, in their relations with each other, derogate from or vary the effect of any of the provisions of this Protocol except Article VIII (2) – (4).

Article IV – Representative capacities

A person may, in relation to equipment, enter into an agreement, effect a registration as defined by Article 16(3) of the Convention and assert rights and interests under the Convention in an agency, trust or representative capacity.

Article V – Identification of equipment

1. For the purposes of Article 7(c) of the Convention and Article XXI, a description of equipment is sufficient to identify the equipment if it contains:
   (a) a description of the equipment by item;
   (b) a description of the equipment by type;
   (c) a statement that the agreement covers all present and future equipment; or
   (d) a statement that the agreement covers all present and future equipment except for specified items or types.
2. For the purposes of Article 7 of the Convention, an interest in future equipment identified in accordance with the preceding paragraph shall be constituted as an international interest as soon as the chargor, conditional seller or lessor acquires the power to dispose of the equipment, without the need for any new act of transfer.

Article VI – Choice of law

1. This Article applies only where a Contracting State has made a declaration pursuant to Article XXVIII(1).
2. The parties to an agreement or a related guarantee contract or subordination agreement may agree on the law which is to govern their contractual rights and obligations, wholly or in part.
3. Unless otherwise agreed, the reference in the preceding paragraph to the law chosen by the parties is to the domestic rules of law of the designated State or, where that State comprises several territorial units, to the domestic law of the designated territorial unit.

Article VII – Association with immovable property

1. Where immovable-associated equipment is situated in a non-Contracting State, this Protocol does not affect the application of any law of that State that determines whether an international interest in the immovable-associated equipment cannot be created, has ceased to exist, is subordinated to any other rights or interests in the immovable-associated equipment, or is otherwise affected by the association of the equipment with immovable property.
2. A Contracting State shall, at the time of ratification, acceptance, approval of, or accession to this Protocol, declare that the entirety of Alternative A, B, or C of this Article will apply in relation to an international interest in immovable-associated equipment which is situated in the Contracting State.

Alternative A

3. If immovable-associated equipment is severable from the immovable property, its association with the immovable property does not affect the application of this Protocol, including the creation, existence, priority or enforcement of any international interest in that equipment. This Protocol does not apply to immovable-associated equipment that is not severable from the immovable property.
4. Immovable-associated equipment is severable from the immovable property only if its estimated value after physical disconnection of the equipment from the immovable property would be greater than the estimated cost of the disconnection and of any restoration of the immovable property.
5. If immovable-associated equipment is severable from the immovable property at the time it becomes immovable-associated equipment or the time an international interest in the equipment is created, whichever is the later, there is a rebuttable presumption that it continues to be severable from that immovable property.

Alternative B

3. This Protocol does not affect the application of any law of the State where immovable property is situated that determines whether an international interest in immovable-associated equipment cannot be created, has ceased to exist, is subordinated to any other rights or interests in the immovable-associated equipment, or is otherwise affected by the association of the equipment with immovable property if the equipment has lost its individual legal identity in accordance with the law of that State.
4. Where equipment subject to a registered international interest is immovable-associated equipment and has not lost its individual legal identity in accordance with the law of the State where the immovable property is situated, an interest in the immovable property that extends to that equipment has priority over the registered international interest in the equipment only if the following conditions are fulfilled:
   (a) the interest in the immovable property has been registered in accordance with the requirements of domestic law prior to the time of registration of the international interest in the equipment under this Protocol and registration of the interest in the immovable property continues to be effective; and
   (b) the equipment became associated with the immovable property prior to the time of registration of the international interest in the equipment under this Protocol.

Alternative C

3. This Protocol does not affect the application of any law of the State where immovable property is situated that determines whether an international interest in immovable-associated equipment cannot be created, has ceased to exist, is subordinated to any other rights or interests in the immovable-associated equipment, or is otherwise affected by the association of the equipment with immovable property.

CHAPTER II – DEFAULT REMEDIES AND PRIORITIES

Article VIII – Modification of default remedies provisions

1. In addition to the remedies specified in Chapter III of the Convention, the creditor may, to the extent that the debtor has at any time so agreed and in the circumstances specified in that Chapter, procure the export and physical transfer of equipment from the territory in which it is situated.
2. The creditor shall not exercise the remedies specified in the preceding paragraph without the prior consent in writing of the holder of any registered interest ranking in priority to that of the creditor.
3. Article 8(3) of the Convention shall not apply to equipment. Any remedy given by the Convention in relation to equipment shall be exercised in a commercially reasonable manner. A remedy shall be deemed to be exercised in a commercially reasonable manner where it is exercised in conformity with a provision of the agreement except where such a provision is manifestly unreasonable.
4. A chargee giving fourteen or more calendar days' prior written notice of a proposed sale or lease to interested persons as provided by Article 8(4) of the Convention shall be deemed to satisfy the requirement of giving the "reasonable prior notice" specified therein. The foregoing shall not prevent a chargee and a chargor or a guarantor from agreeing to a longer period of prior notice.
5. Subject to any applicable safety laws and regulations, a Contracting State shall ensure that the relevant administrative authorities expeditiously co-operate with and assist the creditor to the extent necessary for the exercise of the remedies specified in paragraph 1.
6. A Contracting State may, at the time of ratification, acceptance, approval of, or accession to this Protocol, declare that it will not apply the preceding paragraph.
7. A chargee proposing to procure the export of equipment under paragraph 1 otherwise than pursuant to a court order shall give reasonable prior notice in writing of the proposed export to:
   (a) interested persons specified in Article 1(m)(i) and (ii) of the Convention; and

(b) interested persons specified in Article 1(m)(iii) of the Convention who have given notice of their rights to the chargee within a reasonable time prior to the export.

Article IX – Modification of provisions regarding relief pending final determination

1. This Article applies only in a Contracting State which has made a declaration pursuant to Article XXVIII(2) and to the extent stated in such declaration.
2. For the purposes of Article 13(1) of the Convention, "speedy" in the context of obtaining relief means within such number of calendar days from the date of filing of the application for relief as is specified in a declaration made by the Contracting State in which the application is made.
3. Article 13(1) of the Convention applies with the following being added immediately after sub-paragraph (d):

"(e) if at any time the debtor and the creditor specifically agree, sale of the object and application of proceeds therefrom",

and Article 43(2) applies with the insertion after the words "Article 13(1)(d)" of the words "and (e)".

4. Ownership or any other interest of the debtor passing on a sale under the preceding paragraph is free from any other interest over which the creditor's international interest has priority under the provisions of Article 29 of the Convention.
5. The creditor and the debtor or any other interested person may agree in writing to exclude the application of Article 13(2) of the Convention.
6. With regard to the remedies in Article VIII(1):
   (a) they shall be made available by the administrative authorities in a Contracting State no later than seven calendar days after the creditor notifies such authorities that the relief specified in Article 13 of the Convention is granted or, in the case of relief granted by a foreign court, recognised by a court of that Contracting State, and that the creditor is entitled to procure those remedies in accordance with the Convention; and
   (b) the applicable authorities shall expeditiously co-operate with and assist the creditor in the exercise of such remedies in conformity with the applicable safety laws and regulations.
7. Paragraphs 2 and 6 shall not affect any applicable safety laws and regulations.

Article X – Remedies on Insolvency

1. This Article applies only where a Contracting State that is the primary insolvency jurisdiction has made a declaration pursuant to Article XXVIII(3).

2. References in this Article to the "insolvency administrator" shall be to that person in its official, not in its personal, capacity.
3. Upon the occurrence of an insolvency-related event, the insolvency administrator or the debtor, as applicable, shall, subject to paragraph 7, give possession of the equipment to the creditor not later than the earlier of:
   (a) the end of the waiting period; and
   (b) the date on which the creditor would be entitled to possession of the equipment if this Article did not apply.
4. For the purpose of this Article, the "waiting period" shall be the period specified in a declaration of the Contracting State which is the primary insolvency jurisdiction.
5. Unless and until the creditor is given the opportunity to take possession under paragraph 3:
   (a) the insolvency administrator or the debtor, as applicable, shall preserve the equipment and maintain it and its value in accordance with the agreement; and
   (b) the creditor shall be entitled to apply for any other forms of interim relief available under the applicable law.
6. Sub-paragraph (a) of the preceding paragraph shall not preclude the use of the equipment under arrangements designed to preserve the equipment and maintain it and its value.
7. The insolvency administrator or the debtor, as applicable, may retain possession of the equipment where, by the time specified in paragraph 3, it has cured all defaults other than a default constituted by the opening of insolvency proceedings and has agreed to perform all future obligations under the agreement and related transaction documents. A second waiting period shall not apply in respect of a default in the performance of such future obligations.
8. With regard to the remedies in Article VIII(1):
   (a) they shall be made available by the administrative authorities in a Contracting State no later than seven calendar days after the date on which the creditor notifies such authorities that it is entitled to procure those remedies in accordance with the Convention; and
   (b) the applicable authorities shall expeditiously co-operate with and assist the creditor in the exercise of such remedies in conformity with the applicable safety laws and regulations.
9. No exercise of remedies permitted by the Convention or this Protocol may be prevented or delayed after the date specified in paragraph 3.
10. No obligations of the debtor under the agreement may be modified without the consent of the creditor.
11. Nothing in the preceding paragraph shall be construed to affect the authority, if any, of the insolvency administrator under the applicable law to terminate the agreement.
12. No rights or interests, except for non-consensual rights or interests of a category covered by a declaration pursuant to Article 39(1) of the Convention, shall have priority in insolvency proceedings over registered interests.
13. The Convention as modified by Article VIII shall apply to the exercise of any remedies under this Article.

Article XI – Insolvency assistance

1. This Article applies only in a Contracting State which has made a declaration pursuant to Article XXVIII(1).
2. The courts of a Contracting State in which equipment is situated shall, in accordance with the law of that State, co-operate to the maximum extent possible with foreign courts and foreign insolvency administrators in carrying out the provisions of Article X.

Article XII – Provisions relating to inventory

1. This Article applies only where a Contracting State has made a declaration pursuant to Article XXVIII(4).
2. An interest in inventory created or provided for by an agreement under which the dealer is the debtor is not an international interest if the dealer is situated in the Contracting State referred to in the preceding paragraph at the time the interest is created or arises.
3. Article 29(3)(b) and 29(4)(b) of the Convention do not apply to a buyer, conditional buyer or lessee of inventory from a dealer if the dealer is situated in the Contracting State referred to in paragraph 1 at the time that a buyer, conditional buyer or lessee acquires its interest in or rights over the inventory.
4. For the purposes of this Article a dealer is situated in a State where it has its place of business or, if it has more than one place of business in different States, its principal place of business.

Article XIII – Debtor provisions

1. In the absence of a default within the meaning of Article 11 of the Convention, the debtor shall be entitled to the quiet possession and use of the equipment in accordance with the agreement as against:
   (a) its creditor and the holder of any interest from which the debtor takes free pursuant to Article 29(4)(b) of the Convention unless and to the extent that the debtor has otherwise agreed; and
   (b) the holder of any interest to which the debtor's right or interest is subject pursuant to Article 29(4)(a) of the Convention, but only to the extent, if any, that such holder has agreed.
2. Nothing in the Convention or this Protocol affects the liability of a creditor for any breach of the agreement under the applicable law in so far as that agreement relates to equipment.

CHAPTER III – REGISTRY PROVISIONS RELATING TO INTERNATIONAL INTERESTS IN EQUIPMENT

Article XIV – The Supervisory Authority and the Registrar

1. The Supervisory Authority shall be the international entity designated pursuant to a resolution of the Diplomatic Conference for the adoption of this Protocol provided that such Supervisory Authority is able and willing to act in such capacity.
2. Where the international entity referred to in the preceding paragraph is not able and willing to act as Supervisory Authority, a Conference of Signatory and Contracting States shall be convened to designate another Supervisory Authority.
3. The Supervisory Authority and its officers and employees shall enjoy such immunity from legal and administrative process as is provided under the rules applicable to them as an international entity or otherwise.
4. The Supervisory Authority shall establish a commission of experts from among persons nominated by Signatory and Contracting States having the necessary qualifications and experience, and entrust it with the task of assisting the Supervisory Authority in the discharge of its functions.
5. The first Registrar of the International Registry shall be appointed for a period of five years from the date of entry into force of this Protocol. Thereafter, the Registrar shall be appointed or reappointed at regular five-yearly intervals by the Supervisory Authority.

Article XV – First regulations

The first regulations shall be made by the Supervisory Authority so as to take effect on the entry into force of this Protocol.

Article XVI – Designated entry points

1. A Contracting State may at any time designate an entity or entities as the entry point or entry points through which there shall or may be transmitted to the International Registry information required for registration other than registration of a notice of a national interest or of a right or interest under Article 40 of the Convention in either case arising under laws of another State. The various entry points shall be operated at least during working hours in their respective territories.
2. A designation made under the preceding paragraph may permit, but not compel, use of a designated entry point or entry points for information required for registrations in respect of notices of sale.
3. A registration shall not be invalid by reason of being made otherwise than in conformity with any requirement imposed by a Contracting State under paragraph 1.

Article XVII – Identification of equipment for registration purposes

A description of equipment that contains its manufacturer's serial number and such additional information as required to ensure uniqueness is necessary and sufficient to identify the object for the purposes of Article 18(1)(a) of the Convention. The Regulations shall specify the format of the manufacturer's serial number and provide what additional information is required to ensure uniqueness.

Article XVIII – Additional modifications of Registry provisions

1. For the purposes of Article 19(6) of the Convention, the search criterion for equipment shall be its manufacturer's serial number.
2. The fees referred to in Article 17(2)(h) of the Convention shall be determined so as to recover:
   (a) the reasonable costs of establishing, operating and regulating the International Registry, and the reasonable costs of the Supervisory Authority associated with the performance of the functions, exercise of the powers and discharge of the duties contemplated by Article 17(2) of the Convention; and
   (b) the reasonable costs of the Depositary associated with the performance of the functions, exercise of the powers and discharge of the duties contemplated by Article 62(2)(c) of the Convention and Article XXXVII(2)(c) to (f) of this Protocol.
3. The centralised functions of the International Registry shall be operated and administered by the Registrar on a twenty-four hour basis.
4. The Registrar shall be liable under Article 28(1) of the Convention for loss caused up to an amount not exceeding the value of the equipment to which the loss relates. Notwithstanding the preceding sentence, the liability of the Registrar shall not exceed 5 million Special Drawing Rights in any calendar year, or such greater amount, computed in such manner, as the Supervisory Authority may from time to time determine by regulations.
5. The preceding paragraph shall not limit the Registrar's liability for damages for loss caused by gross negligence or intentional misconduct of the Registrar and its officers and employees.
6. The amount of the insurance or financial guarantee referred to in Article 28(4) of the Convention shall be not less than the amount determined by the Supervisory Authority to be appropriate, having regard to the prospective liability of the Registrar.
7. Nothing in the Convention shall preclude the Registrar from procuring insurance or a financial guarantee covering events for which the Registrar is not liable under Article 28 of the Convention.

Article XIX – Modifications of discharge provisions

1. Article 25 of the Convention applies:

(a) as if references to the debtor in paragraphs 1 and 3 were references to any of the interested persons referred to in Article 1(m)(i) and (iii);
(b) with paragraph 4 being replaced by the following:

4. Where a registration ought not to have been made or is incorrect or should otherwise be discharged in cases not within any of the preceding paragraphs, the person in whose favour the registration was made shall, without undue delay, procure its discharge or amendment after written demand by any of the interested persons referred to in Article 1(m)(i) and (iii) delivered to or received at the address of the person in whose favour the registration was made as stated in the registration"; and

(c) with the following being added immediately after paragraph 4:

"5. Where the holder of the interest referred to in paragraph 1 or 3 of this Article or the person in whose favour the registration was made as provided by paragraph 4 has ceased to exist or cannot be found the court may, on the application of any of the interested persons referred to in Article 1(m)(i) and (iii), make an order directed to the Registrar requiring the Registrar to discharge the registration.
6. Where the intending creditor or intending assignee referred to in paragraph 2 of this Article has ceased to exist or cannot be found the court may, on the application of the intending debtor or assignor, make an order directed to the Registrar requiring the Registrar to discharge the registration."

2. For the purposes of Article 25(2) of the Convention and in the circumstances there described, the holder of a registered prospective international interest or a registered prospective assignment of an international interest shall take such steps as are within its power to procure the discharge of the registration no later than ten calendar days after the receipt of the demand described in such paragraph.

Article XX – Notices of sale

The regulations shall authorise the registration in the International Registry of notices of sale of equipment. The provisions of this Chapter and of Chapter V of the Convention shall, in so far as relevant, apply to these registrations. However, any such registration and any search made or certificate issued in respect of a notice of sale shall be for the purposes of information only and shall not affect the rights of any person, or have any other effect, under the Convention or this Protocol.

CHAPTER IV – JURISDICTION

Article XXI – Waivers of sovereign immunity

1. Subject to paragraph 2, a waiver of sovereign immunity from jurisdiction of the courts specified in Article 42 or Article 43 of the Convention or relating to

enforcement of rights and interests relating to equipment under the Convention shall be binding and, if the other conditions to such jurisdiction or enforcement have been satisfied, shall be effective to confer jurisdiction and permit enforcement, as the case may be.

2. A waiver under the preceding paragraph must be in writing and contain a description of the equipment as specified in Article V(1).

CHAPTER V – RELATIONSHIP WITH OTHER CONVENTIONS

Article XXII – Relationship with the UNIDROIT Convention on International Financial Leasing

The Convention on International Interests in Mobile Equipment as applied to mining equipment, agricultural equipment and construction equipment shall supersede the UNIDROIT Convention on International Financial Leasing in respect of the subject matter of this Protocol, as between States Parties to both Conventions.

CHAPTER VI – FINAL PROVISIONS

Article XXIII – Signature, ratification, acceptance, approval or accession

1. This Protocol shall be open for signature in Pretoria on 22 November 2019 by States participating in the Diplomatic Conference to Adopt a Protocol to the Convention on International Interests in Mobile Equipment on Matters specific to Mining, Agricultural and Construction Equipment held at Pretoria from 11 to 22 November 2019. After 22 November 2019, this Protocol shall be open to all States for signature at the Headquarters of the International Institute for the Unification of Private Law (UNIDROIT) in Rome until it enters into force in accordance with Article XXV.
2. This Protocol shall be subject to ratification, acceptance or approval by States which have signed it.
3. Any State which does not sign this Protocol may accede to it at any time.
4. Ratification, acceptance, approval or accession is effected by the deposit of a formal instrument to that effect with the Depositary.
5. A State may not become a Party to this Protocol unless it is or becomes also a Party to the Convention.

Article XXIV – Regional Economic Integration Organisations

1. A Regional Economic Integration Organisation which is constituted by sovereign States and has competence over certain matters governed by this Protocol may similarly sign, accept, approve or accede to this Protocol. The Regional Economic Integration Organisation shall in that case have the rights and obligations of a Contracting State, to the extent that that Organisation has competence over matters governed by this Protocol. Where the number of

Contracting States is relevant in this Protocol, the Regional Economic Integration Organisation shall not count as a Contracting State in addition to its Member States which are Contracting States.

2. The Regional Economic Integration Organisation shall, at the time of signature, acceptance, approval or accession, make a declaration to the Depositary specifying the matters governed by this Protocol in respect of which competence has been transferred to that Organisation by its Member States. The Regional Economic Integration Organisation shall promptly notify the Depositary of any changes to the distribution of competence, including new transfers of competence, specified in the declaration under this paragraph.
3. Any reference to a "Contracting State" or "Contracting States" or "State Party" or "States Parties" in this Protocol applies equally to a Regional Economic Integration Organisation where the context so requires.

Article XXV – Entry into force

1. This Protocol enters into force between the States which have deposited instruments referred to in sub-paragraph (a) on the later of:
   (a) the first day of the month following the expiration of three months after the date of the deposit of the fifth instrument of ratification, acceptance, approval or accession; and
   (b) the date of the deposit by the Supervisory Authority with the Depositary of a certificate confirming that the International Registry is fully operational.
2. For other States this Protocol enters into force on the first day of the month following the later of:
   (a) the expiration of three months after the date of the deposit of its instrument of ratification, acceptance, approval or accession; and
   (b) the date referred to in sub-paragraph (b) of the preceding paragraph.

Article XXVI – Territorial units

1. If a Contracting State has territorial units in which different systems of law are applicable in relation to the matters dealt with in this Protocol, it may, at the time of ratification, acceptance, approval or accession, declare that this Protocol is to extend to all its territorial units or only to one or more of them, and may modify its declaration by submitting another declaration at any time.
2. Any such declarations are to be notified to the Depositary and shall state expressly the territorial units to which this Protocol applies.
3. If a Contracting State has not made any declaration under paragraph 1, this Protocol shall apply to all territorial units of that State.
4. Where a Contracting State extends this Protocol to one or more of its territorial units, declarations permitted under this Protocol may be made in respect

of each such territorial unit, and the declarations made in respect of one territorial unit may be different from those made in respect of another territorial unit.

5. If by virtue of a declaration under paragraph 1, this Protocol extends to one or more territorial units of a Contracting State:
   (a) the debtor is considered to be situated in a Contracting State only if it is incorporated or formed under a law in force in a territorial unit to which the Convention and this Protocol apply or if it has its registered office or statutory seat, centre of administration, place of business or habitual residence in a territorial unit to which the Convention and this Protocol apply;
   (b) any reference to the location of the object in a Contracting State refers to the location of the object in a territorial unit to which the Convention and this Protocol apply;
   (c) any reference to the administrative authorities in that Contracting State shall be construed as referring to the administrative authorities having jurisdiction in a territorial unit to which the Convention and this Protocol apply; and
   (d) for the purposes of Article XII(4), a dealer is considered to be situated in a Contracting State if it has its place of business or, if it has more than one place of business, its principal place of business, in a territorial unit where the Convention and this Protocol apply.

Article XXVII – Transitional Provisions

In relation to agricultural equipment, construction equipment and mining equipment Article 60 of the Convention shall be modified as follows:

(a) replace paragraph 2(a) with the following:

> "(a) "effective date of this Convention" means in relation to a debtor the latest of the time when:
>
> (i) this Convention enters into force;
> (ii) the State in which the debtor is situated at the time the right or interest is created or arises becomes a Contracting State; and
> (iii) the Protocol becomes applicable in that State to the equipment which is subject to the pre-existing right or interest."

(b) replace paragraph 3 with the following:

> "3. A Contracting State may in its declaration under paragraph 1 specify a date, not earlier than three years and not later than ten years after the date on which the declaration takes effect, when Articles 29, 35 and 36 of this Convention as

modified or supplemented by the Protocol will become applicable, to the extent and in the manner specified in the declaration, to pre-existing rights or interests arising under an agreement made at a time when the debtor was situated in that State. Any priority of the right or interest under the law of that State, so far as applicable, shall continue if the right or interest is registered in the International Registry before the expiration of the period specified in the declaration, whether or not any other right or interest has previously been registered."

(c) insert the following paragraph:

"4. For the purposes of paragraph 3, a declaration takes effect with respect to a pre-existing right or interest in equipment to which the Protocol to the Convention on International Interests in Mobile Equipment on Matters specific to Mining, Agricultural and Construction Equipment becomes applicable in that State in accordance with Article XXXV and XXXVI of that Protocol at the time the Protocol becomes applicable to that equipment."

Article XXVIII – Declarations relating to certain provisions

1. A Contracting State may, at the time of ratification, acceptance, approval of, or accession to this Protocol, declare that it will apply either or both of Articles VI and XI of this Protocol.
2. A Contracting State may, at the time of ratification, acceptance, approval of, or accession to this Protocol, declare that it will apply Article IX of this Protocol, wholly or in part. If it so declares, it shall specify the time-period required by Article IX(2).
3. A Contracting State may, at the time of ratification, acceptance, approval of, or accession to this Protocol, declare that it will apply Article X of this Protocol and, if so, shall specify the types of insolvency proceeding, if any, to which Article X will apply. A Contracting State making a declaration pursuant to this paragraph shall specify the time-period required by Article X.
4. A Contracting State may, at the time of ratification, acceptance, approval of, or accession to this Protocol, declare that it will apply Article XII.
5. Any declaration made pursuant to this Protocol shall apply to the entirety of the equipment to which this Protocol applies.
6. A Contracting State that makes a declaration in respect of any Alternative provided for in Article VII shall choose the same Alternative regarding the entirety of the equipment to which this Protocol applies.
7. The courts of Contracting States shall apply Article X in conformity with the declaration made by the Contracting State which is the primary insolvency jurisdiction.

Article XXIX – Declarations under the Convention

Declarations made under the Convention, including those made under Articles 39, 40, 50, 53, 54, 55, 57, 58 and 60, shall be deemed to have also been made under this Protocol, unless stated otherwise.

Article XXX – Reservations and declarations

1. No reservations may be made to this Protocol but declarations authorised by Articles II, VII, VIII, XXVI, XXVIII, XXIX and XXXI may be made in accordance with these provisions.
2. Any declaration or subsequent declaration or any withdrawal of a declaration made under this Protocol shall be notified in writing to the Depositary.

Article XXXI – Subsequent declarations

1. A State Party may make a subsequent declaration, other than a declaration made in accordance with Article XXIX under Article 60 of the Convention, at any time after the date on which this Protocol has entered into force for it, by notifying the Depositary to that effect.
2. Any such subsequent declaration shall take effect on the first day of the month following the expiration of six months after the date of receipt of the notification by the Depositary. Where a longer period for that declaration to take effect is specified in the notification, it shall take effect upon the expiration of such longer period after receipt of the notification by the Depositary.
3. Notwithstanding the previous paragraphs, this Protocol shall continue to apply, as if no such subsequent declarations had been made, in respect of all rights and interests arising prior to the effective date of any such subsequent declaration.

Article XXXII – Withdrawal of declarations

1. Any State Party having made a declaration under this Protocol, other than a declaration made in accordance with Article XXIX under Article 60 of the Convention, may withdraw it at any time by notifying the Depositary. Such withdrawal is to take effect on the first day of the month following the expiration of six months after the date of receipt of the notification by the Depositary.
2. Notwithstanding the preceding paragraph, this Protocol shall continue to apply, as if no such withdrawal of declaration had been made, in respect of all rights and interests arising prior to the effective date of any such withdrawal of declaration.

Article XXXIII – Denunciations

1. Any State Party may denounce this Protocol by notification in writing to the Depositary.
2. Any such denunciation shall take effect on the first day of the month following the expiration of twelve months after the date of receipt of the notification by the Depositary.
3. Notwithstanding the previous paragraphs, this Protocol shall continue to apply, as if no such denunciation had been made, in respect of all rights and interests arising prior to the effective date of any such denunciation.
4. A subsequent declaration made by a State Party under Article II declaring that the Protocol does not apply to one or more Annexes, shall be deemed a denunciation of the Protocol in relation to that Annex.

Article XXXIV – Review conferences, amendments and related matters

1. The Depositary, in consultation with the Supervisory Authority, shall prepare reports yearly, or at such other time as the circumstances may require, for the States Parties as to the manner in which the international regime established in the Convention as amended by this Protocol has operated in practice. In preparing such reports, the Depositary shall take into account the reports of the Supervisory Authority concerning the functioning of the international registration system.
2. At the request of not less than twenty-five per cent of the States Parties, Review Conferences of the States Parties shall be convened from time to time by the Depositary, in consultation with the Supervisory Authority, to consider:
   (a) the practical operation of the Convention as amended by this Protocol and its effectiveness in facilitating the asset-based financing and leasing of the objects covered by its terms;
   (b) the judicial interpretation given to, and the application made of the terms of this Protocol and the regulations;
   (c) the functioning of the international registration system, the performance of the Registrar and its oversight by the Supervisory Authority, taking into account the reports of the Supervisory Authority; and
   (d) whether any amendments to this Protocol, including the Annexes, or the arrangements relating to the International Registry are desirable.
3. Any amendment to this Protocol under this Article shall be approved by at least a two-thirds majority of States Parties participating in the Conference referred to in the preceding paragraph and shall then enter into force in respect of States Parties which have ratified, accepted or approved such amendment when it has been ratified, accepted or approved by five States Parties in accordance with the provisions of Article XXV relating to its entry into force.

Article XXXV – Adjustments to the Harmonized System codes in the Annexes following a Harmonized System revision

1. Upon the acceptance of a Harmonized System revision, the Depositary shall consult the World Customs Organization and the Supervisory Authority in relation to any Harmonized System codes listed in the Annexes that might be affected by the revision.
2. Not later than three months after the acceptance of a Harmonized System revision, the Depositary shall send to all Contracting States a notification of the Harmonized System revision. The notification shall state whether any Harmonized System codes in the Annexes will be affected by the revision and shall propose adjustments to the Harmonized System codes in the Annexes that are needed to ensure that the Annexes remain aligned with the Harmonized System and that minimise changes to the application of the Protocol to equipment resulting from the Harmonized System revision. The notification must specify the date by which objections to the Depositary proposal must be made pursuant to paragraph 3.
3. Each adjustment to the Harmonized System codes in the Annexes proposed by a Depositary proposal, if made within the time provided by the preceding paragraph, is deemed to have been adopted by Contracting States unless within nine months after the acceptance of the Harmonized System revision the Depositary receives objections to that proposed adjustment from one-third or more of the Contracting States. An objection must specify each adjustment to which it applies and must apply to the entirety of the adjustment.
4. If the Depositary receives objections to a proposed adjustment from one-third or more of the Contracting States within the period specified in the preceding paragraph, the Depositary shall convene a meeting of Contracting States to consider that adjustment. The Depositary shall endeavour to convene the meeting within three months following the expiration of the period specified in the preceding paragraph.
5. Contracting States participating at a meeting convened under the preceding paragraph shall make every effort to reach agreement by consensus. If no agreement is reached, an adjustment shall only be adopted if it is approved by a two-thirds majority vote of the Contracting States participating and voting at the meeting. Subject to paragraphs 7 and 8, agreements and decisions by the meeting of Contracting States shall be binding on all Contracting States
6. Following the expiration of the period specified in paragraph 3 or, if applicable, following the conclusion of a meeting of Contracting States pursuant to paragraph 4, the Depositary shall send to all Contracting States a notification that indicates which of the proposed adjustments have been adopted and which have not been adopted. Subject to paragraphs 7 and 8, the adopted adjustments shall enter into force on the later of twelve months from the date the Depositary sends the notification of adopted adjustments to Contracting States and the date of entry into force of the Harmonized System revision.
7. During the implementation period a Contracting State may, by notification received by the Depositary not less than thirty days before expiration of the implementation period, extend the date on which adjustments enter into force

in relation to that State for a period of six months. A Contracting State may make successive extensions of the entry into force for six-month periods by notification received by the Depositary not less than thirty days before expiration of the current period.

8. During the implementation period or during any subsequent six-month extension period provided by the preceding paragraph, a Contracting State, by notification received by the Depositary not less than thirty days before expiration of the implementation period or such subsequent period, may identify one or more adjustments to the Harmonized System codes in the Annexes which will not enter into force in relation to that State. A Contracting State that has so notified the Depositary may at any time thereafter withdraw its notification under this paragraph as to one or more adjustments by notification to the Depositary in which case such adjustment or adjustments shall enter into force in relation to that State thirty days after receipt by the Depositary of the notification.
9. A new Contracting State will have all rights and benefits of Contracting States under this Article, including the rights to object under paragraph 3, participate and vote in a meeting under paragraphs 4 and 5, extend dates under paragraph 7, and send notifications under the preceding paragraph. Notwithstanding the preceding sentence, a new Contracting State has only the time, if any, remaining to other Contracting States for taking any action, under this Article.
10. Subject to Article 60 of the Convention and Article XXVII of this Protocol, any adjustment to the Harmonized System codes in the Annexes under this Article shall not affect rights and interests arising prior to the date the adjustment enters into force.

Article XXXVI – Modifications of the Annexes

1. This article applies to modifications of the Annexes other than adjustments to the Harmonized System codes in the Annexes governed by Article XXXV.
2. If at any time after the entry into force of this Protocol the Depositary receives a Contracting State proposal, the Depositary shall, at the time provided in paragraph 3 or paragraph 5, send to all Contracting States a notification of the Contracting State proposal. The notification shall identify the Harmonized System codes, if any, that would be affected by the proposal and describe each proposed modification of the Annexes. The notification must specify the date by which objections to the Contracting State proposal must be made pursuant to paragraph 4 or 5.
3. Subject to paragraph 5, at the time the Depositary sends a Depositary proposal to Contracting States pursuant to Article XXXV(2) it shall send to Contracting States a notification of each Contracting State proposal received by the Depositary and not previously sent to Contracting States.
4. Subject to paragraph 5, each modification of the Annexes proposed by a Contracting State proposal referred to in the preceding paragraph is deemed to have been adopted by Contracting States unless within the time specified for

objections in Article XXXV(3) the Depositary receives objections to that proposed modification from twenty-five per cent or more of the Contracting States. An objection must specify each modification to which it applies and must apply to the entirety of that modification.

5. In its sole discretion the Depositary may elect to send to Contracting States, at a time other than that specified in paragraph 3, a notification of each Contracting State proposal received by the Depositary and not previously sent to Contracting States. In that case, each modification of the Annexes proposed by the Contracting State proposal or proposals is deemed to have been adopted by Contracting States unless within the time specified in the notification the Depositary receives objections to that proposed modification from twenty-five per cent or more of the Contracting States. The time specified in the notification shall be not less than nine months after the Depositary's receipt of the Contracting State proposal most recently received by the Depositary. An objection must specify each modification to which it applies and must apply to the entirety of that modification.
6. If the Depositary receives objections to a proposed modification from twenty-five per cent or more of the Contracting States within the period specified in paragraph 4 or paragraph 5, the Depositary shall convene a meeting of Contracting States to consider that modification. The Depositary shall endeavour to convene the meeting within three months following the expiration of the period specified in paragraph 4 or paragraph 5.
7. Contracting States participating at a meeting convened under the preceding paragraph shall make every effort to reach agreement by consensus. If no agreement is reached, a modification shall only be adopted if it is approved by a two-thirds majority vote of the Contracting States participating and voting at the meeting. Subject to paragraphs 9 and 10, agreements and decisions by the meeting of Contracting States shall be binding on all Contracting States.
8. Following the expiration of the period specified in paragraph 4 or paragraph 5 or, if applicable, following the conclusion of a meeting of Contracting States pursuant to paragraph 6, the Depositary shall send to all Contracting States a notification that indicates which of the proposed modifications have been adopted and which have not been adopted. Subject to paragraphs 9 and 10, the adopted modifications shall enter into force twelve months from the date the Depositary sends the notification to Contracting States.
9. During the implementation period a Contracting State may, by notification received by the Depositary not less than thirty days before expiration of the implementation period, extend the date on which modifications enter into force in relation to that State for a period of six months. A Contracting State may make successive extensions of the entry into force for six-month periods by notification received by the Depositary not less than thirty days before expiration of the current period.
10. During the implementation period or during any subsequent six-month extension period provided by the preceding paragraph, a Contracting State, by notification received by the Depositary not less than thirty days before expiration of the implementation period or such subsequent period, may identify one or more modifications to the Annexes which will not enter into force in relation

to that State. A Contracting State that has so notified the Depositary may at any time thereafter withdraw its notification under this paragraph as to one or more modifications by notification to the Depositary, in which case such modification or modifications shall enter into force in relation to that State thirty days after receipt by the Depositary of the notification.

11. A new Contracting State will have all rights and benefits of Contracting States under this Article, including the rights to object under paragraph 4 or paragraph 5, participate and vote in a meeting under paragraphs 6 and 7, extend dates under paragraph 9, and send notifications under the preceding paragraph. Notwithstanding the preceding sentence, a new Contracting State has only the time, if any, remaining to other Contracting States for taking any action, under this Article.
12. Subject to Article 60 of the Convention and Article XXVII of this Protocol, any modification to the Annexes under this Article shall not affect rights and interests arising prior to the date the modification enters into force.

Article XXXVII — Depositary and its functions

1. Instruments of ratification, acceptance, approval or accession shall be deposited with the International Institute for the Unification of Private Law (UNIDROIT), which is hereby designated the Depositary.
2. The Depositary shall:
   (a) inform all Contracting States of:
      (i) each new signature or deposit of an instrument of ratification, acceptance, approval or accession, together with the date thereof;
      (ii) the date of the deposit of the certificate referred to in Article XXV(1)(b);
      (iii) the date of entry into force of this Protocol;
      (iv) each declaration made in accordance with this Protocol, together with the date thereof;
      (v) the withdrawal or amendment of any declaration, together with the date thereof; and
      (vi) the notification of any denunciation of this Protocol together with the date thereof and the date on which it takes effect;
   (b) transmit certified true copies of this Protocol to all Contracting States;
   (c) provide the Supervisory Authority and the Registrar with a copy of each instrument of ratification, acceptance, approval or accession, together with the date of deposit thereof, of each declaration or withdrawal or amendment of a declaration and of each notification of denunciation, together with the date of notification thereof, so that the information contained therein is easily and fully available and assist in the performance of any related duties to ensure the proper operation of the Registry;
   (d) inform the Supervisory Authority and the Registrar of any pending processes under Article XXXV or Article XXXVI and of the outcomes of any such processes;

(e) inform new Contracting States of any pending process under Article XXXV or Article XXXVI;
(f) perform the functions associated with the amendment of the Annexes, as referred to in Articles XXXIV, XXXV and XXXVI; and
(g) perform such other functions customary for depositaries.

IN WITNESS WHEREOF the undersigned Plenipotentiaries, having been duly authorised, have signed this Protocol.
DONE at Pretoria, this twenty second day of November, two thousand and nineteen, in a single original in the English and French languages, both texts being equally authentic, such authenticity to take effect upon verification by the Secretariat of the Conference under the authority of the President of the Conference within ninety days hereof as to the consistency of the texts with one another.

Annexes

Annex 1. Mining Equipment

As consistent with Article II, the Convention shall apply in relation to mining equipment that falls under the following Harmonized System codes in this Annex.

820713: Interchangeable tools for hand tools, whether or not power-operated, or for machine-tools (for example, for pressing, stamping, punching, tapping, threading, drilling, boring, broaching, milling, turning or screw driving), including dies for drawing or extruding metal, and rock drilling or earth boring tools - Rock drilling or earth boring tools -- With working part of cermets

842831: Other lifting, handling, loading or unloading machinery (for example, lifts, escalators, conveyors, teleferics) - Other continuous-action elevators and conveyors, for goods or materials -- Specifically designed for underground use

842911: Self-propelled bulldozers, angledozers, graders, levellers, scrapers, mechanical shovels, excavators, shovel loaders, tamping machines and road rollers - Bulldozers and angledozers -- Track laying

842919: Self-propelled bulldozers, angledozers, graders, levellers, scrapers, mechanical shovels, excavators, shovel loaders, tamping machines and road rollers - Bulldozers and angledozers -- Other

842920: Self-propelled bulldozers, angledozers, graders, levellers, scrapers, mechanical shovels, excavators, shovel loaders, tamping machines and road rollers - Graders and levellers

842951: Self-propelled bulldozers, angledozers, graders, levellers, scrapers, mechanical shovels, excavators, shovel loaders, tamping machines and road rollers - Mechanical shovels, excavators and shovel loaders -- Front-end shovel loaders

842952: Self-propelled bulldozers, angledozers, graders, levellers, scrapers, mechanical shovels, excavators, shovel loaders, tamping machines and road rollers - Mechanical shovels, excavators and shovel loaders -- Machinery with a 360° revolving superstructure

842959: Self-propelled bulldozers, angledozers, graders, levellers, scrapers, mechanical shovels, excavators, shovel loaders, tamping machines and road rollers - Mechanical shovels, excavators and shovel loaders -- Other

843010: Other moving, grading, levelling, scraping, excavating, tamping, compacting, extracting or boring machinery, for earth, minerals or ores; pile-drivers and pile-extractors; snow-ploughs and snow-blowers - Pile-drivers and pile-extractors

843031: Other moving, grading, levelling, scraping, excavating, tamping, compacting, extracting or boring machinery, for earth, minerals or ores; pile-drivers and pile-extractors; snow-ploughs and snow-blowers - Coal or rock cutters and tunnelling machinery -- Self-propelled

843039: Other moving, grading, levelling, scraping, excavating, tamping, compacting, extracting or boring machinery, for earth, minerals or ores; pile-drivers and pile-extractors; snow-ploughs and snow-blowers - Coal or rock cutters and tunnelling machinery -- Other

843041: Other moving, grading, levelling, scraping, excavating, tamping, compacting, extracting or boring machinery, for earth, minerals or ores; pile-drivers and pile-extractors; snow-ploughs and snow-blowers - Other boring or sinking machinery -- Self-propelled

843049: Other moving, grading, levelling, scraping, excavating, tamping, compacting, extracting or boring machinery, for earth, minerals or ores; pile-drivers and pile-extractors; snow-ploughs and snow-blowers - Other boring or sinking machinery -- Other

843050: Other moving, grading, levelling, scraping, excavating, tamping, compacting, extracting or boring machinery, for earth, minerals or ores; pile-drivers and pile-extractors; snow-ploughs and snow-blowers - Other machinery, self-propelled

843061: Other moving, grading, levelling, scraping, excavating, tamping, compacting, extracting or boring machinery, for earth, minerals or ores; pile-drivers and pile-extractors; snow-ploughs and snow-blowers - Other machinery, not self-propelled -- Tamping on compacting machinery

843069: Other moving, grading, levelling, scraping, excavating, tamping, compacting, extracting or boring machinery, for earth, minerals or ores; pile-drivers and pile-extractors; snow-ploughs and snow-blowers - Other machinery, not self-propelled -- Other

847410: Machinery for sorting, screening, separating, washing, crushing, grinding, mixing or kneading earth, stone, ores or other mineral substances, in solid (including powder or paste) form; machinery for agglomerating, shaping or moulding solid mineral fuels, ceramic paste, unhardened cements, plastering materials or other mineral products in powder or paste form; machines for forming foundry moulds of sand - Sorting, screening, separating or washing machines

847420: Machinery for sorting, screening, separating, washing, crushing, grinding, mixing or kneading earth, stone, ores or other mineral substances, in solid (including powder or paste) form; machinery for agglomerating, shaping or moulding solid mineral fuels, ceramic paste, unhardened cements, plastering materials or other mineral products in powder or paste form; machines for forming foundry moulds of sand - Crushing or grinding machines

847431: Machinery for sorting, screening, separating, washing, crushing, grinding, mixing or kneading earth, stone, ores or other mineral substances, in solid (including powder or paste) form; machinery for agglomerating, shaping or moulding solid mineral fuels, ceramic paste, unhardened cements, plastering materials or other mineral products in powder or paste form; machines for forming foundry moulds of sand - Mixing or kneading machines -- Concrete or mortar mixers

870130: Tractors (other than tractors of heading 8709) - Track-laying tractors

870192: Tractors (other than tractors of heading 8709) - Other, of an engine power -- Exceeding 18 kW but not exceeding 37 kW

870193: Tractors (other than tractors of heading 8709) - Other, of an engine power -- Exceeding 37 kW but not exceeding 75 kW

870194: Tractors (other than tractors of heading 8709) - Other, of an engine power -- Exceeding 75 kW but not exceeding 130 kW

870195: Tractors (other than tractors of heading 8709) - Other, of an engine power -- Exceeding 130 kW

870410: Motor vehicles for the transport of goods - Dumpers designed for off-highway use

Annex 2. Agricultural Equipment

As consistent with Article II, the Convention shall apply in relation to agricultural equipment that falls under the following Harmonized System codes in this Annex.

842449: Mechanical appliances (whether or not hand-operated) for projecting, dispersing or spraying liquids or powders; fire extinguishers, whether or not charged; spray guns and similar appliances; steam or sand blasting machines and similar jet projecting machines - Agricultural or horticultural sprayers -- Other

842482: Mechanical appliances (whether or not hand-operated) for projecting, dispersing, or spraying liquids or powders; fire extinguishers, whether or not charged; spray guns and similar appliances; steam or sand blasting machines and similar jet projecting machines - Other appliances -- Agricultural or Horticultural

842911: Self-propelled bulldozers, angledozers, graders, levellers, scrapers, mechanical shovels, excavators, shovel loaders, tamping machines and road rollers - Bulldozers and angledozers -- Track laying

842919: Self-propelled bulldozers, angledozers, graders, levellers, scrapers, mechanical shovels, excavators, shovel loaders, tamping machines and road rollers - Bulldozers and angledozers -- Other

842920: Self-propelled bulldozers, angledozers, graders, levellers, scrapers, mechanical shovels, excavators, shovel loaders, tamping machines and road rollers - Graders and levellers

842930: Self-propelled bulldozers, angledozers, graders, levellers, scrapers, mechanical shovels, excavators, shovel loaders, tamping machines and road rollers - Scrapers

842940: Self-propelled bulldozers, angledozers, graders, levellers, scrapers, mechanical shovels, excavators, shovel loaders, tamping machines and road rollers - Tamping machines and road rollers

842951: Self-propelled bulldozers, angledozers, graders, levellers, scrapers, mechanical shovels, excavators, shovel loaders, tamping machines and road rollers - Mechanical shovels, excavators and shovel loaders -- Front-end shovel loaders

842952: Self-propelled bulldozers, angledozers, graders, levellers, scrapers, mechanical shovels, excavators, shovel loaders, tamping machines and road rollers - Mechanical shovels, excavators and shovel loaders -- Machinery with a 360° revolving superstructure

842959: Self-propelled bulldozers, angledozers, graders, levellers, scrapers, mechanical shovels, excavators, shovel loaders, tamping machines and road rollers - Mechanical shovels, excavators and shovel loaders -- Other

843049: Other moving, grading, levelling, scraping, excavating, tamping, compacting, extracting or boring machinery, for earth, minerals or ores; pile-drivers and pile-extractors; snow-ploughs and snow-blowers - Other boring or sinking machinery -- Other

843050: Other moving, grading, levelling, scraping, excavating, tamping, compacting, extracting or boring machinery, for earth, minerals or ores; pile-drivers and pile-extractors; snow-ploughs and snow-blowers - Other machinery, self-propelled

843210: Agricultural, horticultural or forestry machinery for soil preparation or cultivation; lawn or sports-ground rollers - Ploughs

843221: Agricultural, horticultural or forestry machinery for soil preparation or cultivation; lawn or sports-ground rollers - Harrows, scarifiers, cultivators, weeders and hoes -- Disc harrows

843229: Agricultural, horticultural or forestry machinery for soil preparation or cultivation; lawn or sports-ground rollers - Harrows, scarifiers, cultivators, weeders and hoes -- Other

843231: Agricultural, horticultural or forestry machinery for soil preparation or cultivation; lawn or sports-ground rollers - Seeders, planters and transplanters -- no-till direct seeders, planters and transplanters

843239: Agricultural, horticultural or forestry machinery for soil preparation or cultivation; lawn or sports-ground rollers - Seeders, planters and transplanters -- Other

843241: Agricultural, horticultural or forestry machinery for soil preparation or cultivation; lawn or sports-ground rollers - Manure spreaders and fertiliser distributors -- Manure spreaders

843242: Agricultural, horticultural or forestry machinery for soil preparation or cultivation; lawn or sports-ground rollers - Manure spreaders and fertiliser distributors -- Fertiliser distributors

843320: Harvesting or threshing machinery, including straw or fodder balers; grass or hay mowers; machines for cleaning, sorting or grading eggs, fruit or other agricultural produce, other than machinery of heading 8437 - Other mowers, including cutter bars for tractor mounting

843330: Harvesting or threshing machinery, including straw or fodder balers; grass or hay mowers; machines for cleaning, sorting or grading eggs, fruit or other agricultural produce, other than machinery of heading 8437 - Other haymaking machinery

843340: Harvesting or threshing machinery, including straw or fodder balers; grass or hay mowers; machines for cleaning, sorting or grading eggs, fruit or other agricultural produce, other than machinery of heading 8437 - Straw or fodder balers, including pick-up balers

843351: Harvesting or threshing machinery, including straw or fodder balers; grass or hay mowers; machines for cleaning, sorting or grading eggs, fruit or other agricultural produce, other than machinery of heading 8437 Other harvesting machinery; threshing machinery Combine harvester threshers

843353: Harvesting or threshing machinery, including straw or fodder balers; grass or hay mowers; machines for cleaning, sorting or grading eggs, fruit or other agricultural produce, other than machinery of heading 8437 - Other harvesting machinery; threshing machinery -- Root or tuber harvesting machines

843359: Harvesting or threshing machinery, including straw or fodder balers; grass or hay mowers; machines for cleaning, sorting or grading eggs, fruit or other agricultural produce, other than machinery of heading 8437 - Other harvesting machinery; threshing machinery -- Other

843360: Harvesting or threshing machinery, including straw or fodder balers; grass or hay mowers; machines for cleaning, sorting or grading eggs, fruit or other agricultural produce, other than machinery of heading 8437 - Machines for cleaning, sorting or grading eggs, fruit or other agricultural produce

843410: Milking machines and dairy machinery - Milking machines

843680: Other agricultural, horticultural, forestry, poultry-keeping or bee-keeping machinery, including germination plant fitted with mechanical or thermal equipment; poultry incubators and brooders - Other machinery

843710: Machines for cleaning, sorting or grading seed, grain or dried leguminous vegetables; machinery used in the milling industry or for the working of cereals or dried leguminous vegetables, other than farm-type machinery - Machines for cleaning, sorting or grading seed, grain or dried leguminous vegetables

870130: Tractors (other than tractors of heading 8709) - Track-laying tractors

870192: Tractors (other than tractors of heading 8709) - Other, of an engine power -- Exceeding 18 kW but not exceeding 37 kW

870193: Tractors (other than tractors of heading 8709) - Other, of an engine power -- Exceeding 37 kW but not exceeding 75 kW

870194: Tractors (other than tractors of heading 8709) - Other, of an engine power -- Exceeding 75 kW but not exceeding 130 kW

870195: Tractors (other than tractors of heading 8709) - Other, of an engine power -- Exceeding 130 kW

870410: Motor vehicles for the transport of goods - Dumpers designed for off-highway use

871620: Trailers and semi-trailers; other vehicles, not mechanically propelled; parts thereof -Self-loading or self-unloading trailers and semi-trailers for agricultural purposes

Annex 3. Construction Equipment

As consistent with Article II, the Convention shall apply in relation to construction equipment that falls under the following Harmonized System codes in this Annex.

820713: Interchangeable tools for hand tools, whether or not power-operated, or for machine-tools (for example, for pressing, stamping, punching, tapping, threading, drilling, boring, broaching, milling, turning or screw driving), including dies for drawing or extruding metal, and rock drilling or earth boring tools - Rock drilling or earth boring tools -- With working part of cermets

841340: Pumps for liquids, whether or not fitted with a measuring device; liquid elevators - Concrete pumps

842620: Ships' derricks; cranes, including cable cranes; mobile lifting frames, straddle carriers and works trucks fitted with a crane - Tower cranes

842641: Ships' derricks; cranes, including cable cranes; mobile lifting frames, straddle carriers and works trucks fitted with a crane - Other machinery, self-propelled -- On tyres

842649: Ships' derricks; cranes, including cable cranes; mobile lifting frames, straddle carriers and works trucks fitted with a crane - Other machinery, self-propelled -- Other

842911: Self-propelled bulldozers, angledozers, graders, levellers, scrapers, mechanical shovels, excavators, shovel loaders, tamping machines and road rollers - Bulldozers and angledozers -- Track laying

842919: Self-propelled bulldozers, angledozers, graders, levellers, scrapers, mechanical shovels, excavators, shovel loaders, tamping machines and road rollers - Bulldozers and angledozers – Other

842920: Self-propelled bulldozers, angledozers, graders, levellers, scrapers, mechanical shovels, excavators, shovel loaders, tamping machines and road rollers - Graders and levellers

842930: Self-propelled bulldozers, angledozers, graders, levellers, scrapers, mechanical shovels, excavators, shovel loaders, tamping machines and road rollers - Scrapers

842940: Self-propelled bulldozers, angledozers, graders, levellers, scrapers, mechanical shovels, excavators, shovel loaders, tamping machines and road rollers - Tamping machines and road rollers

842951: Self-propelled bulldozers, angledozers, graders, levellers, scrapers, mechanical shovels, excavators, shovel loaders, tamping machines and road rollers - Mechanical shovels, excavators and shovel loaders -- Front-end shovel loaders

842952: Self-propelled bulldozers, angledozers, graders, levellers, scrapers, mechanical shovels, excavators, shovel loaders, tamping machines and road rollers - Mechanical shovels, excavators and shovel loaders -- Machinery with a 360° revolving superstructure

842959: Self-propelled bulldozers, angledozers, graders, levellers, scrapers, mechanical shovels, excavators, shovel loaders, tamping machines and road rollers - Mechanical shovels, excavators and shovel loaders – Other

843010: Other moving, grading, levelling, scraping, excavating, tamping, compacting, extracting or boring machinery, for earth, minerals or ores; pile-drivers and pile-extractors; snow ploughs and snow-blowers - Pile-drivers and pile-extractors

843031: Other moving, grading, levelling, scraping, excavating, tamping, compacting, extracting or boring machinery, for earth, minerals or ores; pile-drivers and pile-extractors; snow-ploughs and snow-blowers - Coal or rock cutters and tunnelling machinery -- Self-propelled

843039: Other moving, grading, levelling, scraping, excavating, tamping, compacting, extracting or boring machinery, for earth, minerals or ores; pile-drivers and pile-extractors; snow-ploughs and snow-blowers - Coal or rock cutters and tunnelling machinery -- Other

843041: Other moving, grading, levelling, scraping, excavating, tamping, compacting, extracting or boring machinery, for earth, minerals or ores; pile-drivers and pile-extractors; snow-ploughs and snow-blowers - Other boring or sinking machinery -- Self-propelled

843049: Other moving, grading, levelling, scraping, excavating, tamping, compacting, extracting or boring machinery, for earth, minerals or ores; pile-drivers and pile-extractors; snow-ploughs and snow-blowers - Other boring or sinking machinery -- Other

843050: Other moving, grading, levelling, scraping, excavating, tamping, compacting, extracting or boring machinery, for earth, minerals or ores; pile-drivers and pile-extractors; snow-ploughs and snow-blowers - Other machinery, self-propelled

843061: Other moving, grading, levelling, scraping, excavating, tamping, compacting, extracting or boring machinery, for earth, minerals or ores; pile-drivers and pile-extractors; snow-ploughs and snow-blowers - Other machinery, not self-propelled -- Tamping or compacting machinery

843069: Other moving, grading, levelling, scraping, excavating, tamping, compacting, extracting or boring machinery, for earth, minerals or ores; pile-drivers and pile-extractors; snow-ploughs and snow-blowers - Other machinery, not self-propelled -- Other

847410: Machinery for sorting, screening, separating, washing, crushing, grinding, mixing or kneading earth, stone, ores or other mineral substances, in solid (including powder or paste) form; machinery for agglomerating, shaping or moulding solid mineral fuels, ceramic paste, unhardened cements, plastering materials or other mineral products in powder or paste form; machines for forming foundry moulds of sand - Sorting, screening, separating or washing machines

847420: Machinery for sorting, screening, separating, washing, crushing, grinding, mixing or kneading earth, stone, ores or other mineral substances, in solid (including powder or paste) form; machinery for agglomerating, shaping or moulding solid mineral fuels, ceramic paste, unhardened cements, plastering materials or other mineral products in powder or paste form; machines for forming foundry moulds of sand - Crushing or grinding machines

847431: Machinery for sorting, screening, separating, washing, crushing, grinding, mixing or kneading earth, stone, ores or other mineral substances, in solid (including powder or paste) form; machinery for agglomerating, shaping or moulding solid mineral fuels, ceramic paste, unhardened cements, plastering materials or other mineral products in powder or paste form; machines for forming foundry moulds of sand - Mixing or kneading machines -- Concrete or mortar mixers

847432: Machinery for sorting, screening, separating, washing, crushing, grinding, mixing or kneading earth, stone, ores or other mineral substances, in solid (including powder or paste) form; machinery for agglomerating, shaping or moulding solid mineral fuels, ceramic paste, unhardened cements, plastering materials or other mineral products in powder or paste form; machines for forming foundry moulds of sand - Mixing or kneading machines -- Machines for mixing mineral substances with bitumen

847910: Machines and mechanical appliances having individual functions, not specified or included elsewhere in this Chapter - Machinery for public works, building or the like

847982: Machines and mechanical appliances having individual functions, not specified or included elsewhere in this Chapter - Other machines and mechanical appliances -- Mixing, kneading, crushing, grinding, screening, sifting, homogenising, emulsifying or stirring machines

870130: Tractors (other than tractors of heading 8709) - Track-laying tractors

870192: Tractors (other than tractors of heading 8709) - Other, of an engine power -- Exceeding 18 kW but not exceeding 37 kW

870193: Tractors (other than tractors of heading 8709) - Other, of an engine power -- Exceeding 37 kW but not exceeding 75 kW

870194: Tractors (other than tractors of heading 8709) - Other, of an engine power -- Exceeding 75 kW but not exceeding 130 kW

870195: Tractors (other than tractors of heading 8709) - Other, of an engine power -- Exceeding 130 kW

870410: Motor vehicles for the transport of goods - Dumpers designed for off-highway use

870510: Special purpose motor vehicles, other than those principally designed for the transport of persons or goods (for example, breakdown lorries, crane lorries, fire fighting vehicles, concrete-mixer lorries, road sweeper lorries, spraying lorries, mobile workshops, mobile radiological units) - Crane lorries

870540: Special purpose motor vehicles, other than those principally designed for the transport of persons or goods (for example, breakdown lorries, crane lorries, fire fighting vehicles, concrete-mixer lorries, road sweeper lorries, spraying lorries, mobile workshops, mobile radiological units) - Concrete-mixer lorries

Selected Bibliography

Akseli, N. Orkun. *International Secured Transactions Law, Facilitation of Credit and International Conventions and Instruments*. 2011, 112, 113, 115, 117, 121–123.

Akseli, N. Orkun, 'The Principle of Debtor's Protection under the UN Convention on the Assignment of Receivables'. In *International Arbitration and International Commercial Law*, edited by S. Kröll, L. A. Mistelis, P. Perales Viscasillas & V. Rogers. 2011, 510.

Assi, Eugène Assepo. 'La Cour commune de justice et d'arbitrage de l'OHADA: un troisième degré de jurisdiction?', *Revue international de droit comparé* Vol. 57(4) (2005): 943–955.

Atwood, John. 'The Cape Town Convention: The New Dublin International Registration System in Practice', *Uniform Commercial Code Law Journal* Vol. 43(2) (2011): 637–653.

Bazinas, Spiros V. 'Uniform Receivables Financing Law: Key Policy Aspects of the United Nations Convention on the Assignment of Receivables in International Trade', *Revue hellénique de droit international* (2011): 37.

Bazinas, Spiros. 'UNCITRAL's Contribution to the Unification of Receivables Financing Law: The United Nations Convention on the Assignment of Receivables in International Trade', *Uniform Law Review* Vol. 7(1) (2002): 55 and 57, 63.

Berends, André J. *The UNCITRAL Model Law on Cross-Border Insolvency* (1998), 319.

Bodungen, Benjamin B. von. *Mobiliarsicherungsrecht an Luftfahrzeugen und Eisenbahnrollmaterial im nationalen und internationalen Rechtsverkehr, Zugleich ein Beitrag zur internationalen Vereinheitlichung des Rechtes nationaler Mobiliarsicherheiten durch das Kapstadt-Übereinkommen*. 2009, 385.

Böger, Ole. 'A Possible Protocol to the Cape Town Convention on Renewable Energy Equipment', *Uniform Law Review* Vol. 23(2) (1 June 2018): 242–269.

Böger, Ole. 'The Case for a New Protocol to the Cape Town Convention Covering Security Over Ships', *Cape Town Convention Journal* Vol. 5(1) (2016): 73–102.

Brydie-Watson, William. 'The MAC Protocol, Legal Operation and Benefits'. In *Unidroit y la codificación internacional del derecho privado*, edited by Calvo Caravaca, Alfonso Luis (2020) pp. 331–343.

Buxbaum, Richard M. Montesquieu and the Cape Town Convention, of Bankruptcy and Civil Procedure. Kronke, Herbert, National, International, Transnational: Harmonischer Dreiklang im Recht (2020) pp. 733–742.

Selected Bibliography

Clark, Lorne S. 'The 2001 Cape Town Convention on International Interests in Mobile Equipment and Aircraft Protocol: Internationalising Asset-Based Financing Principles for the Acquisition of Aircraft and Engines', *Journal of Air Law and Commerce* Vol. 69 (2004): 15.

Crocq, Pierre. 'Le nouvel acte uniforme portant organisation de sûretés', *La réforme du droit des sûretés de l'Ohada* (2012).

Deschamps, Michel. The Impact of the Cape Town Convention on the Assignment of Receivables. Kronke, Herbert, National, International, Transnational: Harmonischer Dreiklang im Recht (2020) pp. 769–784.

Diarrah, Boubacar S. 'Les innovations introduites dans l'Acte uniforme portant organisation des sûretés', *Revue de droit uniforme africain* (2011): 3–7.

Didenko, Anton N. The Cape Town Convention: A Documentary History, in Hart Studies. Commercial and Financial Law (2021) pp. xxii–215.

Dubovec, Marek. 'Accessions and Non-accessions under the Cape Town Convention: Special Focus on MAC Equipment', *Cape Town Law Journal* Vol. 6 (2017): 55 and 56.

Glaister, William J., Robert Murphy, Marisa Chan, Dunne Elie & Juliand Acratopulo. 'Lex Situs after Blue Sky: Is the Cape Town Convention the Solution?', *Cape Town Law Journal* (2013): 3–23.

Gopalan, Sandeep. 'Harmonization of Commercial Law: Lessons on the International Interests in Mobile Equipment', *Law and Business Review of the Americas* Vol. 9 (2003): 256.

Honnebier, B. Patrick. 'The Convention on International Interests in Mobile Equipment and Aircraft Equipment Protocol Encourages European Property Law Reform', *Edinburgh Law Review* Vol. 8(1) (2004): 124.

Isham, Sara. 'UNCITRAL's Model Law on Cross-Border On Solvency, a Workable Protection for Transnational Investment at Last', *Brooklyn Journal of International Law* (2001): 1204.

Kenfack Douajni, Gaston. 'L'expérience internationale de la Cour commune de justice et d'arbitrage (CCJA) de l'Organisation pour l'harmonisation en Afrique du droit des affaires (OHADA)', *Revue camerounaise de l'arbitrage* (2007): 4 and 5.

Kozuka, Sôichirô. *The Cape Town Convention and the 'Fitness' to the Context*, 2020, 1005–1015.

Kreuzer, Karl F. 'Jurisdiction and Choice of Law under the Cape Town Convention and the Protocols Thereto', *Cape Town Law Journal* (2013): 149–164.

Kronke, Herbert. 'Financial Leasing and Its Unification by UNIDROIT', *General Report on the XVIIIth Congress of the International Academy of Comparative Law* (2012): 331 and 332.

Kuhne, Hans. 'Zur Neuordnung der grenzüberschreitenden Forderungsabtretung im Einheitsrecht UN-Abtretungsrecht', *Schweizerische Zeitschrift für Wirtschaftsrecht* (2002): 140 and 141.

Labitey, Dalé Hélène. 'Quel droit des sûretés réelles pour l'Ohada?', *Revue congolaise de droit et des affaires* (2011): 66.

Mauri, Giulia. 'La Convenzione di Città del Capo e il protocollo aeronautico'. Contratta e Impresa (2009), p. 509.

Nussbaumer, Michel & Frédérique Dahan. 'Promoting Legal Reform in Eastern Europe: The EBRD Approach'. In *Private Law in the Eastern Europe*, 2010, 40–67.

Pritchard, John & David Lloyd. 'Analysis of Non-Consensual Rights and Interests under Article 39 of the Cape Town Convention', *Cape Town Law Journal* Vol. 2(1) (2013): 3–40.

Riffard, Jean-François. La ratification de la convention du Cap et de son Protocole ferroviaire – la délicate alchimie du choix des déclarations (ou du bon usage du sur-mesure d'un point de vue français). Uniform Law Review (2020) pp. 92–108.

Rodríguez de las Heras Ballell, Teresa. 'Complexities Arising from the Expansion of the Cape Town Convention to Other Sectors', *Uniform Law Review* Vol. 23(2) (1 June 2018): 214–241.

Rosen, Howard. Commentary on 'A Comparison of the Position of Buyers under the Cape Town Convention, the Three Existing Protocols and the Draft MAC Protocol'. *Cape Town Law Journal* Vol. 6 (2017): 123 and 135.

Rosen, Howard. 'Public Service and the Cape Town Convention'. *Cape Town Law Journal* Vol. 2(1) (2013): 131–144.

Saidova, Sanam. 'The Cape Town Convention: Repossession and Sale of Charged Aircraft Objects in a Commercially Reasonable Manner', *Lloyd's Maritime and Commercial Law Quarterly* (2013): 180–197.

Sanchez Lorenzo, Sixto. 'Aspectos Reales delw Leasing Internacional', *Revista de la Corte Española de Arbitraje* (1992): 73–75.

Schütze, Elisabeth. *Zession und Einheitsrecht,* 2005, 128.

Sir Roy Goode. 'Creativity and Transnational Commercial Law, from Carshemish to Cape Town', *International and Comparative Law Quarterly* (2021): 1–28.

Sir Roy Goode. 'Official Commentary on the Convention on International Interests in Mobile Equipment and Protocol Thereto on Matters Specific to Mining, Agricultural and Construction Equipment' (2021).

Sir Roy Goode. 'Official Commentary on the Convention on International Interests in Mobile Equipment', no. 4.195 (2014), pp. 227 and 228, nos 4.301 4.302, pp. 269 and 270.

Sir Roy Goode, 'Official Commentary on the Convention on International Interests in Mobile Equipment', no. 4.27 p. 162, no. 4.84, p. 185, no. 4.101 p. 187, nos 4.190 and 4.191 (2014), p. 226.

Sir Roy Goode. 'Official Commentary on the Protocol to the Convention on International Interests in Mobile Equipment on Matters Specific to Aircraft Equipment', nos 5.3 to 5.5 p. 304, no. 5.19 p. 310, no. 5.23 p. 311, no. 5.30 p. 314, no. 5.33 p. 315, no. 5.39 p. 317, no. 5.72 p. 334, no. 5.106 p. 347, no. 5.108 p. 348 nos 5.110 and 5.111 p. 349 (2013).

Sir Roy Goode. 'Official Commentary on the Protocol to the Convention on International Interests in Mobile Equipment on Matters Specific to Aircraft Equipment and Corrigenda' (2019).

Sir Roy Goode. 'Official Commentary on the Protocol to the Convention on International Interests in Mobile Equipment on Matters Specific to Aircraft Equipment and Corrigenda'. (2022).

Sir Roy Goode. 'Official Commentary on the Protocol to the Convention on International Interests in Mobile Equipment on Matters Specific to Railway Rolling

Stock', no. 5.3 p. 395 and no. 5.6 p. 397, no. 5.10 p. 399, nos 5.12 and 5.15 p. 402, no. 5.13 p. 402, no. 5.72 p. 439 (2014).

Sir Roy Goode. 'Official Commentary on the Protocol to the Convention on International Interests in Mobile Equipment on Matters Specific to Space Assets', no. 5.12 p. 422, no. 5.31 p. 433, no. 5.48 p. 439, no. 5.125 p. 483 (2014).

Sir Roy Goode. 'Security Interests in Mobile Equipment: Law Making Lessons from the Cape Town Convention', *Adelaide Law Review* Vol. 35(1) (2014): 65, 67, 68.

Sir Roy Goode. 'Security Interests in Mobile Equipment: Law Making Lessons from the Cape Town Convention', *Adelaide Law Review* Vol. 35(1) (2014): 65.

Sir Roy Goode. 'The Treatment of Intangible Assets under the Cape Town Convention and Protocols', *Cape Town Journal* (2013): 41–49.

Smith, Lesley Jane. 'The Principles of International Space Law and their Relevance to Space Industry Contracts'. In *Contracting for Space, Contract Practice in the European Space Sector*, 2011, 46.

Stanford, Martin J. 'The Availability of a New Form of Financing Space Activities: The Extension of the Cape Town Convention to Space Assets', *Cape Town Convention* (2013): 109–123.

Stanford, Martin. 'From Ottawa to Cape Town: UNIDROIT's Role in the Modernisation of the Law Governing Leasing and the Taking of a Security'. In *Secured Interests in Mobile Equipment*, edited by Iwan Davies. 2002, 491.

Stanford, Martin. 'International Financial Leasing: The Status of the UNIDROIT Convention and an Analysis of its Provisions', *Uniform Commercial Law Journal*, Vol. 32 (1999): 191.

Stanford, Martin. 'The UNIDROIT Convention on International Financial Leasing and the Preliminary Draft UNIDROIT Convention on International Interests in Mobile Equipment: Two Examples of UNIDROIT in Its Law-Making Role', *International Journal of Legal Information* (1999): 189.

Sundahl, Mark J. *The Cape Town Convention, Its Application to Space Assets and Relation to the Law of Outer Space*, 2013, 132, 148–158, 162, 163, 166, 167–177, 180, 181, 184.

Traunmüller, Karin. 'The Declaration of Legal Principles Governing the Activities of States in the Exploration of Outer Space: The Starting Point for the United Nations' Law of Outer Space'. In *Soft Law in Outer Space, The Function of Non-binding Norms in International Space Law*, edited by Irmgard Marboe. 2012, 153.

Veneziano, Anna. 'Advanced Relief under the Cape Town Convention and the Aircraft Protocol: A Comment on Gilles Cuniberti's Interpretative Proposal', *Cape Town Law Journal* (2013): 185–190.

Veneziano, Anna. 'The Cape Town Convention, General Presentation', *Unidroit y la codificación internacional del derecho privado* (2020): 281–288.

Index

The numbers here refer to paragraph numbers.

www.ingramcontent.com/pod-product-compliance
Lightning Source LLC
Chambersburg PA
CBHW071442230926
51846CB00001B/316
9789403536170